D1217091

The Family of Flowers

The Family

Mea Allan

# of Flowers

Illustrated by
Julia Morland and Andrew Crane

PITMAN

Pitman Publishing Limited
39 Parker Street, London WC2B 5PB

Associated Companies
Copp Clark Limited, Toronto
Fearon-Pitman Publishers Inc., Belmont, California
Pitman Publishing New Zealand Ltd., Wellington
Pitman Publishing Pty Ltd., Melbourne

Text and illustrations copyright © 1979
Pitman Publishing Limited

First published in Great Britain 1979

All rights reserved. No part of this publication may
be reproduced, stored in a retrieval system, or
transmitted, in any form or by any means, electronic,
mechanical, photocopying, recording and/or
otherwise without the prior written permission of the
publishers. This book may not be lent, resold, hired
out or otherwise disposed of by way of trade in any
form of binding or cover other than that in which it is
published, without the prior consent of the
publishers. This book is sold subject to the Standard
Conditions of Sale of Net Books and may not be
resold in the UK below the net price.

Reproduced, printed and bound in Great Britain by
Fakenham Press Limited, Fakenham, Norfolk

ISBN 0 273 01400 5

Other Books by Mea Allan

Fiction
Lonely
Change of Heart
Rose Cottage
Base Rumour

Biography
The Tradescants
The Hooker of Kew
Tom's Weeds
Palgrave of Arabia
E. A. Bowles and his garden
Plants that changed our gardens
Darwin and his flowers
Fison's Guide to Gardens
Gardens of East Anglia
The Gardener's Book of Weeds

Contents

List of Illustrations

The Family of Flowers

The word 'family' in the title of this book is used as a collective noun, as one would say a pride of lions and a muster of peacocks. Botanically a family is one division in the hierarchy of the vegetable kingdom.

This hierarchy developed because the plants themselves developed, over millions of years, from the primitive to the sophisticated, the blue-green algae and giant horsetails to the orchids in all their dazzling variety of form and colour.

The few plants increased to many, and when man took an interest in them for his own use as food and fodder, for weaving his clothes and building his dwellings, it became necessary to identify them by giving them descriptive names. Eventually Latin, as the international language, was used; but descriptions tended to be cumbersome and in the eighteenth century the great Swedish botanist Carl Linnaeus undertook the classification of both the animal and vegetable kingdoms. His binomial system of genus and species descends from the greater classes like a family tree.

Foreword

This book is intended as an introduction to the many families of flowering plants we grow in our gardens. From these the author has selected ten families covering a wide range of plants of all kinds, further selecting for description over 1,000 of the best species and varieties, these illustrated by more than 200 botanical drawings. Included are bulbous plants, greenhouse plants and ones specially suited for the rock garden and for shade and woodland conditions, though mainly they are for the open border. Unless stated otherwise, the soil will be ordinary good garden soil.

Each of the ten families occupies a chapter which has an introduction to the family and some hints on the care and culture of individual species and how and where they can be grown for best effect. This is followed by a descriptive catalogue of members of the family, making the gardener's choice of plants an easy one. Appended to each chapter is a useful bibliography for further reading.

The nomenclature used is according to the Royal Horticultural Society's *Dictionary of Gardening*, with some names updated, and to L. H. Bailey's *The Standard Cyclopedia of Horticulture*.

There will be those who progress from 'weekend' gardening to a more intense study of particular plants or kinds of plants such as alpines, lilies, orchids, hardy plants, daffodils, chrysanthemums. Specialist societies exist which cater for these. Their addresses can be had from the Royal Horticultural Society, Vincent Square, London, England, SW1P 2PE, for both British and European societies; Brooklyn Botanic Garden for societies in the United States of America.

Publications of these societies have been invaluable in the compilation of this book, and the author also acknowledges the help of Graham Stuart Thomas's most excellent *Perennial Garden Plants*, Will Ingwersen's *Manual of Alpine Plants*, Patrick M. Synge's *Collins Guide to Bulbs*, and for information on plant families *Flowering Plants of the World* edited by V. H. Heywood. The author is personally grateful to those horticulturists and others who have given kind advice. Particularly she is grateful to A. Gavin Brown for useful suggestions and for his meticulous reading of the typescript.

Author's Introduction

When one loves plants, to write about them in their families is as fascinating as meeting a family of humans to whom one is instantly attracted—parents, children and their cousins. Discovering the family thing, a common likeness, is a good way of getting to know plants, a starting-point in the process of identification.

The more we know about plants, their relationship to one another, the climate of their native home and whether valley or mountainside, wetland, woodland or plain, the better gardeners shall we be. So that, when we buy a new plant, it will be like welcoming a special guest into our home, for whose comfort and likes we have catered to the last detail.

Identification is not only the answer to how and where plants are happy to grow: it is the key to a door that opens on a world of friendship with them. Henceforward our garden is no longer just a pleasant place to wander in (thus rewarding ourselves by having removed the obvious weeds), decorated with pretty flowers perfumed for our further enjoyment: it is now a home where they are the welcoming ones. Oh no, it is not enough to know at what depth to plant a daffodil bulb, or that such-and-such is tender and needs the protection of a sun-warmed wall or greenhouse: not until one has sensed a communion with them, as real as the touch of a hand, and gives oneself to it, shall we know the full enjoyment of plants.

People walking round a garden—along by herbaceous and shrub borders, in and out of the kitchen garden—recognise (if they are perceptive though not knowledgeable) that a strawberry flower resembles that of, for instance, a potentilla. If they have counted the number of petals, finding that the strawberry has five, the potentilla five, and even the dog-rose growing in the hedge five; and, at some time, seen that a

buttercup has nearly escaped detection because it has grown up beside a similar-leaved delphinium, they may think that God ran out of ideas. But when they learn that the strawberry, the potentilla and the dog-rose belongs to a plant-family, and the buttercup and delphinium to another family, plant-life will begin to make sense, and they will be half-way to understanding evolution and the beginnings of life itself.

It was Charles Darwin who put the facts together of how life in its various forms had evolved through the millions of years it took for man to crawl—metaphorically—out of the primeval mud; for the marvellous partnership to develop between the orchid *Angraecum sesquipedale*, whose nectaries measure $11\frac{1}{2}$ in. (290 mm), and its pollinator the Sphinx moth *Xanthopan morgani praedicta*, whose proboscis measures exactly the same length.

Darwin pieced the story together through his penetrating studies of plants. The theme was "Survival". He found that after a wet and cold spring when few insects were about, the violet developed a second kind of flower called cleistogamic, which did not require the intervention of a pollinator. He traced plants backwards through time to their original forms. Comparing the seedlings of different plants and finding similarities between them gave him a clue to their common ancestry. Variation was a corner-stone of his evolutionary theory: in more thousands of experiments, carried out over a period of eleven years, he discovered how plants had become modified and improved.

So can we by our own observations of the strawberry and dog-rose, buttercup and larkspur, look behind time to see how these things have come about, and even catch a glimpse of tomorrow, whither they, and we, are going.

PEDIGREE OF A COLUMBINE

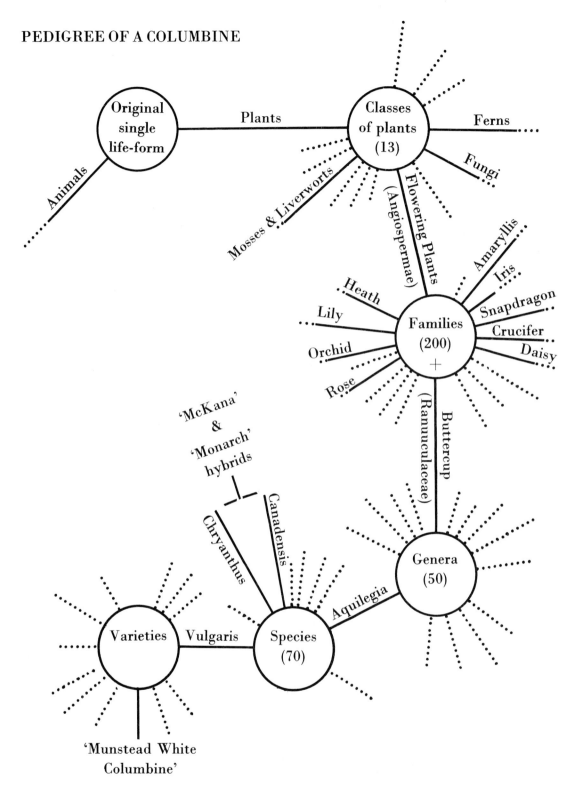

This graph has been devised to help the reader understand how plants are classified.

It takes the form of a pedigree; for just as a family tree shows descent from the earliest-known ancestor, so the pedigree of a plant traces its evolutionary development, reaching back to that single life-form or cell that divided into two – the animal kingdom and the vegetable kingdom.

Polly Carswell
The Amaryllis Family

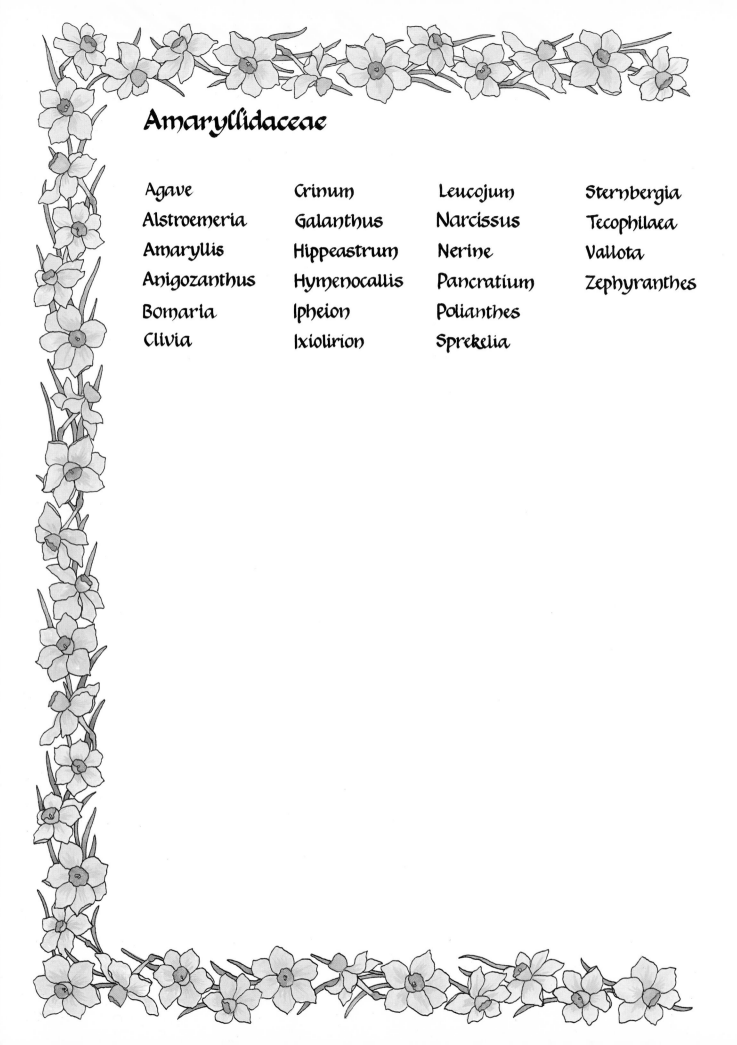

Amaryllidaceae

Agave	Crinum	Leucojum	Sternbergia
Alstroemeria	Galanthus	Narcissus	Tecophilaea
Amaryllis	Hippeastrum	Nerine	Vallota
Anigozanthus	Hymenocallis	Pancratium	Zephyranthes
Bomaria	Ipheion	Polianthes	
Clivia	Ixiolirion	Sprekelia	

The Amaryllis Family

These are mainly showy bulbous flowers, taking their family name from the Greek shepherdess Amaryllis whose beauty was sung in classical poetry and by the English pastoral poets of the sixteenth and seventeenth centuries. There are 85 genera in the family and about 1,000 species, among them two of our best-known and best-loved spring flowers—snowdrops and daffodils in all their variety of green-tipped white and chaliced and trumpeted gold—while others, like the flowers of the genus *Alstroemeria*, the Herb Lilies, should be better known.

Daffodils belong to the genus *Narcissus*, from the name of the beautiful youth of Greek mythology who slighted the fair Echo by falling in love with his own shadow, and was changed into the flower as punishment.

What beauty indeed the Amaryllis family gives us! such colours and nuances of colour—from the bright crimson dusted-with-gold flowers of *Nerine sarniensis*, the Guernsey Lily, to the stunning white trumpets of the *album* form of the Crinum Lily. There is the Chilean Crocus, *Tecophilaea cyanocrocus*, which is not a crocus at all. An astonishing blue, it is the bluest of all spring flowers, intense as any gentian. Another crocus-like flower is *Sternbergia*. Its several species are all bright yellow, varying from canary to deep golden stars when they open to the autumn and winter sunshine. The Spring Starflower is an earlier riser, blooming outdoors in April. There are 25 species in its genus, though only the charming *Ipheion uniflorum* is in general cultivation.

The Common Snowdrop, *Galanthus nivalis*, grows in woods all over Europe, from Spain in the south-west as far east as the Caucasus. A popular name for it is Fair Maids of February, from the white blossoms opening about the second day of that month when maidens dressed in white walked in procession at the Feast of the Purification.

In complete contrast some of the showy members of the family do best as pot plants indoors. One is the gorgeous hippeastrum of many hybrids, familiarly (though incorrectly) known as the Amaryllis.

Amaryllis belladonna
var. *parkeri*

Many of these plants are called Lilies, such as the Kaffir Lily (*Clivia*) and the Spider Lily (*Hymenocallis*), but although all have lily-like flowers and leaves they are not true lilies. Look for the difference between them: the members of the Amaryllis family have the ovary or seed-vessel *below* the other flower-parts (petals, sepals and stamens); the lilies have theirs *above*.

4

CARE AND CULTURE

Although most of the Amaryllis family are bulbous plants, the Agave which inhabits the North American and Mexican desert lands has a fibrous-rooted crown and alstroemerias tuberous roots that form fleshy crowns and run on again.

So we shall mainly be concerned with bulbous plants, accommodating in their liking for and tolerance of varied situations and soils. Some at least will be equally happy in grass as in a border, in a woodland or in the open, in troughs and window-boxes, outdoors or in. This applies to snowdrops, snowflakes, daffodils and the ipheion, for these are hardy subjects able to withstand frost and snow, as can the outdoor species of alstreomerias. A protected garden or one with a mild climate can add crinums, pancratiums, nerines, sternbergias, and the Zephyr Flower *alias* Jamestown Lily (*Zephyranthes*).

Snowdrops are both the earliest and latest of all hardy bulbs, some species starting to bloom in September and others flowering throughout the winter till March. They multiply readily from seed, and the sight of a wood carpeted with their white is never to be forgotten. The loveliest array I ever saw was a winding drift of them flowing down a sloping lawn like a river. There were thousands upon thousands, of many species and varieties. For don't think there is only one kind of snowdrop, *Galanthus nivalis*: see how many fascinating variations of the green **V** you can find on the inner petals. Each difference denotes a different species.

The taller Snowflake, *Leucojum*, is equally at home in any soil and position, with the exception of a few species which prefer to grow in a greenhouse. The flowering period ranges from January through September, according to kind.

Daffodils are seen at their best when naturalised in grass in open woodland, but a corner in even the smallest garden can be transformed by an irregular splash of their sunshine.

Rock gardens provide a perfect home for sternbergias, the smaller snowdrops, and dwarf daffodils: *Narcissus minimus*, smallest of the species at 3 in. (75 mm) high; the little *Narcissus cyclamineus* looking like a Christmas cracker; and the charming Hoop Petticoat, *Narcissus bulbocodium*.

For sheer magnificence the crinums can hardly be surpassed. They bring their

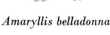

Galanthus nivalis 'Regina Olgae'

Amaryllis belladonna

Alstromeria ligtu hybrid

Sternbergia Intea

Leucojum aestivum

heady scent and white and pink perfections in the late summer when almost everything else is jaded. Varieties of the hybrid *C. × powellii* are reckoned to be hardy or nearly hardy, but are best grown in the shelter of a sunny wall.

Desirable in its deep blue form is the Corn Lily, *Ixiolirion montanum*, though it needs a warm border. There is no difficulty with the alstroemerias. Best to grow is St Martin's Lily, *A. ligtu* and its hybrids which produce small and enchanting lily-like flowers beautifully marked and ranging through coral to salmon and orange. Their running roots make alstroemerias invasive and they can become a nuisance, but on the other hand they need little care and die down unobtrusively after flowering. They are good for cutting and are long-lasting in water.

Queen of the family is the Amaryllis itself. This, *Amaryllis belladonna*, the Belladonna Lily (an old favourite with many forms), is the sole species of its genus. It throws up à tall leafless flower-stem in autumn bearing sweetly scented rose trumpets. Protection from cold winds and plenty of feeding are needed and Amaryllis will reward you.

The name of the 'other Amaryllis', *Hippeastrum*, means 'a knight on horse-back', from the Greek *hippeus*, a rider; and long ago Samuel Curtis pointed out that the spathe was composed of two leaves standing up like ears, giving the whole flower a fancied resemblance to a horse's head. Two species, *advenum* and *pratense*, are hardy enough outdoors *if* planted in warm favoured places. The native home of both is Chile. Easy to grow indoors are the hybrid hippeastrums, flowers striking in colour and size, with white to blood-red trumpets nearly six inches across.

Closely related and always welcome is the attractive outdoor nerine (*bowdenii*) with its bunched heads of pink frilly petals, coming at a time—September, October and November—when little else in the garden is in bloom. There are several good forms, and a miniature species (*masonorum*) for a warm pocket in the rock garden. The nerines are South African plants, good for cutting and looking their loveliest under artificial light.

Between the outdoor and indoor species the Amaryllis family gives us great variety and colour all the year round.

Crinum 'powellii'

Hybrid daffodil 'Kingscourt'

Ipheion uniflorium

Nerine bowdenii

Hippeastrum

Propagating

Because most of the Amaryllis family are bulbous plants we can increase our stock by separating the offsets from the base of the parent bulbs and growing them on.

Mature clumps should be lifted and divided every five to six years because not only do the parent bulbs go on increasing in size, their progeny at the base also increase in size, thus overcrowding and exhausting the soil. That great gardener E. A. Bowles when asked for his recipe for successful snowdrop-growing replied: "Stir 'em up!" A clump of snowdrops broken up and replanted singly while they are in flower will quickly make new clumps. Daffodils will 'die back' by going more to leaf than bloom if they are not lifted and separated occasionally. Do this in June when the leaves have withered.

There is no general rule for the depth at which to plant mature bulbs. Each kind needs its own depth above it, but plant deeper in sandy soil. Corms should be planted no more than 2 in. (50 mm) deep.

Save even the smallest bulblets, for all will develop. Plant these in boxes, or in a frame, or in prepared beds in the open ground. Cormlets should be planted out in spring after wintering in a dry place. Feed with dilute manure water once a week in midsummer. They will flower the following year.

To increase alstroemerias (which need a well-drained sun-warmed soil) dig out a square piece of your existing colony after flowering and place it in a prepared hole, disturbing the roots as little as possible.

Through the ages Nature has perfected her methods of growing and sowing, and I have always believed in following her practices as far as possible. Seeds when ripe fall to the ground, find a place to settle, and start the process of germination. Sow then at the same seasons as those

Narcissus bulbocodium

chosen by Nature. The seeds of bulbs are no exception: when the capsule becomes dry and hard and the chambers split open, this is the time to harvest. Scatter the seeds evenly and thinly in pans filled with a reliable sowing-compost, and if the seeds are from hardy bulbs the pans can be plunged in the cold frame. Exposure to frost and snow will do no harm and may even hasten germination.

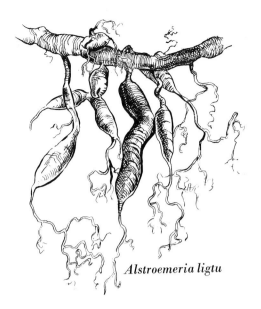

Alstroemeria ligtu

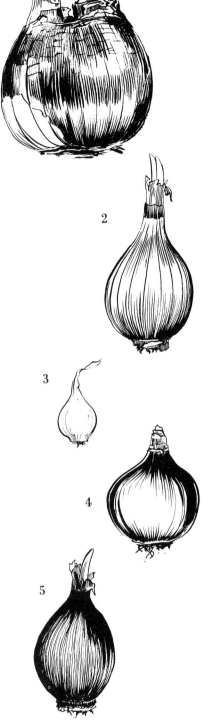

Bulbs of the family showing comparative sizes

1   A garden daffodil, large-cupped form

2   A Tazetta daffodil

3   *Narcissus minimus*, a wild miniature daffodil

4   *Narcissus canaliculatus*, a wild Tazetta

5   A Jonquilla daffodil

6   A Triandrus daffodil

7   *Galanthus nivalis*, the Common Snowdrop, with bulblets

8   *Leucojum vernum*, the Spring Snowflake

9   *Nerine bowdenii*

10 *Amaryllis belladonna*

The rhizomatous root of *Alstroemeria ligtu*

FLOWERS OF THE FAMILY

Alstroemeria. The Peruvian Lily or St Martin's Flower is a valuable perennial with a range of exquisite colour—creamy-white to reddish-pink, violet-mauve, rose-pink, yellow and orange, their lily-like flowers being beautifully marked.

Alstroemeria ligtu

Best to grow are *A. ligtu* and its hybrids. The species, like most of the genus, comes from Chile; its flowers are from reddish-pink to blush and bloom in June and July. Height 2–4 ft (600 mm–1 m). Hybrids are pink, salmon, flame, coral, and orange.

aurantiaca. Umbels of golden-orange flowers streaked with brown, from June to September. Height 3 ft (900 mm). It will thrive in semi-shade.

pelegrina. Lilac flowers decorated with rose-purple spots and a yellow throat, from June to September. Height 2 ft (600 mm). *A.p. alba*, a beautiful white form with dark markings, is the Lily of the Incas, suitable for a mild climate.

pulchella. A Brazilian species with dark-red flowers tipped with bright green and powdered with brown, the strange colouring earning it the name of Parrot Lily, A plant for maximum sun, flowering June to September. Height 2½ ft (750 mm).

violacea. For a favoured climate and to be tried in sheltered gardens. The flowers are a warm violet-mauve, the middle petals nearly white but spotted with purple. Summer-flowering, it is about 1 ft (300 mm) tall.

New varieties of these superb flowers are always being developed. We shall soon be enjoying a series of lovely hybrids of *aurantiaca* being developed in Holland, all of rich and varied colours, some dramatic with contrasting flashes.

Amaryllis Belladonna. This beautiful bulb from the Cape of Good Hope is worth the patience it takes to establish it, for it was well named Belladonna or Pretty Lady. Its leafless scape unfolds in September to show a head of pink trumpets shading paler in the throat, as many as ten flowers to the head if well established in a rich deep soil and thoroughly watered around late July. It grows 2–2½ ft (600–750 mm) tall, the bright-green strap-shaped leaves appearing in winter and early spring. The bulbs should be planted at least 5 in. (130 mm) deep and protected from frost.

Improvements on the original plant have produced some fine forms. One is the vigorous 'Parkeri', with up to 12 flowers to

Crinum × powellii

the head, deep pink with yellow at the throat. 'Hathor' is a superb white form with a yellow throat and large heads of flowers. The late-flowering 'Kewensis' is a dark pink form.

Crinum. The hybrid *Crinum × powellii* is my recommended plant for this genus. Hardy in Britain, Northern Europe and North America it bears large lily-like trumpets in umbels of 6 to 10, opening one after another from July to September and thus giving a long flowering season. Rose-pink is the usual colour, the *album* form is strikingly pure-white, and *krelagei* has blooms of deeper pink. All are sweetly scented. Their height is $2\frac{1}{2}$ ft (750 mm). The bulbs should be planted in October, with the neck 6 in. (150 mm) below the surface of the soil.

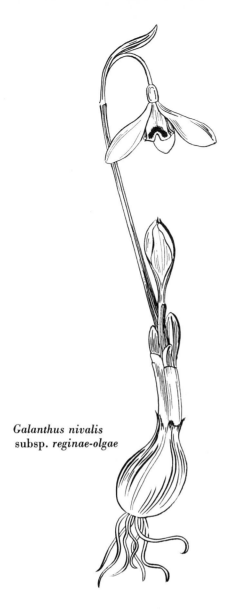

Galanthus nivalis
subsp. *reginae-olgae*

Galanthus caucasicus

Galanthus. The Snowdrop. The single *nivalis* is the commonest kind but there are about 15 species in the genus and many more subspecies and varieties. The bulbs should be planted 3–4 in. (75–100 mm) deep and 3 in. (75 mm) apart, as early as possible in the autumn. Once planted, snowdrops should be left undisturbed until they are obviously overcrowding each other, when they should be lifted and separated *while still in flower.* Ground where snowdrops grow should never be manured, for this is a sure way to kill them.

Starting with autumn-flowering snowdrops, we have *Galanthus nivalis* subsp. *reginae-olgae* and *G. corcyrensis*,

both liking open places. The first is from the mountains of Greece and it generally flowers in October, sometimes in September. The leaves appear about a month later. This is a tall snowdrop, just under 6 in. (150 mm). The inner segments of the flower are marked with a broad upside-down **U**, and the pure-white outer petals stand free, making a most graceful flower. *G. corcyensis* has an even broader green marking, is not quite so tall and flowers from late November to early December. The leaves, then only about an inch long, develop later.

From early January to mid-February two species which flower are *caucasicus*

Galanthus byzantinus

Galanthus nivalis
var. *scharlokii*

(tall with bluish leaves prominently recurved), and *graecus* (twisted leaves and two different markings on the inner segments: a cuneate inverted **V** with deep green above).

By mid-January *nivalis* 'Atkinsii' and the two species *byantinus* and *elwesii* are in flower. E. A. Bowles, the great authority on snowdrops, gave 'Atkinsii' first prize for possessing every virtue: it was robust; it improved the size and beauty of its parent; it increased rapidly and flowered both before and after *nivalis*. It is one of the tallest of snowdrops. The larger forms of *byzantinus* are among the finest and they grow equally well in sun and shade. The

flower is easily recognised by the well-marked inverted **V** and the distinct band above it. G. *elwesii* has silver-grey leaves and large flowers on robust stems. It has been known to start flowering at Christmas.

Galanthus nivalis itself comes at the end of January to February with its charming double form which is a prolific spreader. An early-flowering variant is the unusual 'Scharlokii' with twin spathes standing up like asses' ears. A late-flowering variety raised in Ireland is 'Straffan' which remains in flower for a long period. Strong bulbs will produce a second flowering. This was the late E. A. Bowles's third choice among snowdrops.

Hippeastrum 'Minerva'

Hippeastrum. A genus providing magnificent flowers for house and greenhouse. Its hybrids, ranging from pure white to deep blood-red, are often called 'Amaryllis', and this is the plant that may come to you as a Christmas gift: a very large bulb in a box with growing instructions. Two species—*advenum*, of bright crimson-scarlet trumpets in late summer, and *pratense*, also bright scarlet and flowering in June and July—may be grown outside in a warm situation, otherwise hippeastrums are subjects for a

greenhouse or warm window ledge. Some have their own common name: *equestre* is often known as the Barbados Lily, *reginae* as the Mexican Lily.

The hippeastrums bloom in late winter or early spring according to the amount of heat they are given. They do best in a minimum temperature of 55°F (13°C). After flowering they should be kept growing till the foliage begins to die down, when they should be rested on their sides for 2–3 months. They need feeding with liquid manure during growth.

Hymenocallis. This is a large genus of South American bulbs; none of the species is completely hardy, though *amancaes* and *narcissiflora* may be grown outside in a warm border in summer if lifted and kept dry during the winter. On his *Beagle* voyage Charles Darwin was disappointed with the flora around Lima, Peru's capital, but wrote delightedly that the hills near the town were carpeted with the beautiful yellow lily-like *amancaes*. *H. narcissiflora* used to be known as the 'Chalice-crowned sea Daffodil', although it does not grow by the sea shore.

Both species are very fragrant, flowering in June and growing to a height of 1½ ft (450 mm). Plant in March or April in a temperature of 55°–60°F (13°–16°C). They need copious watering in the summer, even after flowering, and an occasional feed of dilute liquid manure until the foliage dies back in autumn.

Ipheion has only one species in general cultivation—*uniflorum*, the Spring Star Flower, a most attractive early bulb as well as one of the easiest to grow. The dainty flowers in April and May are white, pale lavender or bright lilac-blue, sweetly scented and striped with green on the back. They grow singly on a 6 in. (150 mm) stalk from among grass-like leaves, will spread happily in sun or partial shade and

Ipheion uniflorum

Leucojum aestivum 'Gravetye Giant'

can also be increased by offsets.
Inexpensive to buy, the little Spring Star
Flower should be planted 4 in. (100 mm)
deep and the same distance apart. Not long
ago it was known as *Triteleia uniflora*. It
has also been classed as *Milla* and *Brodiaea*.

Ixiolirion. Plants with good blue flowers
tend to be scarce in the garden. Here is one
species, *montanum*, which has lovely open
flowers of a vivid violet-blue in June. It
grows on slender 16 in. (400 mm) stems, the
flowers with their six pointed petals in a
graceful umbel. Increase by removing the
offsets after the bulbs have flowered.

Leucojum, the Snowflake, differs from the
snowdrop by having its six petals of equal
length, while in the snowdrop the three
inner petals are much shorter than the
outer ones. Visibly it is not at all the same
plant, and nobody could mistake the
distinguishing yellow or green dots on the
pointed ends of the petals. There are three
flowering seasons.

aestivum, the Summer Snowflake, is the
largest species, 2 ft (600 mm) tall and
flowering from mid-April to early May. It
has a fine form known as 'Gravetye' or
'Gravetye Giant' with larger flowers than
the species, up to 1 in. (25 mm) long and
across. William Robinson, the great
advocate of natural gardening, found it
growing in his garden at Gravetye Manor,
Sussex. The flowers hang bell-like in
bunches of 2–5 flowers and have green dots.

vernum blooms in late winter and early
spring. Though only 8 in. (200 mm) tall
it has big flowers of the same size as the
'Giant' which are also tipped with green.
The flowers usually grow singly on the
stem, but occasionally there are two. A
variety named 'Carpathicum' has yellow
or yellowish-green dots.

autumnale is a dainty species blooming
in September. The flowers, small and bell-
like, white tinged with pink, have no
coloured dots. They appear before the
leaves and also usually grow singly on the

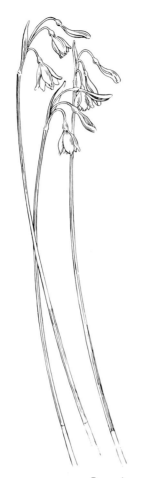

Leucojum autumnale

Leucojum roseum

stem which is up to 8 in. (200 mm) tall.
The bulbs of the Spring and Summer
Snowflakes should be planted in September,
the Autumn Snowflake in March, 3 in.
(75 mm) deep and 6 in. (150 mm) apart in
groups. To increase, lift and divide the
clumps after flowering and replant
immediately, having removed the smaller
bulbs. These can be grown on in boxes of
sandy compost for 2 years, when they are
at flowering size and ready to be planted
out.

There are some delightful species for
growing in a cool greenhouse or alpine
house.

roseum, as its name tells you, has pink
flowers. It grows to about 5 in. (125 mm)
high and usually flowers at the end of
August.

nicaeënse is a charming plant only
2–5 in. (50–125 mm) high. It flowers early
in April and often has two flowers to its
stem. These are white and grow from
among grass-like leaves.

trichophyllum is early flowering, January
to April, taller at 10 in. (250 mm), with
white flowers sometimes four to a stem.

Narcissus. All daffodils belong to the
genus *Narcissus*. As John Parkinson
wrote in 1640:

"Many idle and ignorant gardeners . . .
doe call some of these Daffodills
Narcissus, when as all know that know
any Latine that Narcissus is the same
thing."

15

Yet people still make the uncompromising distinction: the one with the long yellow trumpet is the daffodil; the fragrant white flat-eyed is the narcissus.

All are narcissi, but so varied are they that they have been divided into twelve groups, the first nine being of garden origin:

I Trumpet Narcissi.
II and III Large- and small-cupped.
IV With double flowers.
V Triandrus Narcissi. Small and dainty, height 3–9 in. (75–230 mm).

VI Cyclamineus Narcissi. With the petals swept back like a cyclamen.
VII Jonquilla Narcissi. Rush-like leaves, 2–6 flowers in a cluster, strongly scented.
VIII Tazetta Narcissi. Also bunch-flowered but with flat leaves.
IX Poeticus Narcissi. With a flat wheel-shaped corona.
X Species and wild forms and wild hybrids.
XI Split-corona Narcissi.
XII All Narcissi not falling into any of the other groups.

When we come to study the name Narcissus we find Pliny upsetting the legend about the beautiful Greek youth by stating that 'narce' was the origin, "which betokeneth numbedness or dulnesse of sense", as his translator explained. Caspar Bauhin, the sixteenth-century Swiss botanist, defined it as from 'Narkosis', the condition induced by a narcotic.

But none of this will spoil our appreciation of the beautiful narcissi or detract one iota from the beauty of the flowers themselves. We have a galaxy of poets to sing their praises. Shakespeare, Herrick, Keats, Shelley and others all wrote of the fair Narcissus, the "Daffodils that come before the swallow dares, and take the winds of March with beauty."

To choose which daffodils to plant in one's garden is bewildering, and I would like to advise the new gardener to specialise in some way, perhaps choosing a few from the twelve groups we have listed, to see which kind most appeals. It could be that your favourite plants are alpines, those small mountain flowers that grow among rocks. The choice here is easy: such treasures as the little *cyclamineus*; *bulbocodium*, the Hoop Petticoat Daffodil; and *triandrus albus*, the adorable Angel's Tears with clusters of creamy bells and hanging stamens. There are other miniatures for the rock garden and indeed for any small corner where a few bulbs can grow.

For a bolder display in a border there is an almost endless list of garden hybrids to choose from among Groups I to IX, from the superb 'King Alfred' with its deep golden-yellow trumpet, a favourite since 1899, to the latest Award of Merit daffodil listed in the catalogues of the specialist bulb firms. 'Golden Harvest' (prolific and deep yellow), 'Kingscourt' (deep pure gold and one of the most lovely), 'Cromarty' (a fine yellow trumpet

Narcissus: 'Kingscourt'

growing strongly in the garden), and 'Ulster Prince' (a very fine deep golden-yellow trumpet) have each won one or several Awards of Merit at the shows of the Royal Horticultural Society, and there are plenty of others.

A favourite among the white trumpets is 'Mount Hood', and there are bicoloured trumpets—the creamy-white of 'Rushlight with a lemon frill, and 'Trousseau' whose blue-green foliage sets off the pure white perianth and flanged trumpet which opens a soft yellow and passes to rosy cream.

The search for the blue rose is one of horticulture's pet passions. In the daffodil world the search is for a pink daffodil. This, named 'Mrs R. O. Backhouse', was achieved some years ago with the first truly pink trumpet, though still with a white perianth.

Narcissus 'Binkie'

Narcissus: Tazetta

Some people prefer the cupped flowers of '*the* Narcissus' persuasion, and again there is a wide selection. 'Krakatoa' caused a sensation when it was first exhibited in 1945: its flame-coloured cup against the yellow flames of its perianth might have been the volcano itself! Since then many other wonderful cupped narcissi have appeared. Probably 'Carlton', clear golden-yellow, and 'Fortune' with its deep yellow perianth and large fiery cup are two of the best.

Of the double narcissi some lovely ones are 'Camellia', a soft primrose-yellow; the pure white 'Snowball' ('Shirley Temple'); 'Santa Claus'; and 'Texas' which is an immense early-blooming flower with broad petals of cream, gold and tangerine.

The Jonquils with their clusters of small

Narcissus: Poeticus

flowers are the sweetest scented, and excellent hybrids from them have been raised, some less than 8 in. (200 mm) high suitable for the rock garden and alpine house. Recommended for general planting are the free-flowering 'Cherie' of ivory-white perianth and pinkish cup; 'Orange Queen', a showy variety in a pastel orange colour; and 'Trevithian' which carries a large cluster of pale lemon flowers.

Very alike in their habit of bunching the flowers are the Tazettas. The flowers are larger, 1–2 in. (25–50 mm) across, almost flat with a shallow corona, and circular. They are white, the corona is pale yellow and they are sweetly scented and borne, 4–8, on a 12 in. (300 mm) stem. 'Cragford' of creamy-white perianth and rich orange eye can be brought into bloom by Christmas if grown in a bowl.

Other good varieties for growing in bowls for later blooming are the white 'Cheerfulness', and 'Geranium' with a pure white perianth and geranium-red cup.

Another name for the Tazetta Narcissi is Poetaz, not to be confused with our last group.

This is the Poet's Narcissus (*the* Narcissus, at last!), the well-known Pheasant Eye of snow-white perianth and saucer-shaped pale yellow corona edged with red, blooming in May and early June and renowned for its fragrance. It has some wonderful hybrids: 'Actaea'. 'White Rose', 'Queen of Narcissi' and other beauties.

Grow narcissi in bowls, in pots in the cool greenhouse, in borders and in the rock garden; but, where you can, grow them in groups, the more massed the better, outdoors in a meadow or in a corner of a smaller garden where they can naturalise.

Nerine. This is a genus of 30 species, of which *bowdenii* is the hardiest and one of the best bulbs for autumn. It has several outstanding varieties: recommended are

Nerine bowdenii

'Blush Beauty' with flowers of soft shell-pink, and 'Pink Triumph' with flowers of silvery-pink. The leaves come later.

We have remarked on the beauty of nerines under artificial light. They have an iridescence caused by the surface cells being like a prism directing the light on to drops of pink sap at the base of the flower.

Among indoor species for pots are *angustifolia*, *appendiculata*, and *sarniensis*, the Guernsey Lily, the most beautiful with its wide petals varying in colour from pure white through pale pink and orange-scarlet to pale purple-magenta. Three dwarfs for indoors are *filifolia*, *lucida* and *masonorum*. Outdoors, *humilis* is almost as hardy as *bowdenii*.

The bulbs should be planted in late summer or after flowering, with their necks showing above the soil. They are sun-lovers, so find them a warm place under a south-facing wall. They grow up to 2 ft (600 mm) tall.

Sprekelia. With its dramatic scarlet flower looking like some large exotic insect, *Sprekelia formosissima* is mainly an indoor plant, but it can be a challenge for outdoors where the bulbs should be planted early in September to a depth of 4 in. (100 mm), 6 in. (150 mm) apart in a warm border. They need copious watering while growing. The flowers appear in July and August on 12 in. (300 mm) stems, the leaves following later. Indoors the bulbs should be planted in not too large a pot, in a rich loamy compost with some sand. They will bloom in April and May.

Sternbergia. A small genus of four species, three of which are autumn-flowering and one spring-flowering, but only *lutea* is generally cultivated and is one of the two producing leaves at the same time as the flower. Brilliantly golden-yellow, the flowers closely resemble a crocus but are easily distinguished by having 6 stamens to the 3 of the crocus. It blooms early in the autumn, 6 in. (150 mm) at most above the ground.

The bulbs should be planted 4–6 in. (100–150 mm) deep, never less. They flower best after a baking-hot summer.

Tecophilea. Unless you live in a specially favoured climate the rich-blue Chilean Crocus (*cyanocrocus*) is not for you—in the garden, that is. As an alpine house plant it is more easily grown. It flowers in March or April.

Zephyranthes. The species of this genus are likewise tender with the exception of the autumn-blooming *candida*, Flowers of the Western Wind, a charming plant sending up starry white flowers on 8 in. (200 mm) stems from among rush-like leaves. It blooms August to October and multiplies rapidly from offsets.

The Jamestown Lily (*atamasco*) can be hardy in some gardens in a well-drained sunny place. Blooming in spring and early summer the flower is white with pale pink stripes flushed green at the base, the stem up to 10 in. (250 mm) tall. This bulb also multiplies by offsets. After lifting and dividing replant them immediately.

When grown in a greenhouse or in a pot on a window sill, zephyranthes bulbs should be allowed to become pot-bound: they are likely to flower better.

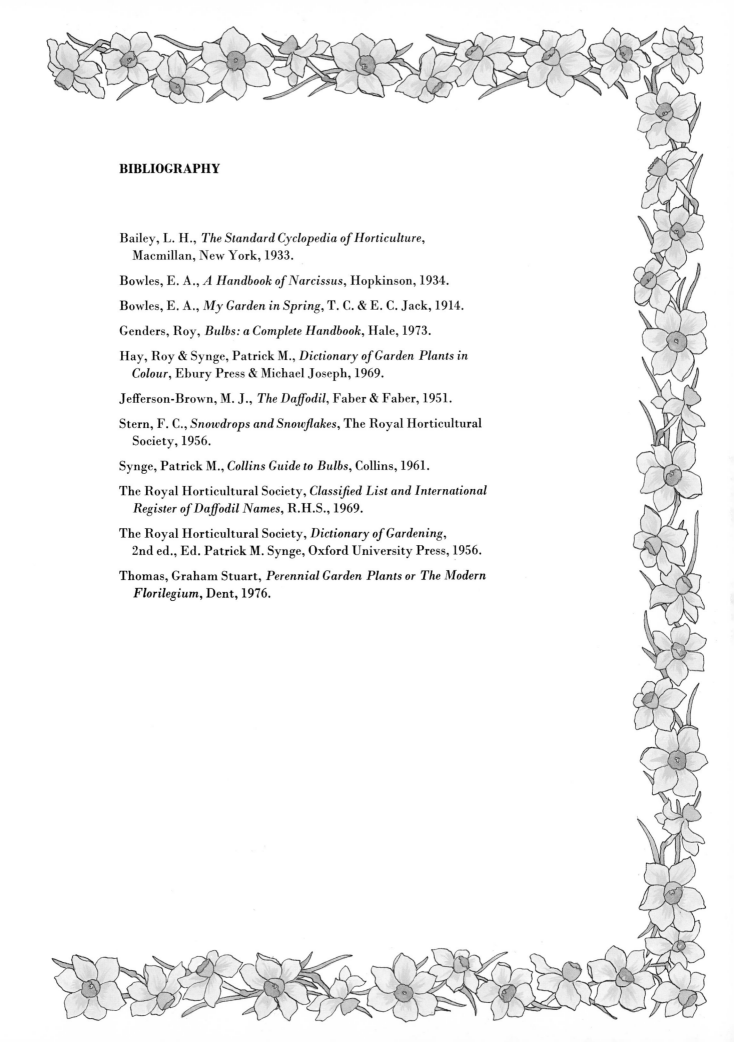

BIBLIOGRAPHY

Bailey, L. H., *The Standard Cyclopedia of Horticulture*, Macmillan, New York, 1933.

Bowles, E. A., *A Handbook of Narcissus*, Hopkinson, 1934.

Bowles, E. A., *My Garden in Spring*, T. C. & E. C. Jack, 1914.

Genders, Roy, *Bulbs: a Complete Handbook*, Hale, 1973.

Hay, Roy & Synge, Patrick M., *Dictionary of Garden Plants in Colour*, Ebury Press & Michael Joseph, 1969.

Jefferson-Brown, M. J., *The Daffodil*, Faber & Faber, 1951.

Stern, F. C., *Snowdrops and Snowflakes*, The Royal Horticultural Society, 1956.

Synge, Patrick M., *Collins Guide to Bulbs*, Collins, 1961.

The Royal Horticultural Society, *Classified List and International Register of Daffodil Names*, R.H.S., 1969.

The Royal Horticultural Society, *Dictionary of Gardening*, 2nd ed., Ed. Patrick M. Synge, Oxford University Press, 1956.

Thomas, Graham Stuart, *Perennial Garden Plants or The Modern Florilegium*, Dent, 1976.

The Buttercup Family

Ranunculacea

Aconitum	Caltha	Helleborus	Ranunculus
Actaea	Cimicifuga	Hepatica	Semiaquilegia
Adonis	Clematis	Isopyrum	Thalictrum
Anemone	Coptis	Nigella	Trollius
Anemonopsis	Delphinium	Paraquilegia	
Aquilegia	Eranthis	Paeonia	
Callianthemum	Glaucidium	Pulsatilla	

The Buttercup Family

Anemones brighten the landscape in spring with their gay colours; tall and elegant, delphiniums are the queens of herbaceous borders and huge mixed bouquets of summer flowers; in the depth of winter the Clematis will curtain the window of a warm room with trails of pinks and purples. Aquilegias and peonies bring both delicacy and full-bloom splendour to the garden in summer.

All belong to the Buttercup family. You have only to look at their leaves to see the family likeness: palmate, like your hand, and except for some species like the moisture-loving Kingcup (*Caltha palustris*) and the alpines, the leaves are much cut. Free petals, free sepals and free stamens are other characteristics.

Anemones are known as Windflowers, from *anemos*, the Greek word for wind. In mythology Anemone was a nymph loved by Zephyr. Jealous Flora banished her from her court and transformed her into the flower that now bears her name.

The annual delphinium (*Delphinium consolida*) is called the Larkspur from its spur-like nectary and also to distinguish it from the perennial.

Another bird, *aquila* the eagle, gives its name to the aquilegia, whose petals are like an eagle's extended wings, the flower's spurs resembling its neck and head. The dove or pigeon is also associated with this flower, giving us the name Columbine from the Latin *columba*; the nectaries resemble the heads of pigeons in a round dish.

Most of the innocent-looking Buttercup family are poisonous: roots, leaves, seeds, berries, sap. The Monkshood (*Aconitum napellus*) is popular in gardens because of its dark blue flowers and tolerance of shade, but it is cited as one of the most dangerous of all British plants.

Nectaries are the receptacles for the honey which flowers manufacture to

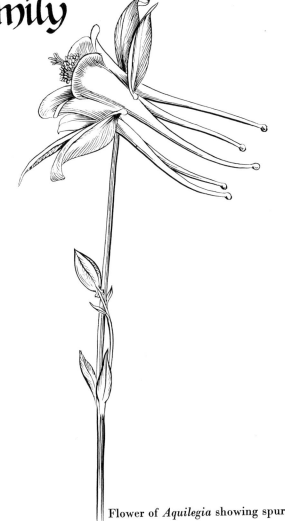

Flower of *Aquilegia* showing spur

attract the insects that fertilise them. But not all the family have their nectaries in a spur: the hellebore uses its petals for storing the honey; the Pasque Flower (*Pulsatilla vulgaris*) secretes its honey in the stamens; the hoods of the monkshood contain nectaries on long stalks.

The flowers range, too, through all the colours of the rainbow: reds in anemone and peony; orange in the double orange form of the Lesser Celandine (*Ranunculus ficaria*); yellow of the sunny Globe Flower (*Trollius*), and Winter Aconite (*Eranthis*); green, hellebores; blue, Love-in-a-Mist (*Nigella*) and delphinium; indigo, Monkshood; violet, the Pasque Flower.

CARE AND CULTURE

Although the plants in this family are so different, most of them have originated in the temperate or even cooler regions of the northern hemisphere, so their culture must be guided by the climate and conditions of their homeland. No cosseting in green-house or hothouse for them, or even on a warm windowsill. Good, open conditions in ordinary garden soil is the general rule. They like plenty of water, hate being dried out.

There are exceptions and variations, of course, even among a single genus like that of *Anemone*. Though called 'flowers of the wind' and very hardy, the de Caen and St Brigid strains of *Anemone coronaria* will flower best in a sheltered, sunny situation. The fibrous-rooted Japanese Anemone (× *hybrida*) is indifferent to shelter; it likes full sun but will tolerate shade. The little Wood Anemone (*nemerosa*) and its charming cultivars like part shade, as does *blanda*, the mountain anemone from Greece and Eastern Europe.

Aquilegias and their humbler cousins the curley-spurred columbines thrive almost anywhere and often grow best if self-seeded. In autumn their attractive leaves turn purplish, and are liked by flower arrangers.

You do not have to have a wall or trellis to grow the climbing clematis successfully. They can be just as lovely draping them-selves over shrubs or climbing up a tree. Culture-note for the latter: do not plant close to the trunk but some feet away and then point the clematis towards it. They can also be used beautifully as ground-cover plants and there are several herbaceous species. What a long season they give us, flowering from mid-winter to autumn according to the species or variety,

Clematis montana rubens

Nigella Damascena

Helleborus corsicus

Aconitum Napellus

attaining heights between 2 and 40 ft
(600 mm–12 m).

The hellebores are like no other plants.
Winter is their domain, and to see them
raise their heads after a severe frost has
bitten them and snow heaped itself on them
is to witness one of the miracles of survival
in the plant world. They are easy to grow
and each species has its own character.

The Winter Aconite brings sunshine in
the darkest days of the year, peeping out
here and there, eventually to form a crowd
of cheerful little faces wrapped in green
ruffs. In England's Lincolnshire they call
it the New Year's Gift.

Pliny called the peony oldest of all
plants. It was named after Paeon who was
worshipped as the God of Healing, a hymn
in his praise becoming known as a paean.
The plants, with magnificent flowers that
can be single or double, and with foliage
often richly tinted in spring and autumn,
and most with a special heavy scent,
deserve plenty of praise.

There are so many beauties of species and
varieties, try planting them as a mixed
group rather than as one among other kinds
of plants. They can tolerate some shade; in
fact they prefer it to full exposure to the
blazing sun.

A peony needs one square yard to spread
to its mature size. Mrs Edward Harding,
an American enthusiast, wrote "No garden
can be really too small to hold a paeony. Had
I but four square feet of ground at my
disposal I would plant a paeony in the
centre and proceed to worship . . ."

From splendour we go to the dwarfs —
buttercups from the alpine regions of the
Mediterranean, Asia Minor, North America
and New Zealand. Your rock garden can
rejoice in their snow-white and glossy
yellow cups.

Aquilegia hybrida

Troiluus Europeaus

Eranthis hyemalis

Anemone de Caen

Delphinium

The genus is called *Ranunculus*, from the Latin diminutive of *rana*, a frog, because so many of the species grow in damp places. Remember this in a hot summer and give them the water they need. If you are lucky enough to have a stream or a damp patch, adorn it with the moisture-loving Kingcup, so that its single or double flowers can be mirrored in the water.

Ranunculus alpestris

The Globe Flower (*Trollius*) is larger, a real bog plant, but will grow in the garden if not dried out.

Of all the buttercup family the tall, regal delphiniums are the queens, almost unique in producing flowers that represent the three primary colours. There are glorious blues, from softest ethereal sky-blue to rich cobalt; and superb red strains and clear yellows. They need an enriched soil, preferably with some lime. There are annual species and charming dwarfs for the rock garden.

The name delphinium comes from the Greek *delphis*, a dolphin; for the flowers, as John Gerard wrote, "especially before they be perfected, have a certain shew and likenesse of those Dolphins, which old pictures and armes of certain antient families have expressed with a crooked and bending figure or shape."

Propagating

Most of the herbaceous members of the family are fibrous-rooted and can be divided in the autumn. Never do this by hacking at the crowns with a spade, but take two forks to prise the clump apart.

Some, for instance the hellebores, are best grown from seed: it is amazing how many perennials indicate this preference by seeding themselves freely, and self-sown plants are usually stronger because the seeds have been sown at the correct time. The annual Larkspur and Adonis and Love-in-a-Mist can only be grown from seed.

Anemones can be increased by growing on their cormlets, pulsatillas by root-cuttings, hepaticas by division, but they are equally easy from seed. Clematis can be layered.

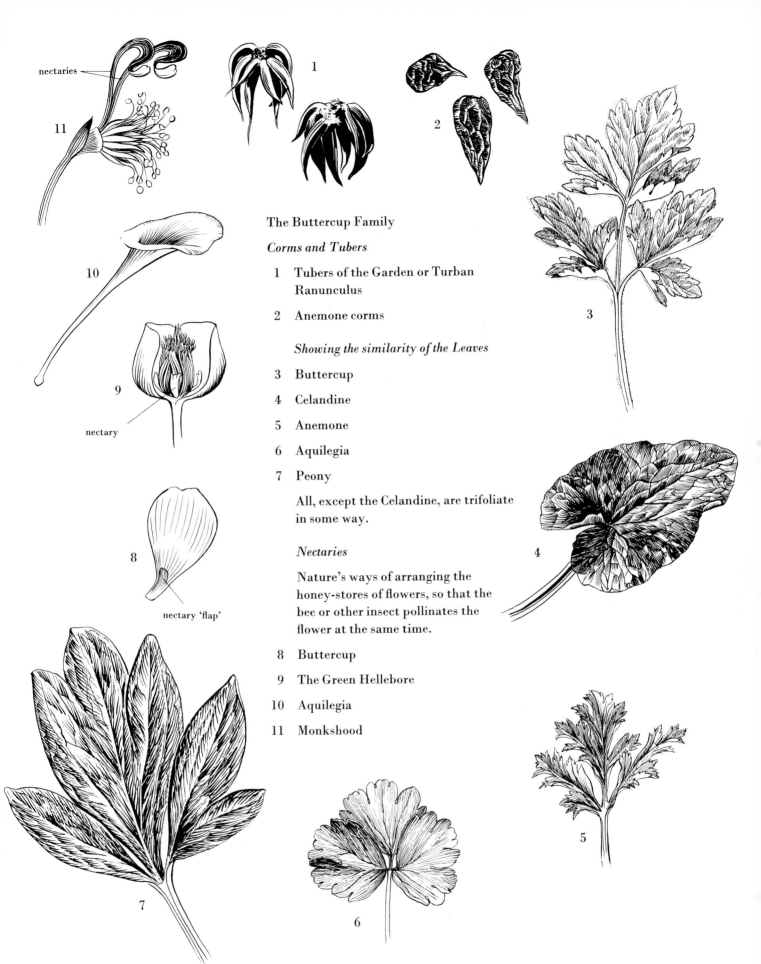

nectaries

11

1

2

10

The Buttercup Family

Corms and Tubers

1 Tubers of the Garden or Turban Ranunculus

2 Anemone corms

Showing the similarity of the Leaves

3 Buttercup

4 Celandine

5 Anemone

6 Aquilegia

7 Peony

All, except the Celandine, are trifoliate in some way.

Nectaries

Nature's ways of arranging the honey-stores of flowers, so that the bee or other insect pollinates the flower at the same time.

8 Buttercup

9 The Green Hellebore

10 Aquilegia

11 Monkshood

9

nectary

8

nectary 'flap'

3

4

5

7

6

FLOWERS OF THE FAMILY

Aconitum. The Monkshood is also called
the Helmet Flower and Wolf's Bane. There
are about 60 species in the genus, all
herbaceous perennials. They have dark
green glossy leaves and the hooded flowers
grow on long spikes. The roots are often
tuberous and need thinning-out every few
years, replanting 5 in. (125 mm) deep.

Aconitum napellus

napellus is the best-known species,
growing up to 5 ft (1.5 m) tall, with light
indigo-blue flowers in late summer. The
variety 'Carneum' has soft flesh-pink
flowers. 'Album' is an off-white form. Other
varieties are 'Blue Sceptre', 2 ft (600 mm)
tall with blue and white flowers;
'Bressingham Spire', violet-blue; 'Newry
Blue', deep blue, and 'Spark's Variety',
deep violet-blue.

carmichaelii comes from Kamtchatka.
The flowers of a light Wedgwood blue, are
borne on short spikes in early autumn.
They will reach about 4 ft (1.2 m). Two
6 ft (1.8 m) varieties are 'Kelmscott' of
violet-blue flowers, and 'Barker's Variety'
which breeds true from its seeds, and both
are extremely attractive.

orientale and *vulparia* are yellow and
yellowish, both summer-flowering and
growing to 5 ft (1.5 m). The latter is the
plant called Wolf's Bane because its
poisonous roots were used as a bait for
wolves.

variegatum has blue or yellowish or
parti-coloured flowers with high helmets
projecting forwards.

Adonis as a genus embraces both annuals
and perennials. The showy crimson and
yellow flowers have five or six petals and
grow singly on stems about 1 ft (300 mm)
tall: *aestivalis* (Pheasant's Eye) and
aleppica are annuals, both crimson and
June-flowering; so is *annua*, the Autumn
or Flos Adonis of intense blood-red flowers,
each petal with a black spot at the base.

The best perennial for a sheltered
corner is *amurensis*. Its fat round buds are
bronze, opening to 20–50 golden-yellow
petals in early spring before the leaves are
fully developed. The Japanese have bred
pink, white, and copper-coloured varieties,
and there is a good double form. Plant in
winter.

Anemone has about 70 species which can be roughly divided into two categories: those with fibrous roots and those with tubers or 'corms'. The first includes both large and small, the tall pink and white Japanese Anemones and the little Wood Anemone (*nemerosa*) and Snowdrop Anemone (*sylvestris*). The second category, of tuberous plants, contains *blanda* in all its bright colours, with the brilliant children of *coronaria*, the single de Caens and the semi-double St Brigids.

The parent of another strain is *pavonina*, also a tuber, the St Bavo Anemone, with a starry flower and a silver centre. As a species in its own right, *pavonina* is the Great Peacock Anemone of Greece.

blanda is the Mountain Windflower of Greece, blooming in March and April, single starry flowers of blue, mauve, pink or white. The stems are short, 4 in. (100 mm), and in time a colony of them will form a gay patchwork quilt. Two of the best forms are the deep blue 'Atrocoerulea' and rich pink 'Rosea'. 'White Splendour' has very large flowers, 'Radar' is large pink with a white centre.

coronaria, the Poppy Anemone we have described as the parent of the de Caens and St Brigids, is a native of Greece and the Eastern Mediterranean. The flowers are up to 3 in. (75 mm) across with six or more wide petal-like tepals, scarlet, crimson, blue, mauve or white, and single, semi-double or double. The flower-stems are 6–18 in. (150–450 mm) long. Recommended single varieties are 'His Excellency' (otherwise 'Hollandia'), crimson-scarlet with a white corona round the bunched stamens; 'Mr Fokker', blue; and 'Sylphide', mauve. A good double is 'The Governor', brilliant scarlet, with 'The Admiral', a deep pink semi-double.

× *hybrida* is the tall pink Japanese Anemone flowering in late summer into autumn and up to 3 ft (900 mm) tall. The leaf is typically that of the buttercup, lobed and serrated as usual but rough and hairy as well.

The name covers three species: *elegans*, *japonica*, and *hupehensis*. Two good varieties are 'Kriemhilde', rose-pink, and 'Margarete', deep pink; both semi-double. There is a superb white sport, 'Honorine Jobert', with a bunch of yellow stamens. It flowers for nearly three months.

Anemone coronaria, de Caen strain

Anemone × *hybrida*

nemerosa, the Wood Anemone, is like a slightly taller *blanda*, with white or pale mauve flowers flushed pale pink or mauve outside and 2 in. (50 mm) across, blooming in spring. It is most graceful and will naturalise in woodland conditions. Some fine varieties have been developed, the best of which is 'Allenii'.

Anemone nemorosa

pavonina, the Great Peacock, is variable in colour: as a species, scarlet with a white eye or with a dark eye flowering pink or mauve; as the St Bavo strain, it has colours ranging through salmon-pink, blush-blue, carmine and brick-red to white. *Pavonina* can be distinguished from the Poppy Anemone by its leaves divided into three lobes, compared with the parsley-like leaves of *coronaria*. It grows 1—1½ ft (300–450 mm) tall and flowers in April-May.

The tuberous-rooted anemones are easily grown from seed, but if you buy them as tubers never choose what are called 'jumbo corms', for these are trade throw-outs. Choose small ones measuring not more than 10 mm.

The fibrous-rooted kinds are best started as grown plants, shallow planted, and can be divided in autumn.

Aquilegia. One of the most charmingly elegant of all garden plants with its beautiful rounded lobed leaves and delicate particoloured flowers poised on long stems. There are two kinds, the Columbine, with short curly spurs, and those with long spurs usually called 'Aquilegias'.

alpina in its 'Deep Violet' form has large flowers of rich royal violet-purple. It grows up to 18 in. (450 mm) tall and blooms in May. Taller is the cross with *vulgaris*, a strain of deep Wedgwood blue but also ranging through all the colours of the old 'Granny's Bonnets'.

chrysantha is a rich yellow with long spurs of paler yellow, vigorous growing when planted in a sunny, well-drained situation, and attaining a height of 3 ft (900 mm).

saximontana is one for the rock garden, a charming dwarf American species with short-spurred blue and white flowers on stems 3–4 in. (75–100 mm).

vulgaris, the Common Columbine, is not to be despised, for its flowers have a wonderful range from palest pink to a dusky maroon, and from blue to indigo. They grow to 3 ft (900 mm) tall. There is also a lovely white form, the 'Munstead White Columbine', a favourite of Gertrude Jekyll, the great gardener of the last century who lived at Munstead Wood in Surrey. It has grey foliage and pale green stems and buds.

Many hybrids have been raised from the long-spurred aquilegias, the best of which are the 'McKana' and 'Monarch' strains. The spurs are 3–4 in. (75–100 mm) long, the flowers up to 4 in. (100 mm) wide. 'Snow Queen' is a beautiful white strain.

Aquilegia vulgaris

Caltha palustris

The colours range from yellow to pink and rich red, purple and mauve. Height 2–3 ft (600–900 mm).

Aquilegias seed freely but are never invasive.

Callianthemum, a small genus for the alpine house or rock garden. They look like the ordinary buttercup but have up to 20 petals, white, pink, soft lilac or china-blue. A good open soil suits them, well-drained but moist during spring and early summer.

Caltha. Here is a member of the buttercup family with heart-shaped or kidney-shaped leaves. The larger species are moisture-loving, the smaller suitable for the rock garden. They are hardy perennials.

palustris is a favourite called the Kingcup or Marsh Marigold; it has large glistening yellow flowers and shining leaves. The variants are attractive, double and semi-double, with colour forms *alba; pallida plena*, pale yellow and double; and *minor*, which is smaller in all its parts.

Cimicifuga, the Bugbane or Black Snake-root, is an unusual plant for cool moist places. It has long white or cream bottle-brush flowers on wiry stalks that twist about like snakes. Most of the species bloom in late summer or autumn and often the leaves turn cream or pale yellow to match. The two usually grown are *racemosa*, which is slightly fragrant; and *ramosa*, useful as an October-flowering plant with pure white narrow spikes 1 ft (300 mm) or more long. The whole plant grows to 7 ft (2.1 m) tall and 4 ft (1.2 m) wide.

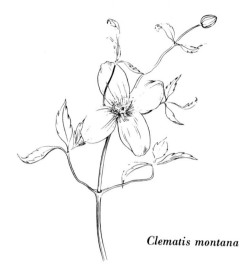

Clematis montana

Clematis has no rival as a decorative climber, with its large-flowering varieties, and species and small-flowering varieties, early-blooming and late-blooming.

Large-flowering varieties blooming early, in May and June, and some will grow happily even on cold exposed north-facing walls. Recommended are 'Barbara Dibley', pansy-violet with deep carmine bars; 'Bees Jubilee', mauve-pink with deep carmine bars, giving a second flowering in September. 'Duchess of Edinburgh' has double white rosette flowers with yellow stamens, and, the best of red Clematis, 'Ernest Markham', glowing petunia-red with golden stamens.

Of the late varieties flowering continuously from June to October, 'Jackmanii', the popular old-fashioned purple; *texensis* 'Countess of Onslow', a semi-herbacious variety from America with pink bell-shaped flowers, from July to October; and 'Madame le Coultre', very beautiful with her large pure white flowers with yellow stamens, June to September.

Clematis 'Bees Jubilee'

The species and small-flowering varieties give us a wide choice between early- and late-flowering kinds and shape of flower.

First we choose *alpina*, 'The Alpine Virgin's Bower', for its blue satiny bells in April and May, with 'Ruby', a profuse rosy-red variety, and 'White Moth' with double white flowers. The evergreen *armandii* has waxy white flowers in clusters in early spring, and needs a

sheltered wall, as does its pale pink variety, 'Apple Blossom'.

For those who do not know that a Clematis can be sweetly scented, there is the 'Elizabeth' variety of *montana*, beautiful, with a profusion of soft pink flowers. All the montanas, species and varieties, are valuable for covering north-facing walls and unsightly sheds: the fast-growing *grandiflora* with its masses of white flowers; *rubens*, deep pink with bronze foliage; and 'Tetra-rose' of lilac-rose flowers.

Two curious species that always cause comment are *orientalis;* orange-coloured nodding flowers with thick sepals have earned it the name of the 'Orange Peel Clematis', and *tangutica*, 'The Russian Virgin's Bower', bright yellow lanterns followed by a silky cloud of seed-heads. Both flower from summer through to autumn.

Plant in autumn in a soil enriched with manure or compost, and only deep enough to leave the crowns $1\frac{1}{2}$ in. (40 mm) beneath the surface. In summer give a liquid fertiliser and plenty of water, in autumn a top dressing of manure or bone meal. Always put some stones around the roots to help retain the moisture.

Most of the species do not need pruning but they can be cut back after flowering if they develop top-heavy growth. Large-flowered varieties like 'Jackmanii' need hard pruning.

Delphinium, a genus of about 200 species, of perennials, annuals, with a few biennials tall as 8 ft (2.4 m), or small as 8 in. (200 mm). We can divide them into delphiniums and larkspurs, as the perennial and annual kinds are usually called.

Most of the perennials we see are the Belladonna Hybrids and the large-flowered hybrids, but the following species are worth including:

brunonianum whose masses of large much-hooded purple flowers in June and July are borne on slender stems, sometimes lilac-blue with a black and yellow 'bee' in the centre. Its height is 9–18 in. (230–450 mm), and it has a musky scent.

grandiflorum, better known in its charming varieties, each 1–2 ft (300–600 mm) in height and giving an exceptionally long display of bloom. The brilliant and prolific 'Blue Butterfly' is the most popular; 'Azure Fairy' has bright Cambridge-blue flowers in the same profusion, and the deep-gentian 'Blue Gem' makes a compact bushy plant. This group, having been weakened by over-breeding, is best treated as annuals.

tatsienense comes from Szechuan and attains 2 ft (600 mm). It has finely cut leaves, and the flowers are of a rich azure blue, blooming from June to August.

The Belladonna Hybrids began their career about 1900. They are medium-sized, 3–5 ft (900 mm–1.5 m) in height, branching in habit and with open spikes. They will go on blooming from mid-summer to autumn provided that the early spikes are removed after flowering. Named varieties are 'Blue Bees', light blue; 'Moerheimi', white; and 'Wendy', gentian blue. 'Pink Sensation', a cross with *ruyii*, was born in 1935, a delightful plant with clear pink flowers.

The large-flowered hybrids were first bred about 1875 and work went on both in

Delphinium 'Mighty Atom'

England and the United States to produce the stately delphinium so much admired in our herbaceous borders. They range in height from 4–8 ft (1.2–2.4 m) and they are now available as doubles and singles in a colour-range from primrose-yellow to cream and white, from pale to dark blue, violet-mauve, dark purple and amethyst to almost pink. Some of the shades are vivid, some opalescent and ethereal. All have a fascinating 'bee' in the centre.

They need staking. Before real growth begins in spring, long twigs should be stuck round the plant. The foliage will grow up through the twigs to support the tall flowering spikes. The rich deep loam they enjoy should not be allowed to dry out in summer.

Most of our annual larkspurs come from the two species *ajacis* and *consolida*. The Rocket Larkspur (*ajacis*) has showy flowers varying from blue to violet, rose-pink to white. From this species the hyacinth-flowered types have been developed in dwarf and tall varieties 1–3 ft (300–900mm) high; *consolida*, the branching larkspur, 1½–2 ft (450–600 mm), has deep violet or purple flowers. From it the Stock-flowered, Giant Imperial and Emperor types have been developed, superb plants for the border and good for cutting. Varieties range from white, soft pink and lilac to deep salmon-rose, rosy-scarlet and violet-blue.

Eranthis. A small genus of seven species of which only *hyemalis* is important—the common Winter Aconite with its single yellow head in a green ruff on a 2–4 in. (50–100 mm) stem. Similar, but not so hardy, is *pinnatifida*, with white flowers.

Eranthis hyemalis

Closely related to *hyemalis* is *cilicica* , with taller stems. From these two has come the hybrid *tubergenii*, larger than its parents and longer lasting, but usually sterile.

Winter Aconite seeds freely, but should it tend to disappear this is a sign of under-nourishment. Give the ground a light mulching or treatment with a liquid fertiliser.

Helleborus. A near relative of the Winter Aconites and, like them, winter flowers. There are about 20 species, all herbaceous perennials. Most familiar are the snow-white Christmas Rose and the Lenten Rose. They will grow in full sun or under trees or in the shade. Attractive accommodating plants, we should not be without them.

Helleborus corsicus

corsicus is the most beautiful of all the hellebores, a study in palest translucent green: the wide hanging cups, nectaries and stamens, the wide lobed leaves with their prickly edges and outstanding veins. Hardy and always evergreen it produces showers of seedlings in a favourable year. It comes from Corsica, as its name tells us, and from Sardinia and the Balearic Islands, grows to 2 ft (600 mm) and flowers at the very beginning of winter through to spring.

niger, the Christmas Rose, was cultivated in Britain by the Romans and there has remained ever since. The name *niger* refers to the blackness of the roots. It is not so beautiful in leaf, but the exquisite white perfection of its blooms filled with golden stamens is more than compensation. Some find it a difficult plant to establish, but this may depend on the stock and I would say keep trying till you find a specimen that is happy, and propagate from its seeds. Old manure and leaf mould in spring will help. The height is 1 ft (300 mm).

orientalis, the Lenten Rose, is a native of Greece and Asia Minor. A very variable plant, its wide-open flowers from December to April ranging in colour from whitish to plum, sometimes beautifully spotted inside and flashed with green. The colours can look muddy and the plant can look sickly or bush out exuberantly. For all that, *orientalis* is well worth having, at 18 in. (450 mm).

foetidus, the Stinking Hellebore, has dark green, beautifully cut leaves with a curious blackish flush. The green flowers edged with maroon are borne in clusters and are with us throughout the winter and into spring. It is a perfect plant for sun and shade, robust, and a good seeder.

Hepatica. A genus of three species, closely related to *Anemone* and used to have this name. *H. triloba* is the wild hepatica usually grown in gardens, with white, deep blue, pale blue and occasionally pink flowers, mostly single but sometimes double. Finest is the hybrid × *ballardii* with pale china-blue flowers up to $1\frac{1}{2}$ in. (40 mm) across. Both bloom in February and March and like woodland conditions or shady nooks in the rock garden.

Nigella. This genus has a variety of common names: Love-in-a-Mist, Devil-in-a-Bush, and the Fennel Flower from its fennel-like foliage surrounding the flowers in a light green mist. It is one of the most charming and fascinating annuals, mixing well with others, perfect in a colony of its

Nigella damascena

own, unsurpassed as a cut flower. *Nigella damascena* is the species popularly grown. Sow the seed freely where it is to grow. The sky-blue flowers with their spiky petals will continue to the end of summer, growing $1\frac{1}{2}$–2 ft (450–600 mm) tall..

Paeonia. There are 33 species in this genus and scores of varieties, for this superb flower has merited the attention of hybridists—mainly in China and Japan—for hundreds of years. Apart from the herbaceous kinds there is the shrubby or 'tree' peony. So we can choose our plants from three categories: species; the Chinese Peonies or garden hybrids derived mainly from the superlative *lactiflora*, and, third, the Moutan or Tree Peony.

cambessedesii is a fantastic plant of deep rose-pink flowers decorated with red filaments and purple stigmas, the foliage deep green above, intense crimson-purple beneath and with crimson stalks. An exotic from the Balearic Islands it enjoys being baked with sunshine. It grows 18 in. (450 mm) tall.

Paeonia
'Kelway's Lovely'

lactiflora is another gem, of most graceful habit and huge white single flowers with a boss of yellow stamens. The flowers are set off by beautiful reddish-brown leaves and stems. Its height is 3 ft (900 mm).

mlokosewitschii, the unpronounceable from the Caucasus has been dubbed 'Molly the Witch'. It is an early-blooming species with large lemon-yellow flowers and golden anthers making a perfect foil for the soft grey-green leaves. It will thrive in any sunny position and grows to a height of 2 ft (600 mm).

officinalis is the popular garden plant, the old double red (var. *rubra plena*) known to everybody. There are good single red forms and beautiful varieties such as 'Paradoxa Rosea', a deep pink, and 'China Rose', a clear salmon-rose with orange stamens, growing to 2 ft (600 mm) tall.

peregrina gives us large single blooms of intense fiery scarlet among fresh green glossy foliage. It has a beautiful form in salmon-scarlet with an orange sheen. The height is 2 ft (600 mm).
All these flower in May or earlier.

Chinese Peonies

These are so bewilderingly many that one can list only a few of them here. The colour-range is from white through pink to deep reddish-crimson and maroon, both single and double flowers.

Doubles: the whites include the incomparable 'Baroness Schroeder' and 'Marie Crousse'; whites with creamy centres, 'Duchesse de Nemours' and 'Kelway's Glorious'. Pale pink: 'British Beauty', 'Sarah Bernhardt'; deeper pinks, 'Kelway's Lovely', 'Carmen' and 'Carnival'. Singles: the best pure white is 'Whitleyi Major'; dark crimson, 'Lord Kitchener' and 'Sir Edward Elgar'.
These flower in June.

Imperial varieties are the single peonies whose stamens have been changed into narrow petals, making a central cluster which sometimes matches the other stamens, other times the petals. The stunning pink 'Bowl of Beauty' is one. As a bonus to these wonderful hybrids their spring foliage is often decoratively a rich mahogany.

Later valuable work in hybridising has been done, notably by the late Dr A. P. Saunders of New York, and some of his hybrids are now finding their way to Europe, such as 'Rose Garland' and two splendid reds, 'Defender' and 'Legion of Honour'. All three are early-blooming and have single flowers. There are two superb single whites, 'Archangel' and 'Chalice'.

The Moutan or Tree Peony

This magnificent flowering shrub which grows up to the small-tree height of 8 ft (2.4 m) gives us a gorgeous display in late spring and early summer of large flowers up to 8 in. (200 mm) across. Two of the finest forms are 'Black Pirate', deep maroon-crimson with a huge boss of golden stamens, and 'Haquo-Jishi', a semi-double white

37

with large leaves deeply divided. They flower in late spring, are valuable as tall subjects in herbaceous beds, and some of them are fragrant.

Pulsatilla vulgaris

Ranunculus asiaticus

Pulsatilla. As with *Hepatica* this genus was once classed as *Anemone*. Best-known is the spring-flowering species *vulgaris*, the Pasque Flower, violet-purple and later a mop-head of silvery fluffy seeds growing from among filigree leaves. There are white, brick-red, maroon and deep shell-pink forms. It is a beauty for the rock garden, 4–8 in. (100–200 mm) in height.

Ranunculus. A large genus of some 250 species of annuals and perennials ranging in height from the 4 ft (1.2 m) of *lyallii*, a white-flowered New Zealand giant, to tiny species for the rock garden.

asiaticus is the Turban Ranunculus of various colours, 9–15 in. (230–380 mm) tall or more, flowering in late spring. There is a red-flowered single form, wild in the Levant, which is yet another supposed 'Lily of the Field' of the Bible.

ficaria, the Lesser Celandine, is well worth growing for its white, orange and lemon, (single and double) forms. The much larger Mediterranean form *grandiflora* is a treasure with its waxy yellow $2\frac{1}{2}$ in. (60 mm) cups flowering in March and April.

gramineus is unusual in having narrow linear leaves, but the flowers, bright yellow, are very buttercup-like and 1–3 on a stem. It will make large clumps in a sunny spot, growing to 8 in. (200 mm) tall and flowering in summer.

lingua, the Great Spearwort, is a plant for boggy ground beside water. It has long narrow leaves and glossy yellow flowers up to 2 in. (50 mm) across. It reaches 2–3 ft (600–900 mm) in sun or light shade.

Some dwarf rock garden species are *acetosellifolius*, cup-shaped white flowers on 4 in. (10 mm) stems; *alpestris*, another lovely little white-flowered alpine species, with heart-shaped leaves; *brevifolius*, solitary yellow flowers on short stems, and grey-green leaves; and *wettsteinii*, snow-white flowers on short stems, with deeply divided leaves at ground level.

Thalictrum. The Meadow Rue, is a genus of dainty plants with heads of fluffy flowers, in colour either mauve, rosy-lilac or yellow, with some white forms. The best species for the garden are *aquilegiifolium* with a cloud of purplish-pink flowers from late spring to mid-summer; *delavayi* with more branching flowers, and *diffusiflorum* with much larger flowers, rich lilac bells. A little beauty is *kiusianum* 4–6 in. (100–150 mm). Two yellows are *minus* and *speciosissimum*, delightful to grow among other plants. Their height is from 1–5 ft (300 mm–1.5 m).

Trollius. Globe Flowers are always attractive with their deeply-cut fresh green leaves and moons of blossom. The species *europaeus* blooms in late spring and early summer. Globe Flowers are most effective beside a pool, and grow to 2 ft (600 mm)

Trollius europaeus

tall. The summer-flowering *ledebourii* has orange cups and deeply lobed and toothed leaves. Both species have good varieties and can be propagated by division in the early autumn.

BIBLIOGRAPHY

Bailey, L. H., *The Standard Cyclopedia of Horticulture*, Macmillan New York, 1933.

Bishop, F., *The Delphinium, a Flower Monograph*, Collins, 1949.

Fisk, J., *The Queen of Climbers* (Clematis), 2nd ed., Fisk, 1978.

Genders, Roy, *Anemones for Market and Garden*, Faber, 1956.

Harding, Mrs Edward, *The Book of the Peony*, Lippincott, 1917.

Hay, Roy & Synge, Patrick M. *Dictionary of Garden Plants in Colour*, Ebury Press & Michael Joseph, 1969.

Ingwersen, Will, *Ingwersen's Manual of Alpine Plants*, Will Ingwersen & Dunnsprint, 1978.

Kelway, James, *Garden Paeonies*, Eyre & Spottiswoode, 1954.

Markham, Ernest, *Clematis and their Cultivation*, 3rd ed., Country Life, 1951.

Matthew, Brian, *A Gardener's Guide to Hellebores*, The Alpine Garden Society, London.

Robinson, William, *The Virgin's Bower: Clematis*, Murray, 1912.

Stern, F. C., *A Study of the Genus Paeonia*, Royal Horticultural Society, 1946.

The Royal Horticultural Society, *Dictionary of Gardening*, 2nd ed., Ed. Patrick M. Synge, Oxford University Press, 1956.

Thomas, Graham Stuart, *Perennial Garden Plants or The Modern Florilegium*, Dent, 1976.

The Crucifer Family

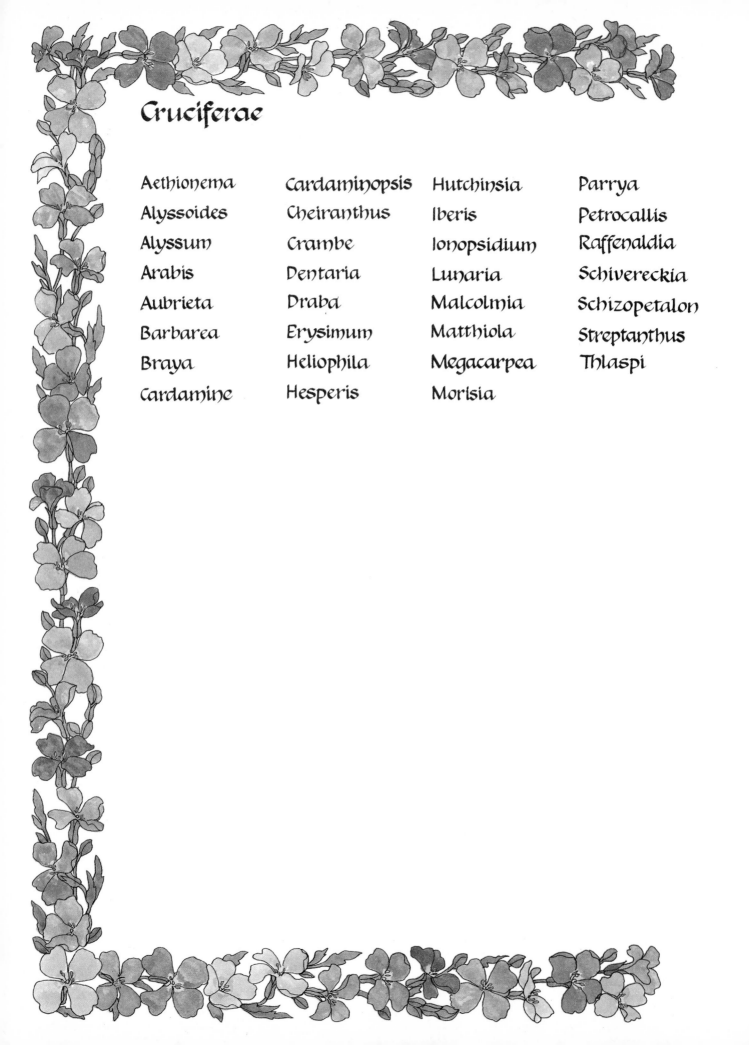

Cruciferae

Aethionema	Cardaminopsis	Hutchinsia	Parrya
Alyssoides	Cheiranthus	Iberis	Petrocallis
Alyssum	Crambe	Ionopsidium	Raffenaldia
Arabis	Dentaria	Lunaria	Schivereckia
Aubrieta	Draba	Malcolmia	Schizopetalon
Barbarea	Erysimum	Matthiola	Streptanthus
Braya	Heliophila	Megacarpea	Thlaspi
Cardamine	Hesperis	Morisia	

The Crucifer Family

Of all the families of plants the Crucifers are probably the easiest to identify: they have four petals and these form a cross. Hence, of course, the name Crucifer. The seeds are contained in pods, and these—of different shapes, called siliquas and siliculas—are characteristic of the family.

The flowers, most of which are fragrant, grow on long stalks up the stem, the lower flowers opening first (as with the wall-flower); but often (as in candytuft) they form a flat cluster at the top, this because the stalks grow longer and longer the farther they are down the stem. In this case the outer ring of flowers opens first, these being from the lowest stalks.

You can fill your garden with scent by growing only some of these Crucifers: *Hesperis matronalis*, the Sweet Rocket; *Cheiranthus cheiri*, the Wallflower; the dramatic white cloud of *Crambe cordifolia*; *Matthiola bicornis*, the Night-scented Stock and, most fragrant of all, the Brompton and Ten-week Stocks. These last two were the Stock Gilliflowers (July flowers) of the nineteenth-century gardeners, but it was John Tradescant who in 1627 first brought home from La Rochelle *Matthiola sinuata*, his "greatest Sea-Stocke Gilloflower" from which the Ten-week Stocks were later developed.

Other Crucifers have long been in our gardens. John Gerard, gardener to Lord Burghley in the sixteenth century, was growing "Arabis, Candie Mustard", in 1599, with "Barbarea, S. Barbaraes woort"; while "double yellow wallflowers" were already familiar.

Hybridists have developed these old friends to give us varieties pastel-shaded and 'brilliant' and 'large-flowered', dwarfer and taller. They have worked wonders with the simple 4-petalled flowers, and we are grateful. But sometimes it is good to look at the originals from which they were bred and find out what it was that attracted the plant hunters when they first saw them growing in the wild.

A large proportion of the family are ground-huggers, among them the drabas, which include some alpine aristocrats for the rock garden, and some common but still to be treasured—the arabis for its snowy cascade down an otherwise dull slope, the yellow alyssum for its sunshine, the so-easy-to-grow aubrietias for their colourful patchworks early in the spring.

The naming of a Crucifer

44

CARE AND CULTURE

The genera of this family come from the cold and temperate parts of both hemispheres, but they are especially abundant in the Mediterranean region, only a few hail from the tropics. So we do not look among them for exotics to fill our glasshouses but in two other directions —the vegetable garden where we grow edible Crucifers like cabbages, cauliflowers and kale; and our flower borders.

The family divides itself into three categories: annuals; small sub-shrubs and perennials suitable for the rock garden; and biennials we use in groups, like wall-flowers and stocks.

Many of them, as well as the annuals, can easily be grown from seed. Others can be increased by cuttings. If both these processes are carried out faithfully, the results should be a very flowery garden.

Let us look first at the annuals. There are not many of them and all are small. Sweet Alyssum (*Alyssum maritimum*) is as popular in America for pot culture and window gardens as it is in Britain for edging and bedding. Among the Cape Stocks (*Heliophila*, 'sun-loving') are some charming blue-flowered annuals, while the annual Candytuft (*Iberis*) is deservedly popular for its show of colour over the long flowering period of May to July.

Virginian Stock (*Malcolmia maritima*) and Night-scented Stock (*Matthiola bicornis*) should always be sown together: the latter fades by day to a drooping half-dead-looking plant, though unnoticed among the kaleidoscopic colours of its companion which helps to prop it up. But what an exquisite fragrance the pale lavender flowers give out at night! Their seeds can be scattered where you want them to grow, and this should always be where you walk in the evening, or by a window or french doors.

Lastly we have the Violet Cress or Diamond Flower (*Ionopsidium acaule*), a delightful little Portuguese annual not 2 in. high, which, once introduced, sows itself over and over and therefore has the virtues of a perennial.

Our second category are the sub-shrubs,

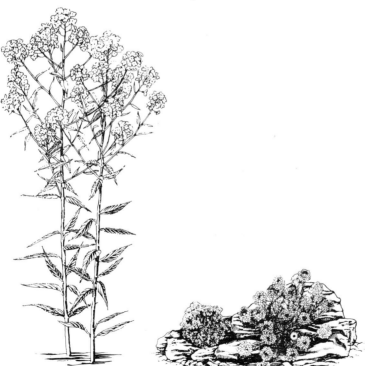

Hesperis matronalis

Thlaspi rotundifolium   *Aethionema*

Heliophila longifolia

Cheiranthus cheiri

the 'nearly-shrubs', perennial plants like the Burnt Candytuft (*Aethionema*) with wiry stems and forming a bush; the yellow alyssum (*saxatile*) with its tough half-woody stems; the perennial candy-tufts (*Iberis*) which form evergreen shrublets. All these species like dry sunny places and can be propagated by cuttings, an unflowered shoot joining a main stem gently torn off and forming a heel, to be dipped in water and then in hormone rooting powder, and planted in a pot or cold frame. *Aethionema* cuttings are taken from the soft growth tips and not from the woody shoots.

All these woody plants are good for the rock garden, as are the soft-foliaged Crucifers like aubrietia and arabis, the Rock Cress: there cannot be many rockeries without them, the first spreading carpets of colour in purple-blues and all the shades of pink to the richest burgundy; with white arabis single and double, and pink arabis from the most delicate to the deepest rose.

Among the drabas (the Whitlow Grass genus of which there are more than 250 species) are some of the choicest of all the alpines. They form mossy mats or charming cushions or tussocks of rosette leaves which usually become completely covered with golden-yellow or clearest-white flowers. North America is particularly rich in drabas. A close relative is *Petrocallis*, another alpine gem, and *Schivereckia* of silvery leaves, allied to *Alyssum*.

The erysimums give us some charmers in yellows and lilacs. *Morisia*, propagating readily from cuttings, forms clusters of evergreen leaves in which sit large golden flowers. The thlaspis from the High Alps have dense heads of fragrant lilac and pinky-lilac flowers.

When moving alpines, it is best—contrary to the accepted rule—to do it when they are in flower or just after. The reason is that the roots are annual: they grow from early spring to seeding time, and then cease to be active. Later, new fibres start to grow, but it is important to transfer the plant at its zenith.

Finally we have the biennials. The faithful Honesty (*Lunaria*) will clothe any

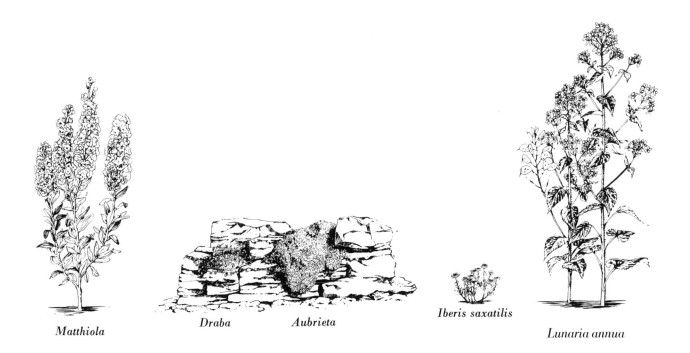

Matthiola   *Draba*   *Aubrieta*   *Iberis saxatilis*   *Lunaria annua*

bare spot with brilliant purple or red-purple heads of flowers and, having shed its seeds, make silvery moons of its empty pods to light up the dull winter days.

Hesperis is a biennial I would not be without, the Sweet Rocket or Dame's Violet. Its fragrance is wonderful and I leave it to seed as it likes.

Why is it that the Crucifers have such scent? Where would our spring borders be without the velvet sweetness of the wallflowers? They come in such glowing colours: golden-yellows and soft pinks, wine-reds and even attractive browns. What a glorious picture they create when massed together: contrasts and complements of colour and shades of colour like a Persian carpet.

Equally the stocks, the Bromptons and Ten-Weeks, are at their loveliest either in a flood of soft pastel colours or in rich pinks and purples. Not to have somewhere in the garden groups or masses of these fragrant beauties is to miss something of what a garden is all about.

Biennials can easily be grown from seed sown in the open, or in boxes, and transplanted to a nursery plot to form good-sized plants, and finally to their places in the border.

Propagating

Almost all the Crucifers can be grown easily from seed—either bought or, thereafter, collected from your own plants. The seeds of this family being contained in pods, you will know when they are ripe when the pods darken and become brittle: they can then be harvested and sown there and then in shallow pots or propagating trays.

The pods, siliquas and siliculas, do not differ essentially from each other: the term *silicula* is merely a diminutive of the other, denoting a very short and broad pod, as in the evergreen Candytuft; whereas a siliqua is long (like a pea-pod)

Matthiola bicornis
and *Malcolmia maritima*

as in the wallflowers, arabis, cardamine and stocks. Siliquas can also be elliptical or round like the pods of the Honesty and erysimum.

Seeds of course vary in size. The smaller they are the nearer the surface they should be sown, and for the very small it is not necessary to cover them with soil but only to press them gently into it. Sowing thinly is the golden rule. The soil should be very fine and neither too dry nor too moist. Never water immediately after sowing. Afterwards, according to need, it can be lightly sprayed.

It is interesting, by the way, that the seedlings of stocks with light leaves will have double flowers, and seedlings with dark leaves single flowers.

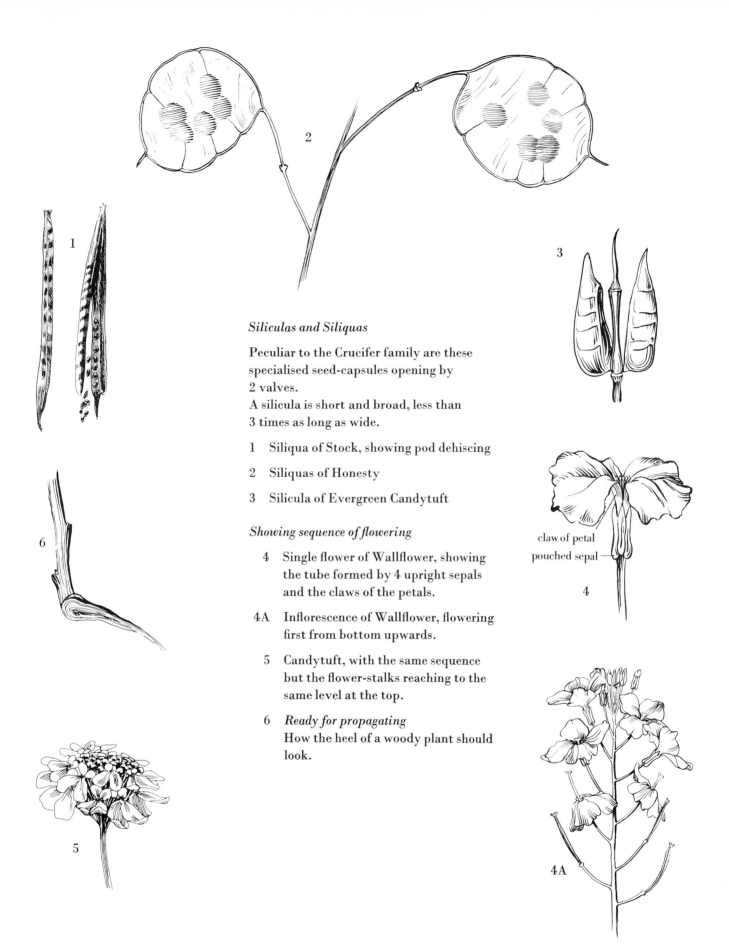

Siliculas and Siliquas

Peculiar to the Crucifer family are these specialised seed-capsules opening by 2 valves.
A silicula is short and broad, less than 3 times as long as wide.

1   Siliqua of Stock, showing pod dehiscing

2   Siliquas of Honesty

3   Silicula of Evergreen Candytuft

Showing sequence of flowering

4   Single flower of Wallflower, showing the tube formed by 4 upright sepals and the claws of the petals.

4A   Inflorescence of Wallflower, flowering first from bottom upwards.

5   Candytuft, with the same sequence but the flower-stalks reaching to the same level at the top.

6   *Ready for propagating*
How the heel of a woody plant should look.

claw of petal
pouched sepal

FLOWERS OF THE FAMILY

Aethionema, Burnt Candytuft or Dwarf Cress, is for the sunniest place in the rock garden. The name is from the scorched appearance of the stamens.

coridifolium from Asia Minor grows 4–6 in. (100–150 mm) high and has bluish foliage and rounded heads of rosy-lilac flowers in June. Good for crevices and troughs.

grandiflorum is a very beautiful plant from the Lebanon and Iran. It has long been a garden favourite in Britain and America, making 12 in. (300 mm) high bushes with crowded racemes of warm pink flowers from May to August.

iberideum from the eastern Mediterranean has mats of blue-grey leaves covered in April and May with spikes of white flowers. It grows 4 in. (100 mm) high.

'Warley Rose' was given an Award of Merit in 1913 by the Royal Horticultural Society (as *Aethionema armenum* 'Warley Hybrid'). It was a selected seedling which arose in the garden of the great Miss Ellen Willmott around 1910, since when it has been a popular shrublet for its beautiful racemes of rich pink flowers in May and June growing from a mound of blue-grey foliage.

Alyssum. There are not just two alyssums, the tiny white annual (*maritimum*) and the familiar yellow perennial (*saxatile*): the genus contains about 80 species of which more than two dozen are attractive rock plants.

alpestre, a tiny shrublet about 3 in. (75 mm) high, with oval silvery leaves and pale yellow flowers in June. It came from the Mediterranean and has been cultivated since 1777.

Aethionema 'Warley Rose'

Alyssum maritimum

pulchellum is a more trailing plant making twiggy mounds of intense blue foliage and sprays of rose-pink flowers. It is slightly taller at 6 in. (150 mm).

argenteum, a dense grower, about 15 in. (380 mm) high, the oblong leaves silvery beneath, yellow flowers up the stem and in a clustered head at the top all summer.

maritimum, Sweet Alyssum, the popular little annual. It is easily grown and a few seeds if sown in September in crevices or paving will make plants flowering early next summer. Once sown it will self-seed for ever. Besides white there are now charming coloured forms.

montanum makes mats of neat ash-grey hairy foliage, or can grow up to 6 in. (150 mm) high, with heads of soft yellow fragrant flowers from May to July.

saxatile, the larger popular alyssum, has some interesting varieties: 'Citrinum' of cool lemon-yellow flowers, April-May, 9 in. (230 mm); 'Gold Ball', dense heads of sweetly-scented brilliant golden-yellow flowers and silvery foliage, April-June; 'Dudley Neville', distinctive for its orange-buff flowers; 'Plenum', a very showy fully double form with golden flowers.

serpyllifolium, with mats of tiny thyme-like leaves of silver-grey and heads of deep yellow flowers April-June, 2 in. (50 mm). It makes a delightful little plant for trailing over the edge of a trough.

Arabis, Rock Cress, is another large genus of mostly small perennials for the rock garden and alpine house, a few tall for the border. They are easily grown.

albida (now *caucasica*), a fragrant early bloomer, January to May, grown in Britain since 1798. It is a variable little plant only a few inches high with white or pink or red flowers and two double forms: a magnificent white, 'Plena', and one tinged with pink.

alpina, one of the best rock plants, its rosettes of leaves adorned with star-shaped hairs, the 6 in. (150 mm) stems bearing clusters of white flowers March-May. There is a new selected variety 'Rose Frost' ('La Fraicheur') with deeper than rose-pink flowers. It is 4 in. (100 mm) high.

Arabis albida 'Flore pleno'

blepharophylla, a Californian species tender in Britain but good for the alpine house where it will flower in January with spikes of rich rosy-purple, pink or white, on 4–6 in. (100–150 mm) stems.

ferdinandi-coburgii from Macedonia forms mats of grey-green leaves in summer which become green in winter. With its mantle of white flowers it is one of the most charming of the species. The variegated-leaved form 'Variegata' is valuable as a compact foliage plant of green and white.

lyallii is a North-west American and Canadian species with pink flowers on foot-high stems which grows happily in Britain.
verna, best of the annuals, grows 3–6 in. (75–150 mm) high and has spikes of small purple flowers with a white claw, May to June. A good seeder for filling cracks and crevices.

Aubrieta is the Latin spelling, Aubrietia the pronunciation and thus spelt for the common name. There are many beautiful hybrids and forms, most of them springing from the species *deltoidea*, with a possible admixture of others such as *erubescens*, *kotschyi*, *libanotica* and perhaps *olympica*, though the last is sometimes regarded as only a form.

Aubrieta deltoidea

deltoidea is very variable, 2–12 in. (50–300 mm) high, with tufts of wedge-shaped toothed and hairy leaves. The colours range from lilac to red-purple. Good varieties are *bougainvillea* (light violet, dwarf and compact); *campbellii* (a large plant with large purple flowers); *eyrei* (flowers large and long, deep violet); *graeca* (a vigorous grower and one of the best, dwarf and compact, large light-purple flowers); *leichtlinii* (profuse pink flowers), and *violacea* (large deep-violet-purple flowers fading to reddish-violet).

Two other outstanding varieties are 'Argenteo-variegata' of striking silver-variegated foliage and lavender flowers; and an old favourite, 'Dr Mules' with vigorous bright-green foliage and rich violet-blue flowers.

erubescens is tall with tufts of small flowers, white at first becoming pink or pale lilac.

kotschyi, of prostrate growth, has hairy grey leaves and profuse small flowers, white to pale lilac or pink.

libanotica has dense tufts of grey-green hairy leaves. The flowers vary in size and colour, white to lilac. The pods are grey.

olympica is usually a dwarf tuft but can have tallish stems. The flowers are a pale soft purple.

Aubrietias can be layered as well as grown from seed or cuttings.

Cardamine. Only the perennial species are worth cultivating, and few of these are of interest to alpine gardeners. I recommend one of these and three suitable for the border.

latifolia has large lilac-pink flowers in June and grows 1–2 ft (300–600 mm) high. It is a handsome plant delighting in moist soil.

macrophylla is not quite as tall and grows from a creeping rootstock, with pale purple flowers in June. It also likes cool places by water.

pratensis is the wild Cuckoo Flower or Lady's Smock, of which the variety 'Plena', seedless and double, is very beautiful and can be increased by cuttings or division. The colours can be white, soft pink or pale purple. The flowers bloom from May to June on 9 in. (230 mm) stems.

trifolia is one for the rock garden in a cool partially shaded place. It has lush mats of rich green trefoil leaves, and the showy little heads of white flowers grow on scapes, that is stems without leaves, 4–6 in. (100–150 mm) high, March-May.

Cheiranthus cheiri

Cheiranthus cheiri 'Harpur Crewe'

Cheiranthus. The Wallflower is very much sold as a bedding plant, so you buy it by the boxful if you do not grow it from seed. Many of the species have been moved by the taxonomists into other genera, leaving us with only two we can definitely call *Cheiranthus*, but with a host of glorious hybrids.

cheiri grows tall, 1–2 ft (300–600 mm), and is erect, bushy and floriferous, the leaves lance-shaped, the fragrant flowers large and mostly in shades of yellow in long racemes. This is the wallflower from which most of our varieties descend, giving us a colour-range from palest pinks and yellows through every shade to glowing reds, goldens and browns.

Well known is 'Harpur Crewe', often grown in rock gardens and deservedly popular for its rounded bushes covered in spring and early summer with clusters of double yellow flowers sweetly fragrant. It asks for plenty of sunshine but poor rather than rich soil.

Another variety, very long-lived, is the lovely 'Moonlight' with its masses of pale lemon-yellow flowers. It grows to a height of 1 ft (300 mm).

semperflorens, a shrubby branching species 2–3 ft (600–900 mm) tall with flowers from January to December, at first cream, becoming purple or striped. A well-known variety is 'Wenlock Beauty' with smoky-purple flowers.

E. A. Bowles, the great gardener of Enfield in Middlesex, grew a mauve Wallflower for which he could not find a name. 'Bowles's Mauve' is now listed as a superb variety forming a vigorous erect bushlet with bluish foliage and large spikes of rich mauve-purple flowers in early summer and at times throughout the year.

× *allionii* is the Siberian Wallflower of bright orange flowers, about 1 ft (300 mm) tall. Although a perennial it is best treated as a biennial because it is apt to flower so freely as to kill itself.

Crambe. Of the 20 species in this genus only one, *cordifolia*, is suitable for the flower border. It makes a handsome and hardy plant, flowering from seed in its third year and thereafter annually. From a base of big heart-shaped leaves it throws up flower-stems which become a cloud of white in June, growing to a height of 3–6 ft (900 mm–1.8 m) and diffusing a honey-like scent. It is easily grown.

Crambe cordifolia

Dentaria. The Toothwort or Coral-root. The 30 or so species are perennials related to *Cardamine* but distinct from them by their leaves being mostly crowded towards the top of the stem, and their reddish flowers. Many are of American origin and some species are cultivated in rock gardens.

digitata is a European about 18 in. (460 mm) high with rich purple or soft-lilac flowers in May.

diphylla, the Pepper-root of North America, is a pretty spring flower whose petals are white inside and pale purple or pinkish outside. It grows 8–16 in. (200–400 mm) tall.

enneaphylla from the sub-alpine woodlands of the Eastern Alps has creamy flowers and bronze young foliage, making it an attractive plant. Its height is about 12 in. (300 mm), and it flowers in May.

macrocarpa has rosy or purple flowers and is a native of North California to British Columbia. It is 4-15 in. (100-380 mm) high.

pinnata, another European, is one of the handsomest species with heads of 12 to 15 pure white or pale purple flowers in May and fresh green palmate leaves. It grows about 1 ft (300 mm) tall.

Draba. Spread across the temperate and arctic regions of the world many of the species inhabit mountains, which makes them true alpine plants. All are dwarf and spring-flowering.

aizoides grows well and is an early flowerer with masses of yellow heads in March and April rising on 2 in. (50 mm) stems from deep-green bristly rosettes.

alpina forms dense patches of rosettes, its heads of yellow flowers carried on short downy stems. Among its many varieties is *glacialis* with sulphur-yellow flowers. The species comes from the arctic regions. *bryoides* var. *imbricata* makes hard mounds of green mossy rosettes and produces showy yellow flowers on thread-like stems. It is even smaller and more compact than the species and is ideal for troughs and screes. Its height is up to 2 in. (50 mm).

mollissima from the Caucasus is for the alpine house where it must grow in soil that

Draba molissima

Erysimum alpinum
'Moonlight'

is gritty but not lacking in humus; water from below by plunging the pot into half a bowl of water. It will reward your care, for it is a gem of domed hummocks of soft stems and tiny grey-haired leaves covered over in spring with a shock of soft-yellow star-like flowers.

polytricha makes a dense rounded hummock of soft grey-green foliage in neat symmetrical rosettes, with clusters of bright yellow flowers in April on frail 2 in. (50 mm) stems.

rigida has hard bright-green pads of minute leaves and thread-like stems 2 in. (50 mm) high, bearing golden-yellow flowers.

rosularia is a choice plant for the alpine house with its grey mounds of foliage smothered with pale yellow flowers in early spring. It grows slightly taller than 3 in. (70 mm).

Erysimum. The perennial dwarf Wallflower. This genus contains, however, both the tall and the small in annuals, biennials and perennials. Some of the species are those transferred from *Cheiranthus*, the true Wallflower, and there are some lovely hybrids.

alpinum is a perennial about 6 in. (150 mm) high, with fragrant sulphur flowers in May. 'Moonlight' has paler flowers over mats of dark green foliage.

linifolium is a rock garden overgreen with slender stems 5–15 in. (120–380 mm) long and dense racemes of fascinating flowers from May to July: the petals purple and violet, the anthers greenish. There is a most attractive variegated-leaved form.

perofskianum, an annual about 1 ft (300 mm) tall with erect leaves and reddish-brown flowers. Sow at different times for a succession of bloom, and in the autumn for spring flowering.

pumilum 'Golden Gem' is a June-October flowerer with heads of deep golden-yellow, seeding itself freely. Height 6 in. (150 mm). Indeed a gem for the rock garden.

Heliophila. The Cape Stock is a native of South Africa, its botanical name meaning sun-loving. There are both annuals and sub-shrubs in the genus, with yellow, white, rosy or blue flowers.

linearifolia is a very variable species 6–24 in. (150–600 mm) high, with flowers from July to September normally sky-blue with a yellow centre but sometimes lilac with yellow. The leaves are hairy or smooth but always narrow and grassy.

Heliophila longifolia

longifolia is an enchanting and half-hardy annual up to 18 in. (450 mm) high, with delicate sprays of bright blue white-eyed flowers among the same grassy leaves. It is easy to grow outdoors and makes an attractive pot for a cool greenhouse.

Hesperis. Was given its name from the Greek word for evening, the time when the flowers are most fragrant.

matronalis, Dame's Violet, Damask Violet or Sweet Rocket, is the popular species, 2–3 ft (600–900 mm) high, providing lovely spikes of flowers in various colours, single and double.

Hutchinsia is a genus of only eight species, of which the tiny *alpina* is a gem for sink gardens, as well as for special nooks in the rock garden, with its shining feathery leaves covered with snow-white spikes of flowers from May to July and often through the summer. It grows 1–4 in. (25–100 mm) high.

Iberis. Candytuft. The three well-known species are easy, useful and decorative—*umbellata*, the Common or Globe Candytuft, a sweet-scented annual, and the evergreen shrublets *saxatilis* and *sempervirens*. In addition, there are others for the border and rock garden.

sempervirens itself is the parent of some charming varieties, all usually dwarfer. Two are compact forms for the rock garden or front of the border—'Snowflake' and 'Little Gem'.

amara, the Rocket or Hyacinth-flowered Candytuft, is distinct in type from the common annual. It produces a spike of flowers, white and fragrant, commencing in a cluster but soon lengthening. Growing erect, 6–15 in. (150–375 mm) high, it flowers throughout the summer, according to autumn or spring sowing.

tenoreana is sometimes called *jucunda*. Whichever name you use it is a superb plant forming neat mounds of glossy dark-green toothed leaves, hidden from May to July under clouds of enormous (relatively) white and soft pink flowers. Its height is 3–4 in. (75–100 mm), and it is very showy and easy to grow.

Iberis saxatilis

Ionopsidium acaule

gibraltarica has larger clusters and larger flowers and is probably the most striking and showy of the perennial kinds. The outer flowers are pink, the inner ones white. Unfortunately what is often sold is not the true species but a form of *sempervirens*. It should be a 9 in. (230 mm) evergreen with dark narrow wedge-shaped leaves toothed at the apex. It flowers in early summer.

Ionopsidium. The Diamond Flower has only two species, of which *acaule* from Portugal can hold its own in beauty with the choicest alpines in the rock garden. The violet, white, or flesh-coloured little flowers among tiny round leaves bloom summer, autumn and winter. Sown where it is to grow, it will flower two months later. Though it seeds freely it is never invasive. It likes growing in the shade.

Matthiola. The fragrant genus of which the two species *incana* and *sinuata* are the parents of our garden stocks. There are two main groups: the Summer Stocks, annuals and usually called Ten-week Stocks because they flower in ten or so weeks from the sowing of the seeds; and the Winter Stocks which include the Intermediate, East Lothian, and Queen or Brompton Stocks. Biennials, these last are sown in one year to flower the next.

The two types cover the entire blooming season, but the winter-flowering stocks are really the more useful, for they may also be grown for summer bedding, and they produce larger plants and finer flowers.

They also make good indoor plants.

To the two types we must now add a sub-type, to include the Trysomic Seven-week Stocks, earliest of all and blooming in seven weeks from sowing. These are branching plants producing 85 percent of double flowers in a brilliant colour blend. They grow 15–18 in. (380–450 mm) tall. It is easy to find which plants will bloom double and which single. With double stocks the results are 50-50 according to whether the seedling leaves are light (double) or dark (single). In the case of the Trysomic seedlings the vigorous ones will be double, the weak ones single.

Matthiola sinuata,
Brompton Stock strain

Matthiola,
Ten Week Stock strain

The original wild species are no longer grown in gardens, and so it is to their hybrids we look for our border plants.

Ten-week Stocks bloom from May to October. There are dwarf varieties and taller kinds 1½–2 ft (450–600 mm). Winter-flowering Brompton Stocks bloom outdoors from March to May, earlier if grown in a cold greenhouse. The East Lothian type if sown in February or March will flower from July to September. These may also be sown in early autumn, wintered in a frame and planted out in spring for summer bedding.

The flowers of both groups of stocks range from white, pink, and yellow to crimson and mauve, and through all the shades between.

Megacarpea. This genus does not offer us in *polyandra* superb blooms; though its heads are covered with hundreds of tiny yellowish-white or violet flowers, it is not for these that we admire this plant, but for its enormous pinnate leaves. It is a robust plant growing up to 6 ft (1.8 m) tall or more, with several stems rising from a crown. The basal leaves are 2½ ft (760 mm) long, and are toothed and slightly softly hairy. Grow it if you have space in a sunny situation.

Petrocallis. Closely related to *Draba* and comprising only a few species, of which *pyrenaica* is a treasure from the high screes of the European Alps. It makes neat mounded cushions of downy shoots, and the innumerable white flowers tinged with lilac and very fragrant are borne on 2 in. (50 mm) stems. Fittingly, its botanical name means Rock Beauty. It flowers in May and can be raised from seed but is best propagated by pieces pulled off the side in late August or early September, and rooted in sand.

Schivereckia. A genus with only two species, and these are both sun-loving dwarf perennials with rosettes of silvery leaves; *doerfleri*, about 2 in. (50 mm) high, and *podolica*, 5–7 in. (120–180 mm) high. Both have white flowers in spring and summer.

Schizopetalon. A half-hardy annual of this genus, *walkeri*, is grown for the almond fragrance of its white evening flowers which are not showy, though the deeply cut petals are dainty and feathery. Sow the seed in April and May for July-September flowering. It grows 9–12 in. (230–300 mm) high.

Streptanthus. The name means 'twisted flower', referring to the sepals which in some species are twisted. Most of the 13 species of annuals and perennials are natives of western North America. The leaves are attractive: long and heart-shaped, and clasping the stem up which the flowers grow alternately.

Megacarpea polyandra

hyacinthoides is an annual species 2–3 ft (600–900 mm) tall with deep-bluish-purple flowers in September.

maculatus is also an annual, less tall at 18 in. (450 mm) or sometimes more, the racemes of flowers with petals deep velvety-purple in the middle and lighter towards the edges. It flowers in August.

Thlaspi. The larger annual species (like *arvense*, the Field Penny Cress) are weeds. The smaller perennials, on the other hand, are "the most precious and charming of high Alpines from the lonely shingles", as Reginald Farrer, that great plantsman, called them. All over the high limestone screes grows *rotundifolium*, one of the loveliest of all alpines, forming a tight tussock 6 in. (150 mm) across, among the stones, covered by the packed heads of its large fragrant rosy-lavender flowers.

The Greek species *bulbosum* can also be recommended for its rich rose-purple flowers on 4–6 in. (100–150 mm) stems and neat rosettes of leathery spoon-shaped leaves.

Thlaspi rotundifolium

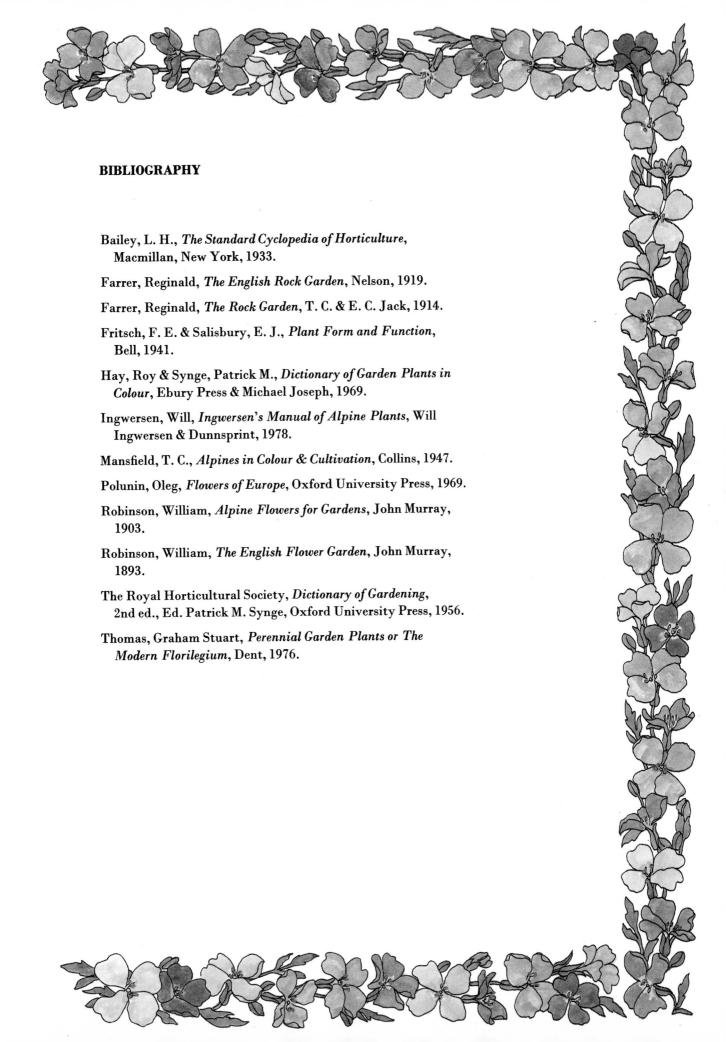

BIBLIOGRAPHY

Bailey, L. H., *The Standard Cyclopedia of Horticulture*, Macmillan, New York, 1933.

Farrer, Reginald, *The English Rock Garden*, Nelson, 1919.

Farrer, Reginald, *The Rock Garden*, T. C. & E. C. Jack, 1914.

Fritsch, F. E. & Salisbury, E. J., *Plant Form and Function*, Bell, 1941.

Hay, Roy & Synge, Patrick M., *Dictionary of Garden Plants in Colour*, Ebury Press & Michael Joseph, 1969.

Ingwersen, Will, *Ingwersen's Manual of Alpine Plants*, Will Ingwersen & Dunnsprint, 1978.

Mansfield, T. C., *Alpines in Colour & Cultivation*, Collins, 1947.

Polunin, Oleg, *Flowers of Europe*, Oxford University Press, 1969.

Robinson, William, *Alpine Flowers for Gardens*, John Murray, 1903.

Robinson, William, *The English Flower Garden*, John Murray, 1893.

The Royal Horticultural Society, *Dictionary of Gardening*, 2nd ed., Ed. Patrick M. Synge, Oxford University Press, 1956.

Thomas, Graham Stuart, *Perennial Garden Plants or The Modern Florilegium*, Dent, 1976.

The Daisy Family

Compositae

Achillea	Celmisia	Gamolepsis	Mutisia
Ageratum	Centaurea	Gazania	Olearia
Ammobium	Charieis	Gerbera	Onopordon
Anacyclus	Chrysanthemum	Grindelia	Osteospermum
Anaphalis	Chrysogonum	Haplopappus	Perezia
Antennaria	Coreopsis	Helenium	Pyrethrum
Anthemis	Cosmos	Helianthus	Raoulia
Arctotis	Crepis	Helichrysum	Rudbeckia
Arnica	Cynara	Heliopsis	Santolina
Artemisia	Dahlia	Helipterum	Sanvitalia
Aster	Dimorphotheca	Homogyne	Senecio
Baeria	Doronicum	Hymenoxis	Serratula
Bellis	Echinops	Inula	Solidago
Boltonia	Emilia	Lasthenia	Stokesia
Brachycome	Erigeron	Layia	Tagetes
Bupthalmum	Eriphyllum	Leontopodium	Tithonia
Calendula	Eupatorium	Leptosyne	Townsendia
Callistephus	Euryops	Leucogenes	Ursinia
Carduncellus	Felicia	Leuzia	Urospermum
Carlina	Gaillardia	Liatris	Xeranthemum
Catananche	Galacites	Ligularia	Zinnia

The Daisy Family

This is the largest of all the families of flowers. Its members can be found growing right across the world in every sort of location. There are more than 14,000 species in over 900 genera, yet they are the most easily recognizable of all flowers.

No one can mistake a daisy. Whether tall or short, splendid in colour or of modest white, single or double, the daisy proclaims itself, its so-called petals radiating out from a central disk, often yellow, which is a collection of flowers, just as the petals are another collection of flowers, each one complete in itself. Hence the name Composite, meaning a composition. The flowers in the centre are called disk-florets, the ones radiating outwards, ray-florets. A few other families have daisy-like flowers, but a single character distinguishes them from Compositae: the daisy's anthers are always joined.

The daisies are important border flowers. What would our September days be without the perennial glories of dahlias, Michaelmas Daisies and chrysanthemums?

And what would flower-arrangers do without the grey and silver foils of Senecios, Anaphalis and Artemesias?

There is one perennial, *Achillea*, whose flowers make the gold plates of its most popular variety. An August border without 'Gold Plate' would be the poorer. The goldfinches would never forgive me if I did not plant Cosmea for its seeds. The name means 'adornment'. How welcome are their white, pink, and crimson daisies throughout the weeks of July till October.

The family has also given us those pretty paper-like flowers we call everlastings or immortelles, the Strawflowers of the African *Helichrysum*, the Australian *Ammobium* and Persian *Xeranthemum*. These were used as mourning flowers for George Peabody, the quiet American who did so much for Anglo-American friendship.

So many daisies from so many places—they would form a floral United Nations. *Brachycome*, the Swan River Daisy, from Australia; *Callistephus*, the China Aster, from China; *Buphthalmum*, the Ox-eye, from Austria; and *Leontopodium*, the Edelweiss, from Switzerland; *Celmisia* from New Zealand; Asters galore from the United States, and a host of delegates from South Africa—an enchanting summer and autumn garden with flowers of every colour, delicate and dazzling, bold and shy.

Celmisia coriacea

64

CARE AND CULTURE

Because of the very similarity of the Composites, if we pulled some hundreds of flower-heads and placed them side by side in a square, such a carpet of daisies would present a bewildering sight, especially if we culled them from a garden sown and planted for autumn colour. Where would *Helenium* begin and *Gazania* end, and what of the ones between—*Gaillardia*, *Heliopsis*, *Coreopsis* and the others? How to know which is which? But each will have some distinction: petals rounded at the tips or pointed; leaf-shape; the arrangement of the flowers on their stems, and so on.

Daisies are not difficult subjects. Most of the annuals can be sown where they are to grow, or if sown under glass they are easily transplantable. The shrubby santolinas and senecios are hardy or require only minimal shelter, while celmisias are happiest in a northerly temperate climate where they will get snow in winter—though the name Snow Daisy refers to its white flowers and leaves. The many perennials from South Africa can withstand a surprising amount of cold, but a warm sunny corner will help if not ensure survival.

Sun the daisies must have. The very name means 'day's eye'. The flower-heads close when the sun goes down, and even during the day when the sun is obscured by clouds. So it is no use planting daisies in a totally shaded border and expecting them

| *Centaurea Cyanus* | *Pompon dahlia* | *Rudbeckia* | *Zinnia* | *Achillea fillipendul* |

to show you smiling faces.

The very first daisy to appear in the garden is *Bellis perennis* that infests our lawns. We would not dream of tolerating that in our gardens, but we might find a place for the pretty daisies developed from it: I have a small corner where I grow double whites among white violets.

But it is in summer when the sun is at its fullest and the days longest that daisies come into their own. Then a flood of them springs into life: the big white Shasta Daisy created from weeds by Luther Burbank, the great American hybridist; the lovely pyrethrums, rosy-pink and crimson, so good for cutting; the marigolds of all kinds and particularly the common

Calendula for its pure-orange sunshine; for a spot of drama *Carlina acanthifolia*, a single yellow sunburst flat against the ground; the African Daisy, *Arctotis*, of brilliant iridescent colours, annual and perennial, with a range of fine hybrids. The catalogue is almost endless.

Year after year the faithful Globe Thistle, *Echinops*, displays its drumstick heads of metallic blue in August, on the threshold of autumn. Then in these golden days we can enjoy more of the sun-heads: the *Helianthus* whose name—from *helios* and *anthos*—literally means sun-flower, and *Helipterum*, one of the Australian everlastings, from *helios* and *pteron*, a wing, to name but two of the sun-lovers.

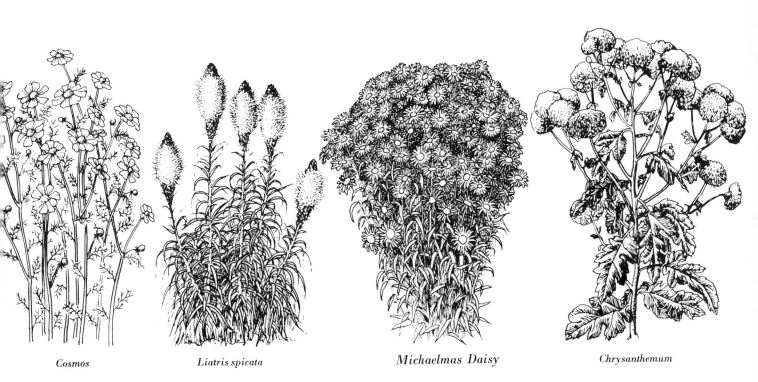

Cosmos

Liatris spicata

Michaelmas Daisy

Chrysanthemum

But of all the autumn daisies none is so glorious as the chrysanthemum, in full beauty when summer is over and winter looms ahead—the flower of the East as the rose is the flower of the West. It began as a wayside weed in China where it was developed into beautiful forms. In Europe and America it has also—deservedly—become a cult, with its devotees of the 'Mop-head', 'Spider', and what is commonly called the garden chrysanthemum.

Second only to the chrysanthemums are the dahlias, half-hardy, and in a temperate zone their tubers will need to be lifted before winter. Good compost is important in their cultivation, and they flourish in a slightly acid soil (pH 6–5). Versatile in form, dahlias range from the Miniature Cactus to the Large Decoratives, as classified by Britain's National Dahlia Society, which lists their varieties in ten divisions of colour: white, yellow, orange or bronze, red, pink, mauve or lavender, wine or purple, blends, bicoloured and variegated. Translate these into a border of dahlias— the result is a stunning spectacle. The dwarf 'bedding' dahlias can be treated as annuals and are good for gap-filling.

Michaelmas Day, the festival of St Michael, is September 29th when

Michaelmas Daisies are giving us their glorious blues, purples, pinks and crimsons. The name loosely covers most of the perennial species and hybrids popularly grown, the genus being *Aster*. The species *tradescantii*, introduced from Virginia in 1633 by the younger John Tradescant, is one of the last flowers of autumn, its myriad small white daisies hovering over the border like a mist. They linger on, past late September, when the annuals of brilliant blues and pinks called China Asters (*Callistephus*) have gone and winter is nearly upon us.

Propagating

Grow the annuals and biennials from seed, the perennials from rootstocks, dahlias by division of the tubers. Propagate the shrubby plants from cuttings, as described in the chapter on Crucifers (page 47). A good tip for the final stage is to plant the cuttings *round the edge* of the pot: they root better this way. Keep moist but do not over-water or the stems will rot, and this applies particularly to cuttings of softer woods. To lessen the risk, let sappy cuttings wither for a day or so or, if planted immediately they are removed from the parent plant, give no water until the second or third day.

Carlina acanthifolia

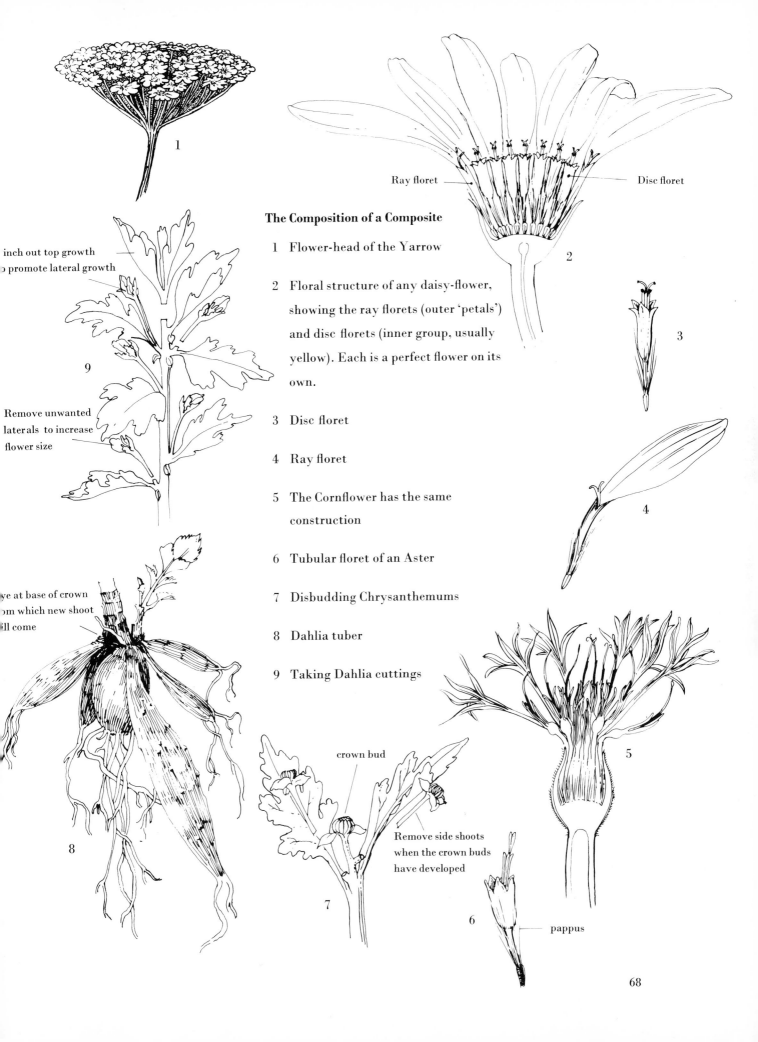

Ray floret

Disc floret

The Composition of a Composite

1 Flower-head of the Yarrow

2 Floral structure of any daisy-flower, showing the ray florets (outer 'petals') and disc florets (inner group, usually yellow). Each is a perfect flower on its own.

3 Disc floret

4 Ray floret

5 The Cornflower has the same construction

6 Tubular floret of an Aster

7 Disbudding Chrysanthemums

8 Dahlia tuber

9 Taking Dahlia cuttings

inch out top growth
promote lateral growth

Remove unwanted
laterals to increase
flower size

e at base of crown
m which new shoot
ll come

crown bud

Remove side shoots
when the crown buds
have developed

pappus

FLOWERS OF THE FAMILY

To aid the gardener in his choice, we have divided the Composites into six groups: Annuals and Biennials; Annuals whose cousins may be Perennials; Perennials; Everlastings; Grey- and Silver-leaved; Alpines and small plants.

Annuals and Biennials

Ageratum. The Floss Flower, *conyzoides*, is the blue fuzzy-headed dwarf plant for bedding and edging, half-hardy and best raised under glass, flowering in July until the first frost. There are purple, pink and white forms. A tall variety attaining 1½ ft (450 mm) is *mexicanum* of soft lavender-blue, useful for cutting.

Arctotis. The African Daisy has only one annual in its genus, *grandis*, with long-stemmed silvery-white flowers in autumn, with mauve centres ringed by a golden band. The strain known as Arctotis Hybrids bear large daisies in a range of brilliant colours, pale yellow to orange and red, pink, bronze and white. Height 1–1½ ft (300–450 mm).

Baeria. Two species, *coronaria* and *gracilis*, have masses of small golden-yellow flowers from July to September, and finely-cut foliage.

Calendula. The Garden or Pot Marigold is distinctive for its pungent scent and for flowering almost throughout the year, the 1–1½ ft (300–450 mm) stems bearing brilliant orange flowers, mainly double, the ray-florets with crimped tips. Hybrids of the species *officinalis* produce daisies of creamy-yellow, clear lemon-yellow, dark orange, light orange with a maroon centre, and shades in between.

Callistephus. The China Aster (*C. chinensis*) of vivid blue, violet and white daisies, commonly called the Aster in Britain, is the parent of a vast range of varieties, single and double, from 6 in. to 2½ ft (150 – 800 mm) in height, and of many colours. They have been classified into groups such as the Ostrich Feather type, the Quilled, and the Pompon. America developed the large-flowered and long-stemmed florists' varieties, valuable for cutting.

Callistephus chinensis

Charieis. This dwarf South African plant has a compact habit, making it suitable for edgings. The species *heterophylla* has deep blue daisies from July till September, with golden or deep-blue centres. There are white, dark violet, violet-red and pink varieties.

Emilia. The name Tassel Flower or Flora's Paint Brush applies to the species *saggitata*, easily grown, with clustered heads of bright scarlet like miniature tassels from June to October. Height 1–2 ft (300–600 mm).

Layia. A distinctive Californian daisy is *elegans* whose yellow flowers are often

69

tipped with white, giving it the name Tidy Tips. It's one of the best-known and generally most useful species, flowering July–September, height 1 ft (300 mm).

Ursinia. These showy plants bear masses of flowers in brilliant shades of orange and yellow, and unlike many other South African daisies remain fully open all day. Two good species are the bushy *anethoides* with bright orange flowers zoned with crimson-purple, and fern-like foliage; and *pulchra*, forming a compact little bush covered with rich orange flowers having a dark central ring. 'Golden Bedder', light orange with a deeper orange centre, is the popular variety.

Zinnia elegans

Zinnia. Mexican and half-hardy, these must be sown in a warm greenhouse and potted singly before transplanting early in June, or when the frosts are over. But their lovely vibrant colours—lilac, scarlet, crimson and rose, pale buff and white, are worth working for. The species *elegans*, called Youth and Old Age, blooms summer to autumn and grows 2–2½ ft (600–800 mm) tall; *haageana*, midsummer to mid-autumn, has single golden-yellow or orange flowers and is the parent of many dwarf double varieties.

Annuals and Perennials

Centaurea. This somewhat thistle-like flower is known under various names, according to the species. As *cyanus*, flowering in May and June, it is the annual Cornflower, Blue Bottle or Batchelor's Button, a fluffy flower with variants in white and pink, and fine varieties in doubles of these colours, all about 3 ft (900 mm) tall and good for cutting, with double dwarf forms about 1 ft (300 mm) high.

Centaurea cyanus 'Julep'

As *moschata*, also an annual, it is the Sweet Sultan, even fluffier, the tips of the ray-florets being much cut. Attractive, with scented flowers from July to September, pinkish-purple, white or yellow, it grows to 1½ ft (450 mm).

The Perennial Cornflower, *dealbata*, is very similar with finely-divided light-green leaves, greyish beneath. Rather a floppy plant but worth growing for its beautiful lilac-pink flowers from midsummer to mid-autumn. Height 3 ft (900 mm).

The Mountain Knapweed, *montana*, is useful because it flowers early, in June. Its flower is more open, deep blue with a reddish centre, with white, pink, deep amethyst and other forms. Height 18 in. (450 mm).

70

Chrysanthemum. This is a large genus containing many garden favourites different from each other. There are both annuals and perennials, and both have been highly hybridised to give us an even wider range of form and colour.

Annuals

These should be sown outdoors where they are to grow, as they do not move well. Four species are recommended.

carinatum (*tricolor*), a Moroccan daisy ringed with yellow at the base and with a purple centre, the ray-florets red, hence its old name of *tricolor*. Among the varieties are the 'Monarch Court Jesters' of many combinations of three colours. Flowering June to September, height 1½–2 ft (450–600 mm).

coronarium, a Mediterranean species with single flowers of pale yellow and finely cut foliage. Good doubles, 'Golden Crown' one of the best with quilled petals of bright yellow. July to October, 1½–3 ft (450–900 mm).

parthenium, an annual or biennial of many synonyms but familiar as Feverfew, in its golden-leaved form Golden Feather, much used for bedding and edging. Height 1 ft (300 mm). A dwarf form, Golden Moss (*aureum crispum*), has parsley-like foliage.

sagetum is the native Corn Marigold of single yellow flowers, from which some excellent varieties have been bred: 'Eastern Star', primrose-yellow with a chocolate centre; the deep-yellow 'Eldorado', and the golden-yellow 'Evening Star'.

Perennials

The perennial outdoor species provide distinctive border flowers.

coccineum, the Pyrethrum of florists and garden, lovely flowers in the early summer,

Chrysanthemum coccineum 'Vanessa'

single and double, white, pink and crimson, excellent for cutting. Height 2 ft (600 mm).

frutescens, the summer-flowering Paris Daisy or French Marguerite—but from the Canary Islands, a shrubby plant with a succession of yellow-centred daisies in white, pink, and yellow forms, singles and doubles. Height 3 ft (900 mm).

maximum, the Shasta Daisy, a must for every garden, with its huge white daisies a perfect foil for lupins, delphiniums, and oriental poppies. The original type is a bold single flower, newer kinds have fringed petals or are doubles like 'Esther Read' and 'Wirral Supreme'. Height 3 ft (900 mm).

nipponicum from Japan gives us pure-white single flowers in autumn into November. Semi-shrubby, height 2 ft (600 mm).

uliginosum, the Hungarian Daisy and another autumn-flowerer, taller at 6 ft (1.8 m) and wonderful for the back of a big border with its large white daisies; also for the wild garden, as it will naturalise in grass.

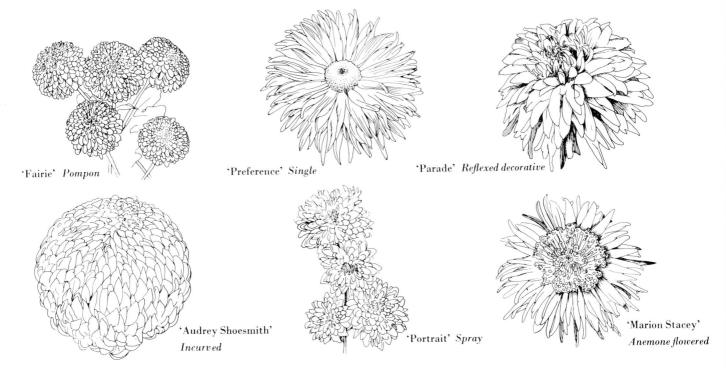

'Fairie' *Pompon*

'Preference' *Single*

'Parade' *Reflexed decorative*

'Audrey Shoesmith'
Incurved

'Portrait' *Spray*

'Marion Stacey'
Anemone flowered

While the annual and perennial species have been extensively hybridised, varieties of the annuals differ little from the type, except in flower-colour and size, and some of these we have already mentioned. It is different with the perennials, bred to such a wide variety that for show purposes they have been classified by chrysanthemum Societies into twenty-four groups and sections according to the type of bloom. This classification includes Exhibition Incurved; Reflexed Decoratives; Anemone-flowered; Spidery-flowered; Pompons; and Sprays, applying chiefly to those for flowering under glass in autumn and winter from cuttings taken in February-March. Some of the classes apply to the outdoor hybrids.

We have selected a few special hybrids for indoor and outdoor growing:

Petals incurved, forming a globe: Indoor, 'Audrey Shoesmith', pink; 'Frances Jefferson', light bronze. Outdoor, 'Topper', golden.

Petals—outer reflexing, inner incurving: Indoor, 'Flash', crimson; 'Parade', red. Outdoor, 'Cherry Glow', bright bronzy-red; 'Headliner', deep pink.

Pompons: Indoor, 'Dresden China'; 'Baby'. Outdoor, 'Glow', golden-orange; 'Bunty', white, shading to orange centre; 'Fairie', deep rose.

Single: Indoor, 'Peggy Stevens', yellow; 'Preference', pink with a pale centre. Outdoor, 'Daphne'; 'Bessie'.

Spray: Indoor, 'Portrait', pink, reflexing. Special American Sprays: 'Tuneful', single, yellow, red, bronze; 'Marble', single, yellow, bronze, pink, white.

The following are for indoors only: the beautiful Anemone-flowered 'Marion Stacey', purple, and 'Yellow Grace Land', both single; the Spidery, Plumed, and Feathery section of increasing popularity— 'King of the Plumes', and the type of which the rosy-purple 'Rayonante' is an exquisite example.

There are also the tall Korean hybrids raised by Alexander Cumming of Bristol, Connecticut, and the much-branched dwarfs recently introduced into Britain. A yet-newer Korean is 'Wedding Day', a single white with a green centre instead of the usual yellow.

Coreopsis. The Tickseed has splendid flowers in yellows, browns and crimsons marked and zoned in contrasting colours. The annual species is usually confused in seed catalogues as *Calliopsis*.

coronata, an annual of branching habit with large orange-yellow flowers marked at the base with maroon. July–September, height 1½ ft (450 mm).

drummondii, one of the best, with large clear yellow flowers marked with maroon. July–September. Height 1½–2 ft (450–600 mm).

tinctoria, yellow flowers zoned with crimson-brown, up to 2½ ft (800 mm) high. There are many fine forms dwarf and compact, marbled and striped.

verticillata, a perennial bushy plant with bright brassy-yellow daisies for months on end. 'Golden Shower', of a warmer yellow, is the best form. Height 1 ft (300 mm).

Cosmos. The tall annual, *C. bipinnatus*, is a charmer, single, white, pink, and crimson, flowering July till October among lacy foliage. The finest variety is 'Gloria', of large bicoloured flowers up to 5 in. (125 mm) across, rose with a maroon-red zone.

A contrasting perennial is *atrosanguineus*, half-hardy with dahlia-like tubers, bearing dark velvety-red flowers, chocolate-scented, continually till autumn. Height 2½ ft (760 mm).

Cosmos bipinnatus

Gaillardia. Blanket Flowers as annuals
are easily grown, though best treated as
half-hardy, and valuable for cutting. Of
these, *amblyodon* from Texas has blood-red
flowers from July to September, height
1–2 ft (300–600 mm); *pulchella*, handsome
crimson-purple flowers tipped with yellow,
July to October, height 15–18 in. (400–
450 mm). Good forms of this are the
bronze-red *picta* 'Indian Chief' and its mixed
strains, with a double in *picta lorenziana*
whose ray-florets, enlarged and tubular,
form a globe. The strain known as 'Blood
Red Giants' has larger and long
stemmed flowers.

Two perennials are *aristata* with yellow
and red flowers and many colourful hybrids
from summer to mid-autumn, while the
large daisies of *grandiflora* are flamboyant
in colours from deep yellow to maroon-red
around a reddish-brown centre. Height
2–3 ft (600–900 mm).

Helianthus. The Sunflower has two annual
species of which *annuus* is the one familiar
in cottage gardens, a huge clock-face of a
daisy. It can attain a height of 12 ft
(3.70 m) and has many hybrids including
double forms and a 'dwarf' 15–18 in.
(400–450 mm) high. Mixed strains have
produced creamy-white, bronze-red and
maroon flowers.

Of the several perennial species,
atrorubens has a notable hybrid in
'Monarch' of gorgeous semi-double
flowers like a cactus dahlia, brilliant deep-
yellow with a black centre; while
scaberrimus with its running roots will
never leave a hole in your borders. Its
decorative bright yellow flowers with dark
brown centres come in late summer.
Height 5 ft (1.5 m).

Tagetes. The many garden varieties have
been developed from four species, and
these, with their hybrids, divide into two
groups: 1. the African Marigold (*erecta*)

Helianthus annuus

with the Sweet-scented Marigold (*lucida*,
the only perennial); and 2. the two species
of French Marigold, *patula* and *tenuifolia*
(*signata*), spreading and bushy plants up to
1½ ft (450 mm) high. Despite their names,
all are natives of Mexico; the annual
species is therefore half-hardy.

Though the flowers of *erecta* are single,
yellow or orange, its varieties include tall
and dwarf doubles and carnation-flowered
doubles, all strongly aromatic. Varieties
with odourless foliage have been bred in
America from the parent *lucida* which has
no garden value compared with the
varieties. The parent of the French
Marigolds is *patula* with flower-heads of
numerous ray-florets usually yellow with
red markings. There are many fine
varieties, single, double, and dwarf.

The freely-branching *tenuifolia* is the
smallest of the species, the compact form
pumila only 9 in. (200 mm) high, but
covering itself with bright yellow starry
flowers.

Perennials

Achillea. The Yarrow of our gardens, the tall decorative plant with bright yellow flower-heads, flat and solid, without ray-florets, with feathery aromatic foliage.

filipendulina is the species we grow at the back of our herbaceous borders, rising to 4 ft (1.25 m) and sometimes even taller. It blooms from late June or July and keeps its colour when cut for the winter. 'Gold Plate' is the most popular form; 'Coronation Gold' is not so tall and has greyish-green leaves.

The hybrid × *clypeolata* has most beautiful silvery jade-green feathery foliage and heads of clear yellow in June, or throughout the summer on freshly-divided plants. It is only 18 in. (450 mm) high.

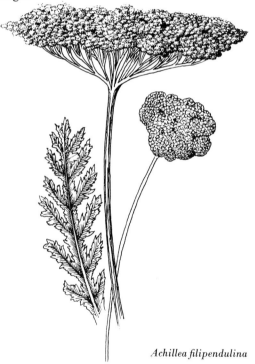

Achillea filipendulina

grandifolia has flat heads of tiny white daisies and lacy ever-grey foliage. It will flower from summer to autumn if the old heads are cut off. Height 2 ft (600 mm).

Aster. Americans call these flowers Hardy Asters. Britons refer to them as Michaelmas Daisies, though strictly speaking, only one species (*novi-belgii*) should bear this name; the others are correctly named Hardy Asters. Under whichever name, these beautiful daisies are one of the most important flowers of the autumn garden.

amellus is less often seen than its hybrids and varieties, which are great improvements on the species. One of the very finest is × *frikartii* 'Moench', clear lavender-blue, long-lasting and freely-branching, height 3 ft (900 mm). 'Sonia' has large clear-pink flowers, height 2 ft (600 mm).

ericoides, though small-flowered, is still attractive in winter and is wilt-free, $2\frac{1}{2}$ ft (800 mm) tall. Two good varieties are 'Ideal' and 'Silver Spray', both 3 ft (900 mm). Good short and compact varieties are 'Blue Star', 'Brimstone' and 'Pink Cloud'.

lateriflorus has a fascinating form, 'Horizontalis', with tiny foliage turning coppery-purple by September, and tiny pale-lilac flowers with pronounced stamens. It grows erect to 2 ft (600 mm).

novae-angliae, the New England Aster, has violet-purple or pink flowers and grows up to 6 ft (1.8 m). It has some good varieties, of which 'Elma Potschke' is of a startling carmine-rose, and 'Barr's Pink', magenta.

novi-belgii, the true Michaelmas Daisy or New York Aster, has escaped from gardens to adorn waste places with its violet-blue flowers. The modern varieties are in glorious colours from white to deep pink and crimson, pale lavender to blues and purples. Height $2\frac{1}{2}$-4 ft (800 mm-1 m).

Unsurpassed for vigour and elegance is the variety 'Climax', with huge pyramids

Aster novi-belgii

Anemone-flowered

Colerette

Pompon

Cactus-flowered

Paeony-flowered

Single-flowered

of Spode-blue single flowers. It grows to 6 ft (1.8 m). 'Winston S. Churchill' has glowing ruby-red flowers, and a tall dark-blue variety is 'Mistress Quickly'. There is also a race of dwarfs, of which 'Little Pink Beauty' is the best semi-double pink; 'Lady in Blue' making compact bushes massed with semi-double blue flowers.

pappei, an adorable shrublet 12–15 in. (300–400 mm) high, gives a summer-long display of clear-blue daisies.

thomsonii has a variety 'Nanus', perpetually in lilac-blue flower from July onwards. Height 18 in. (400 mm).

Dahlia. Named in honour of Andreas Gustav Dahl, the Swedish botanist, the original Mexican dahlias have given rise to so many hybrids that the National Dahlia Society has classified them into eleven main groups, from which we will choose some of the best varieties.

Single-flowered: 'Domingo' (reddish-orange); 'Kokette' (a red and white bicolor).

Anemone-flowered: the dark red 'Comet' with tubular inner florets is best-known; 'Guinea' (golden); 'Roulette' (a pleasing pink).

Colerette: 'Fashion Monger' (pale yellow disk-florets, ray-florets splashed with claret); 'Libretto' (dark red with white inner florets, yellow disk-florets).

Paeony-flowered: 'Bishop of Llandaff' (crimson with dark coppery foliage); 'Morning Glow' (orange blended).

Pompons: 'Willo's Violet' (deep violet); 'Honey' (primrose-yellow).

Cactus-flowered: 'Poetic' (dark pink and cream blend, large); 'Authority' (bronze-orange blend); 'Covenander' (pink-red, this and the previous variety medium); 'Klankstad Kerkrade' (sulphur-yellow, small).

Dimorphotheca. Cape Marigold, Star of the Veldt, and African Daisy are the names bestowed upon this beautiful flower. There are three species, all summer-blooming into autumn.

aurantiaca, bright orange with hybrids in shades of yellow, pale salmon, buff-apricot, and white.

barberiae, bright purplish-pink heads up to 2½ in. (60 mm) across, on stems up to 1 ft (300 mm).

ecklonis, white with blue disk-florets in heads 3 in. (75 mm) on stems up to 2 ft (600 mm).

Doronicum. The Leopard's Bane is one of the earliest flowers of spring, *caucasicum* with deep-yellow daisies growing to 1½ ft (450 mm) tall, the parent of two good varieties: 'Magnificum' and 'Spring Beauty'.

Erigeron. There are two very different forms of Fleabane: *mucronatus*, a great seeder producing shoals of little pink and white daisies on 6 in. (150 mm) stems, flowering all summer and appearing in cracks and crevices; and the wide range of bigger Erigeron Hybrids in many shades of pink, lilac and mauve. Among the best, from 1½–2 ft (450–600 mm) high are 'Charity' (light pink); 'Dignity' (violet-mauve); and 'Festivity' (lilac-pink).

Gazania. Only one is notable, the hybrid × *splendens* with most attractive golden-orange daisies spotted with brown or mauve around the centre, and narrow silky-white leaves. Forms are pink, bronze, and ruby, height 6–9 in. (150–200 mm), flowering through summer into autumn.

Helenium. Best of these are the russet-coloured varieties of *autumnale:* 'Coppelia', a late-flowerer of deep coppery-orange, 3 ft (900 mm) tall, and 'Moerheim Beauty', bronze-red and the same height.

Liatris. This is a most unusual flower for a daisy, producing closely-packed spikes of feathery ray-florets, which unfold first at the top.

callilepis, the Kansas Gayfeather, has spikes of bright purple-rose flowers in summer, height 2–3 ft (600–900 mm).

spicata, the Blazing Star, has long-lasting reddish-purple spikes rising from grassy leaves. 'Alba' is a white form.

Liatris spicata

Ligularia. These are really plants for the waterside where their kidney-shaped leaves can expand: all-green, green above and maroon beneath, or all maroon.

dentata (syns. *clivorum, Senecio clivorum*), loosely-bunched orange-yellow heads on stems 3–5 ft (900 mm—1.5 m) tall. A fine variety is 'Gregynog Gold' with its bronze centre.

hodgsonii, handsome orange flowers on 2 ft (600 mm) stems above dark green leaves.

Rudbeckia fulgida 'Goldsturm'

Rudbeckia. This is generally called the Cone Flower because of the disk-florets forming a rounded pyramid, the ray-florets striking off to make a single daisy. All 2–3 ft (600–900 mm).

fulgida, deep yellow with a maroon centre.

hirta, Black-eyed Susan, golden-yellow with a dark-brown centre; with two good forms, 'Gloriosa' and 'Gloriosa Double'.

purpurea has a striking variety in 'The King', pink with a glowing rosy-red cone.

Solidago. Most American gardeners regard this as a weed, but British gardeners still like a clump or two in their autumn borders. The original species, *canadensis*, has some fine varieties, from the 6 ft (1.8 m) 'Golden Wings' to the 12 in. (300 mm) fluffy-headed 'Golden Thumb'.

Stokesia. Stokes's Aster (*laevis*) is like a beautiful lavender-blue scabious, 1–1½ ft (300–450 mm) tall and flowering from midsummer to late autumn. There is a white form, and two good varieties in 'Blue Star' and the large lavender-blue 'Superba'.

Everlastings

These, also called immortelles, warrant both names; their flower-heads retaining their colour and shape for many years if cut in their prime. Four genera give us a varied supply of these attractive papery flowers.

Ammobium alatum

Ammobium alatum, the Winged Everlasting, has a yellow centre surrounded by silvery-white petal-like bracts, the lance-shaped leaves forming a rosette, with a larger form in *grandiflorum*.

Helichrysum has several charming species with grey or silvery leaves, best-known being *bracteatum*, the Strawflower, its flowers single with pink or yellow bracts, height 2–3 ft (600–900 mm).

Helipterum manglesii has nodding heads of bright rose, pink or white. A double pink form is 'Rosea'.

Xeranthemum annuum of purple or rosy flower-heads has double forms with one or two rows of bracts around a central tuft of tubular florets. In the mixed strains the outer petals are either white, pink or purple, and the centres are usually white.

Senecio cineraria

Leontopodium alpinum

Grey- and Silver-leaved

These are much sought after by flower arrangers and by those concerned with making set displays.

The 'Candicans' variety of *Senecio cineraria* (*Cineraria maritima*), the Dusty Miller, is such a one; its leaves are not only silvery but most attractively cut. If the effect of the foliage only is wanted, the flowers should be pinched off: the plant then becomes more leafy and bushy.

Anaphalis, Pearl Everlasting, is decorative both in its grey leaves and white flowers which can be cut for the winter. The best-known species, *margaritacea* of small pearl-buttons in late summer, makes a charming edging plant. *Celmisia coriacea*, the Snow Daisy, is handsome all over with its long pointed leaves glaucous-white above, woolly-white beneath, silvery woolly stems and large pure-white daisies.

Two shrublets are *Artemisia absinthium* whose varieties 'Lambrook Silver' and 'Lambrook Giant' are to be preferred for their shimmering silky-grey leaves much divided; and *Santolina chamaecyparissus*, Lavender Cotton, with white-felted branches and clustering silvery-grey foliage. A dwarf form is 'Nana'.

Alpines and Small Plants

A great many of the small and true alpine Composites also have their leaves covered with a thick tomentum of grey or silvery-white, their protection against the cold. These plants are *Antennaria*, of which *dioica* is the most commonly grown species, useful as a carpeter for small bulbs, and with two charming pink-flowered varieties; *Anthemis biebersteinii* with tufts of silvery filigree-fine leaves, the species *cupaniana* having foaming masses of grey aromatic foliage; and *Inula candida*, rosettes of wide leaves with a felt of dazzling white and flower-spikes coated with white hairs carrying the clear yellow flowers.

The long pointed leaves of *Leucogenes grandiceps* grow in tufts, are covered with a white tomentum above and beneath, the small yellow daisies surrounded by white woolly bracts. Two others are *Anacyclus depressus*, with prostrate stems carrying grey-green ferny foliage and wide many-rayed daisies, the florets being white on top and crimson beneath, the central disk of florets yellow; and *Leontopodium alpinum*, the Edelweiss, known to everyone who has ever gone to Switzerland in spring, beloved for its grey flannel flowers.

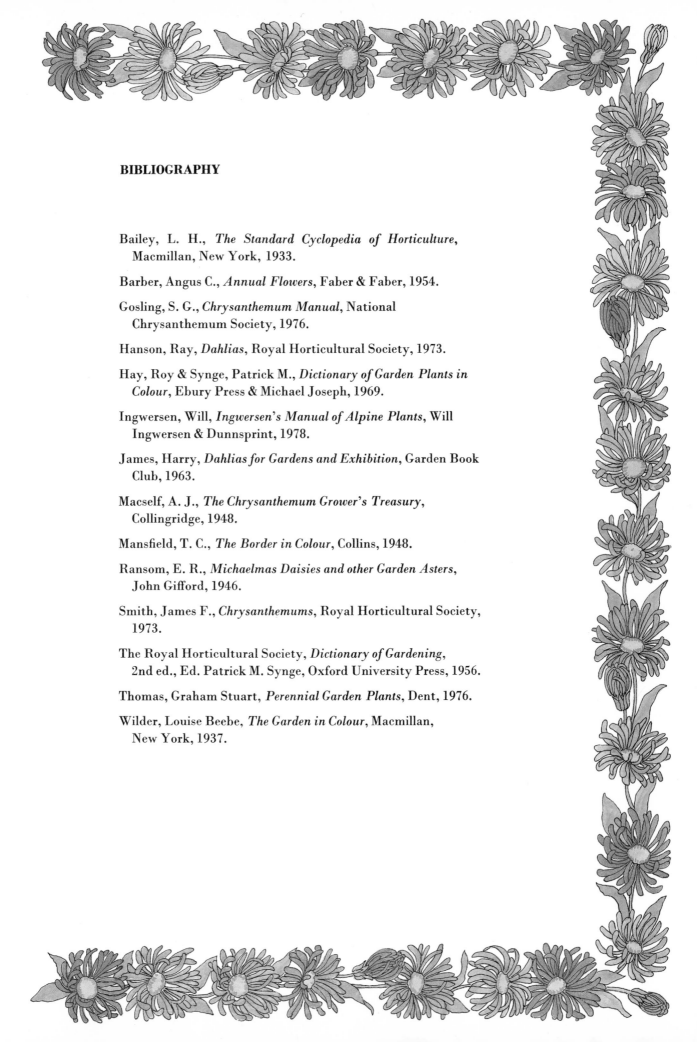

BIBLIOGRAPHY

Bailey, L. H., *The Standard Cyclopedia of Horticulture*, Macmillan, New York, 1933.

Barber, Angus C., *Annual Flowers*, Faber & Faber, 1954.

Gosling, S. G., *Chrysanthemum Manual*, National Chrysanthemum Society, 1976.

Hanson, Ray, *Dahlias*, Royal Horticultural Society, 1973.

Hay, Roy & Synge, Patrick M., *Dictionary of Garden Plants in Colour*, Ebury Press & Michael Joseph, 1969.

Ingwersen, Will, *Ingwersen's Manual of Alpine Plants*, Will Ingwersen & Dunnsprint, 1978.

James, Harry, *Dahlias for Gardens and Exhibition*, Garden Book Club, 1963.

Macself, A. J., *The Chrysanthemum Grower's Treasury*, Collingridge, 1948.

Mansfield, T. C., *The Border in Colour*, Collins, 1948.

Ransom, E. R., *Michaelmas Daisies and other Garden Asters*, John Gifford, 1946.

Smith, James F., *Chrysanthemums*, Royal Horticultural Society, 1973.

The Royal Horticultural Society, *Dictionary of Gardening*, 2nd ed., Ed. Patrick M. Synge, Oxford University Press, 1956.

Thomas, Graham Stuart, *Perennial Garden Plants*, Dent, 1976.

Wilder, Louise Beebe, *The Garden in Colour*, Macmillan, New York, 1937.

The Heath Family

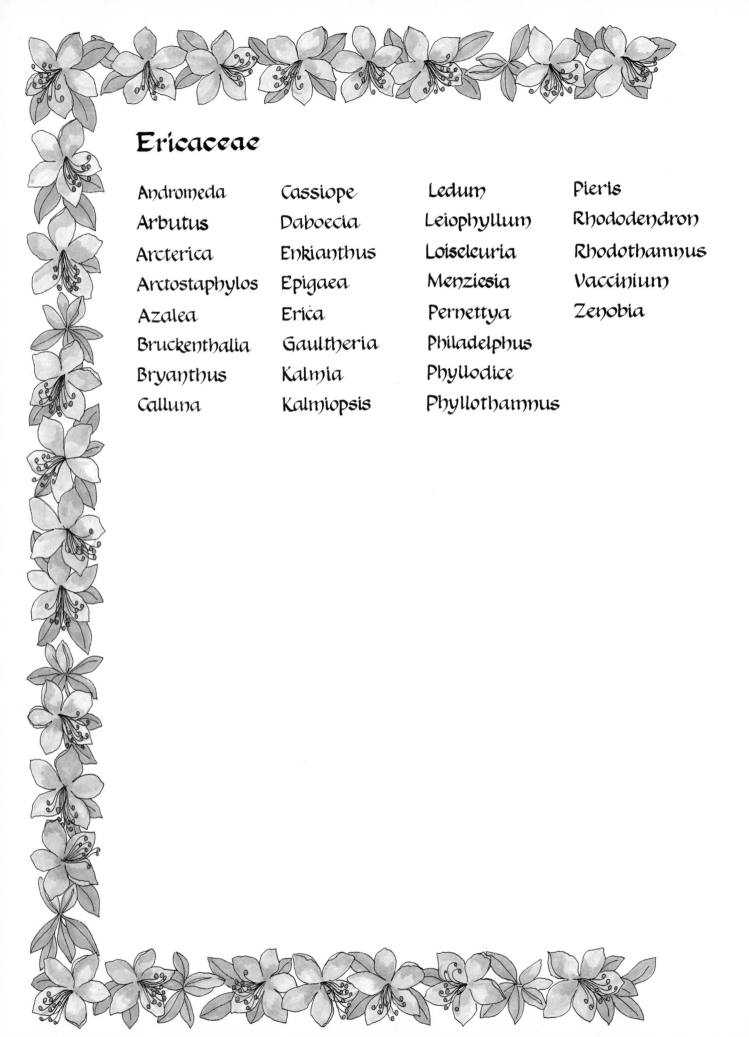

Ericaceae

Andromeda

Arbutus

Arcterica

Arctostaphylos

Azalea

Bruckenthalia

Bryanthus

Calluna

Cassiope

Daboecia

Enkianthus

Epigaea

Erica

Gaultheria

Kalmia

Kalmiopsis

Ledum

Leiophyllum

Loiseleuria

Menziesia

Pernettya

Philadelphus

Phyllodice

Phyllothamnus

Pieris

Rhododendron

Rhodothamnus

Vaccinium

Zenobia

The Heath Family

It was the custom of Carl Linnaeus, the great classifier of animals and plants, to name genera of the Heath family after the nymphs and goddesses of Greek mythology. So we have the beautiful Andromeda who was chained to a rock as an offering to a sea monster; and Cassiope, her mother; Phyllodoce who was a nymph attending Cyrene, and Pieris from Pieria, birthplace of the Muses. And just as the stories of classical mythology are evergreen, so are practically all the plants in this family, and they comprise more ornamental hardy shrubs than any other family in the whole vegetable kingdom.

There are three easy ways to identify them: the petals of the flowers, whether large or tiny, are united in the shape of a tube; the leaves grow alternately up the stem and are leathery or bristly, few being deciduous; the majority obtain some of their food through the help of special fungi which become attached to their roots.

Though called the Heaths, the family includes such important members as the Rhododendrons, Kalmias, and lovely Pieris, which give us flowers in spring and summer, in autumn brilliant foliage.

Kalmia was well-named the Calico Bush, its pink saucer flowers dotted with the scarlet of its anthers is sheer joy, as pretty as a little girl's print frock.

As for the rhododendrons it was young Dr Joseph Hooker who, as a plant collector for Kew climbed the Himalaya from the torrid heat of the plains to the temperate heights where he discovered the glorious shrubs that turned a new page in horticultural history. Rhododendrons there had been before, if few of them, but none to touch scarlet *barbatum*, superb *falconeri*, magnificent *dalhousiae* which Joseph called "the noblest species of the whole race".

Few plants can offer us an entire garden of beauty, but it is true of the *Erica* and *Calluna* genera, the Heaths and Heathers. They range from ground-huggers to small-tree size of nearly 7 feet (2 m). They give us colour in foliage and flower all the year round, and this whether you live on a lime or an acid soil.

From the hills of Scotland they have come, from Spain and Portugal and South Africa, to give you—and the bees—their constant delights.

Kalmia latifolia

CARE AND CULTURE

The members of the Ericaceae family come from the cold and temperate regions of the world, which include not only open heathlands baked by the summer sun and swept by drying winds, but also the uplands of mountains in the tropics.

During the passage of millions of years, evolution has provided plants with various mechanisms for their protection and for the preservation of their race. It has provided ericaceous plants like rhododendrons with the means of conserving their water supply —in leathery evergreen leaves and by pores in the leaves called stomata which can be opened when the plant needs to transpire, and kept shut when the plant needs to retain moisture, which it does throughout the winter, particularly when the temperature of the soil is often so low that absorption of water by the roots practically ceases. So all the Ericaceae, with few exceptions, can do with plenty of water, but in a drought they do not easily wilt.

Again except for a very few, ericaceous plants like an acid soil, and this they get in poor heathland where peat is present, or in places where there is plenty of raw humus—old forest land, for instance, of deciduous trees.

What if your soil is calcareous, limey or chalky? Very many of the Heath family are small shrubs, and these will grow happily in peat beds, bigger shrubs in tubs filled with a good humus from the compost heap, with some peat added.

As an alternative to tubs, raised beds with walls made of bricks, stone or rubble are another way of sequestering the lime-haters, at the same time introducing an architectural feature to the garden. Fill them with a suitable soil mixture. A suggestion is one part each of loam, leaf

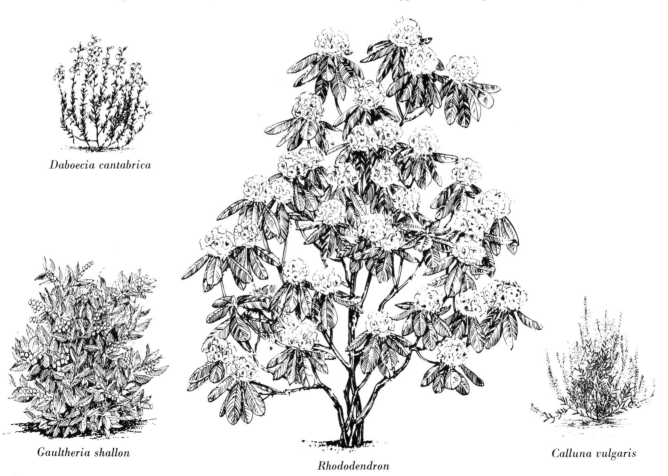

Daboecia cantabrica

Gaultheria shallon

Rhododendron

Calluna vulgaris

mould, and medium sand, all lime-free, and one and a half parts of peat.

So gardeners on a non-acid soil need not despair. Though most of the summer-flowering heathers dislike lime, the addition of quantities of peat and an occasional watering with a solution of Epsom salts will keep them happy. Or you can use a preparation containing sequestrol.

Fortunately there are heathers which tolerate lime: *Erica carnea*, *darleyensis*, and *erigena*, and all their colourful varieties. Tree heaths also (of which there are several species and varieties) are lime-tolerant, and these are magnificent. When mantled with their flowers they can be breathtaking.

Apart from the colour it gives, a heather garden is labour-saving, needing little more than clippers run over each clump when the flowers have faded. This way the heathers will keep their youth and compact growth,

to flower profusely again next year. Peat spread among them will keep down summer weeds. When tree heaths become lanky they may be hard-pruned back to the old wood during April.

Space is a consideration. Those who fall under the spell of rhododendrons may deplore the fact that they have not room enough to display them in great banks or groups. They can take heart, for there are many beautiful miniatures that will give equal pleasure, and of course their cousins the azaleas (which really are rhodo-dendrons) add wonderful colour and can be an outstanding feature. In a small garden they can still be the pride of the gardener, who can create his own colour groupings.

Among the bigger shrubs that make their mark are *Ledum*, Labrador Tea, with handsome foliage and white flowers; the sun-loving *Pernettya*, good as a tidy hedge

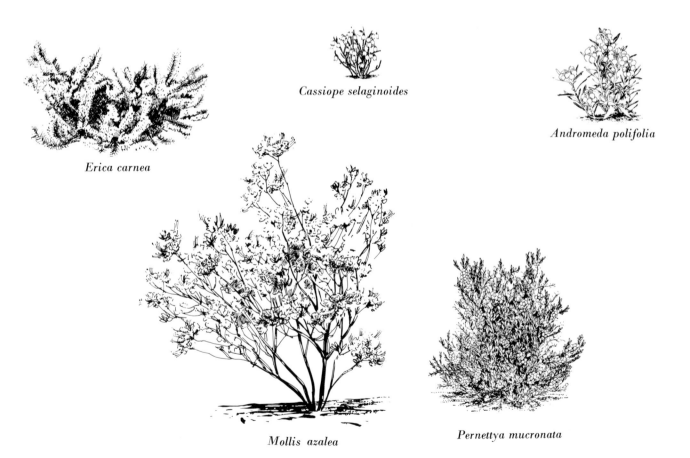

Erica carnea

Cassiope selaginoides

Andromeda polifolia

Mollis azalea

Pernettya mucronata

as well as a free-standing plant, their masses of pure white or vividly coloured berries some of the showiest fruits of the plant world; *Zenobia* of beautiful evergreen foliage and clusters of Lily of the Valley flowers; and, for sheer glory of scarlet leaf in autumn, the deciduous Blueberry, *Vaccinium corymbosum.* A deciduous genus of the family is *Enkianthus* which also gives us brilliant autumn foliage. It can tolerate some shade, as can *Ledum* and *Zenobia.*

The shrubs in this labour-saving Heath family do not need pruning; but if a shrub is overtopping some other precious plant the snippings should follow its original shape; and if this is going to leave the shrub lopsided, it or the other plant should be moved elsewhere. Dead-heading is a different matter, especially with rhododendrons which must have the dead flowers removed if they are to bloom well next year.

Of the smaller shrubs in *Ericaceae* are some exquisite little plants, many with bell-flowers and most of them sun-loving. One must remember that alpines grow in exposed places where there are no trees to shade them. *Cassiope* is one having these tiny bells, with *Arcterica* and the delicate but hardy *Menziesia*, which is a small deciduous shrub from Japan. For those who cannot grow the large *Kalmia latifolia* there is a tiny cousin reaching no taller than 5 in. (125 mm).

Two prostrate shrublets are the Mountain Azalea, *Loiseleuria*, which makes pink drifts of flowers in the mountains of Central Europe, and an *Epigaea* which means much to Americans because it is their Mayflower, said to have been the first New World plant seen by the Pilgrim Fathers and named for their ship.

Menziesia ciliicalyx

Propagating

Propagation of the *Ericaceae* is by seeds, cuttings, and layers, all of which take time. If buying a mature plant, look for a good root system—the roots should be coming out of the bottom of the container. Roots are particularly important to the Heath family and most of them have fibrous ones, fine and hair-like, spreading outwards close to the surface, so as to catch the least rainfall. Plant in this way, not too deeply and giving the roots their full spread—and of course in a bed of humus with an admixture of the peat that they love. This care at the start of their lives will put you in credit for a rewarding show of flowers, and you can then look to your Heaths for years of trouble-free gardening.

Identify Heaths by these individual flowers

1. *Erica cinerea*, Bell Heather
2. *Erica vagans*, Cornish Heath
3. *Erica erigena*, Irish Heath
4. *Erica tetralix*, Cross-leaved Heath
5. *Daboecia cantabrica*, St Dabeoc's Heath
6. *Erica carnea*, Mountain Heath
7. *Calluna vulgaris*, Heather

Rhododendrons have two flower-shapes

8. Open flowers growing in a bunch are typical of rhododendrons from the Himalaya.

9. Funnel-shaped flowers are typical of those from China.

10. *Azalea mollis*

11. Bronze, silver, jade: the aftergrowths of rhododendrons often rival the flowers in their exquisite colours.

88

FLOWERS OF THE FAMILY

Andromeda. The taxonomists have moved into other genera many of the plants previously classed as Andromedas, leaving us only two dwarf species, but both valuable for the rock garden:

glaucophylla is from North-East America and has pale pink pitcher-shaped flowers in clusters in the late spring or early summer. The stems are erect and the narrow leaves are hairy and white on the undersides.

polifolia is the Bog Rosemary and provided it gets a peaty soil is one of the best dwarf shrubs. Again the flowers are pink, borne in compact clusters at the tips of the wiry branches in May and June. It can grow to a height of 18 in. (450 mm), but if a smaller plant is wanted there are several variants. 'Compacta' is slow-growing and forms a mound of grey waxy leaves and large pink flowers in May and June.

Andromeda polifolia

Arcterica. This genus has only one species, *nana*, which means dwarf and always denotes one of the real tinies. This one is usually less than 4 in. (100 mm) high. The thin woody stems bear glossy deep-green leaves in pairs or threes. The creamy-white urn-shaped flowers have a most delicious scent. Hardy, it blooms in March and April and increases by underground runners. A must if ever there was one.

Arctostaphylos. The small species are ideal for ground cover and thrive in sun or light shade. Two are found in Europe, the rest inhabiting North-West America, Mexico and Central America.

hookeri is a Californian species seldom more than 4 in. (100 mm) high. It forms wide mats of shiny evergreen leaves with white pink-flushed bells on the tips of the shoots in spring.

myrtifolia is a vigorous carpeter with crimson-tinged stems and leaves, and clusters of white bell-flowers followed by purple-black berries. A lovely little shrublet.

uva-ursi, the Bearberry, is native to countries all over the world, including northern Britain and North America. This is a creeping shrub with pink-tinted white flowers and red berries.

Azalea. Though classed with *Rhododendron*, it is still Azalea to the gardener, to whom the visible distinctions make reference easy (though unreliable!). Rhododendrons are large, azaleas small; rhododendrons are evergreen, azaleas shed their leaves.

Horticulturists have divided the Azalea series of *Rhododendron* into six species-groups, of which four are important: Luteum, Schlippenbachia, Canadense and Obtusum. The species *Luteum* is deciduous with large deliciously-scented yellow flowers. In its group by far the greatest number of members are natives of the United States,

Rhododendron luteum

and like *luteum* itself almost every one is fragrant, with a scent of lemon, honeysuckle, clove, spicy, or with a hint of Bog Myrtle. The flower-colours are white, yellow to orange, orange to rich red, pale pink and deeper pink, while *occidentale* has almost all the azalea colours in its forms.

The Schlippenbachia group are Asiatic species, are deciduous, and have large tubular flowers. The type species (*R. schlippenbachia*) is one of the best of all azaleas, making a densely branched shrub widely spreading and 8–10 ft (2.5–3 m) high. Its white, pale pink or rich deep-pink flowers come in May at the same time as the leaves. The rest of the species are also tall, *weyrichii* almost tree-like with flowers variously described as red, orange-red with purple blotches, bright pink suffused mauve, and brick-red.

The species in the Canadense group are deciduous and have bell flowers. The type species (*R. canadense*) is a very twiggy shrub, upright but rarely more than 3 ft (900 mm) tall. Attractive are the grey-green leaves and rose-purple flowers in April. It thrives better in colder areas. Equally hardy and a better garden plant is *vaseyi*, whose flowers are usually pale rose-pink, but also white with orange-red spots.

The Obtusum group includes all the evergreen azaleas, several of which have been cultivated by the Japanese for centuries with some triumphant results, most famous being the Kurume Azaleas introduced into Britain and America in 1918 by Ernest Henry Wilson who became Keeper of the Arnold Arboretum. Britain knows them as the 'Wilson Fifty', though actually they numbered fifty-one. The Kurumes are perfectly hardy but must have ample sunshine. The exquisite flowers, in April and May, are single or hose-in-hose and of every colour except yellow, orange, and blue.

Kurume azalea

There are other azalea hybrids. The hardy Ghent Hybrids appeared in Belgium in 1830 and were further developed at Knap Hill in England to produce

90

magnificent plants with large trusses carrying up to thirty flowers, and at Exbury with an even more striking range of flower-colours. The May-flowering Mollis Hybrids are equally hardy if grown on their own roots. There are also evergreen greenhouse hybrids.

In the Eastern States of America the winters are too severe for the general run of evergreen hybrids, including the Kurumes, and a great deal of hybridising has been going on, resulting in a large range called the Glenn Dale Hybrids and the Gable Hybrids. The Glenn Dales have an extraordinary range of flowering time and colour, with a number of stripes and whites with frilled edges of contrasting colours.

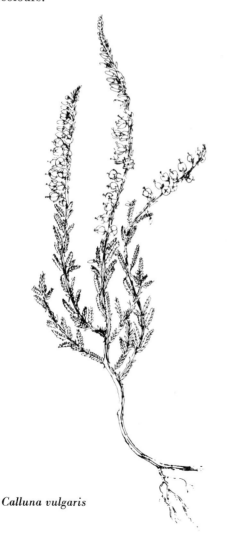

Calluna vulgaris

Calluna. Though there is only one species in this genus—*vulgaris*, the common Heather or Ling—there are so many forms that it is possible to have colour from them all the year. Flowering periods are July to August, August to September, and October to November. Other forms have colourful foliage. All are easily grown in a lime-free soil.

Varieties well-known both in Britain and America are 'Alba' (White Heather), flowering mid-season, and a form 'Aurea' with beautiful golden foliage; 'Alportii' of tall erect growth 2 ft (600 mm), with crimson flowers mid-season; 'Cuprea', mainly for its foliage, young shoots golden in summer, ruddy-bronze in autumn and winter; 'Hammondii', beautiful dark-green foliage with long spikes of pure white flowers in summer, a strong grower useful as a low hedge up to 2 ft 6 in. (800 mm). America has a form producing a profusion of pink flowers, 'Hirsuta Compacta' or 'Sister Anne', making tight mounds of pretty grey foliage and flowering in mid-season.

Cassiope. A group of delightful hardy evergreen shrublets with bristly heather-like leaves and waxy bell flowers. Originating in the mountainous and Arctic regions they thrive in a moist peaty soil with a north aspect. There are some fascinating species and many beautiful varieties.

fastigiata, from the Himalaya, is a dwarf bush up to 9 in. (225 mm) with erect square stems and large Lily of the Valley flowers in May and June. It is one parent of 'Badenoch' which makes a low mound of grey-green foliage smothered with masses of waxy white bells, and of 'Bearsden' with similar flowers but finer light-green foliage.

lycopodioides makes tangled mats of scale-like deep-green foliage, the flowers a profusion of hanging white bells on bright

Cassiope selaginoides

Daboecia cantabrica

red stalks. It is the best of the genus and easily grown. 'Beatrice Lilley' is a form even more compact and holds its white flowers in brilliant red cups (calyces) in April and May.

selaginoides from Tibet has tiny green foliage like a club moss, and bears creamy-white hanging bells in May and June. It grows no more than 6 in. (150 mm) high. A very choice hardy plant.

Daboecia. St Dabeoc's Heath has only one species that can be recommended, *cantabrica* (the *polifolia* of catalogues), producing long sprays of showy flowers, rose-purple and pitcher-shaped, from June to November. It grows 18 in. (450 mm) high. There are good varieties. 'Alba' has large rounded flowers of pure white from June to October, and pale green foliage. Vigorous and hardy, it grows 2 ft (600 mm) tall; 'Atropurpurea' has long spikes of rich purple flowers and glossy green leaves, hardy and long-flowering; 'Bicolor', white, rose-purple and striped flowers, often on the same spike; 'Porter's Variety', a dwarf and compact form with small rich-crimson

flowers from July to September, and dark green foliage; 'Praegerae', long arching spikes of large bright salmon-pink bells. It needs a sheltered spot and grows up to 15 in. (380 mm) high. 'William Buchanan' makes a succession of large deep rosy-crimson bells from June to October above dark-green lustrous foliage. Its height is 9 in. (230 mm).

Enkianthus. This outstanding group of deciduous shrubs from Japan has the same bell flowers hanging in clusters from the tips of the branches in May. They are chiefly attractive for the exquisite colouring of the autumn leaves which turn fiery orange and crimson. They prefer to grow in semi-shade.

campanulatus is an erect branched species attaining 8–10 ft (2.5–3 m), with cream flowers veined and edged with crimson which last for three weeks and are useful for cutting.

cernuus var. 'Rubens' is noteworthy for its deep-red fringed flowers from May to June. It grows 3–5 ft (800 mm–1.5 m) high.

Enkianthus campanulatus

Erica carnea
'King George'

chinensis, a remarkably beautiful small tree or tall narrow shrub reaching 20 ft (6 m) in favourable conditions. The flowers are probably the largest of the genus, yellow and red with darker rings carried in many-flowered umbels. The large leaves usually have red stalks.

perulatus, with its branches divided and arranged in tiers, its hanging white bells in May having constricted mouths. The leaves assume startling colours in the late autumn, the bush appearing to be on fire with brilliant red and fierce orange flames. Its height is 6–8 ft (1.8–2.4 m).

Epigaea. A genus of two species of creeping shrubs which like semi-shade.

asiatica from Japan makes a mat of leathery bronze-green leaves, rough and hairy, oval and pointed. The clusters of sweetly-scented flowers are starry and tubular, bright red in the bud, white to rose when open in April and May.

repens, the Trailing Arbutus or May-flower, is only an inch or so high, with wavy oval leaves and fragrant white or rose-tinted flowers in April.

Erica. The most interesting of the Heath-and-Heather genera, and comprises the Bell Heather and Heaths, as distinct from the heather or ling of the single-species *Calluna*. It is easy to see the difference between them. In *Calluna* the flower petals are separated, and the leaves are opposite and arranged in four rows on the young shoots; in *Erica* the petals are joined, making a globular flower, and the leaves are in whorls around the stem.

There are more than 500 species of *Erica*, many of them not hardy in Britain and only a few of the European ones hardy in America where there are no native Heaths at all. However, there are enough species and varieties to make a round-the-year show of colour in flower and foliage.

Three beautiful species and their varieties thrive without difficulty in a non-acid soil.

carnea, one of the most widely planted in America and Britain, forming dense hummocks and mats covered with rosy-red flowers throughout the winter. Its dozens of cultivars cover a flowering period beginning in November for the earliest,

Erica × *darleyensis*

Erica vagans

April for the latest, the majority between January and March. Heights are 6–9 in. (150–230 mm).

A few choice ones are 'Aurea' of golden foliage in spring and early summer, flowers deep pink paling to almost white, mid-season to late; 'C. J. Backhouse', pale pink deepening with age, late-flowering; 'Eileen Porter', low-growing with rich carmine-red flowers from October to April; 'Praecox Rubra', deep rose-red, early-flowering to mid-season; 'Ruby Glow', large flowers of rich dark red and bronzed foliage, late-flowering; 'Springwood White', still the finest white cultivar, with strong trailing growths packed with flowers in mid-season; 'Winter Beauty' and 'King George', both bright rose-pink, commencing to flower in December.

× *darleyensis*, a most useful group, flowering in winter, excellent for ground cover and averaging $1\frac{1}{2}$–2 ft (450–600 mm). Recommended cultivars are 'Arthur Johnson' for its long dense sprays of magenta flowers, useful for cutting, the most reliable and longest-flowering variety; 'Darley Dale' (formerly *darleyensis*), one of the most popular, with

pale pink flowers over a long period; 'Jack H. Brummage' of soft-yellow foliage and light-pink flowers; 'Silberschmelze' (Silver Beads) with silvery white flowers over a long period.

erigena (*mediterranea*), a dense shrub small to medium-sized covered from March to May with fragrant rose-red flowers. It has some very beautiful cultivars: 'Brightness', compact and bushy, 2–3 ft (600–900 mm), with bronze-red buds opening to rose-pink; 'Nana', a compact form with silvery-pink flowers; 'W. T. Rackliff', charming with emerald foliage and pure white flowers.

vagans, the Cornish Heath, is a species that prefers an acid soil but will tolerate a small amount of lime. It is dwarf and spreading, with pinkish-rose flowers in long sprays from July to October. There are several most attractive varieties: 'Fiddlestone', superb with long sprays of rose-cerise flowers over a long period; 'Mrs D. F. Maxwell', deep cerise, one of the best Heaths; 'Valerie Proudley', a choice golden-foliage form with white flowers, rather slow-growing.

94

Our last two species are lime-haters.

cinerea, Bell Heather, offers some of the brightest and widest range of colours from June to September, with an average height of 9–12 in. (230–300 mm). A few of the many varieties are 'Atrorubens', distinctive with brilliant red flowers in long sprays; 'Cevennes', lavender-rose; 'Domino' with white flowers and ebony calyces, a unique combination; 'Golden Drop', summer foliage golden-copper turning to rust-red in winter; and 'Velvet Night', with extraordinary blackish-purple flowers.

tetralix, the Cross-leaved Heath, is a European species with dense heads of rose-coloured flowers from June to October whose cultivars have fascinating grey-green or silver-grey foliage. Outstanding are 'Alba Mollis' with pretty grey foliage and white flowers; 'L. E. Underwood', silver-grey mounds with flowers a striking terracotta in bud opening to pale pink; and 'Pink Glow' with grey foliage and shining pink flowers.

For those, particularly in America, who must grow heaths and heathers indoors, *Erica hyemalis* is one of the best with its rosy flowers tipped with white. Great numbers of these Cape Heaths are sold at Christmas time.

The Tree Heaths because of their size—some nearly 20 ft (6 m)—are not for every garden, though even one in the right place can be a spectacle. Most are hardy and all are tolerant of lime.

arborea var. *alpina*, up to 7 ft (2 m), has fresh light-green foliage and bears pure white flowers from March till May.

australis 'Mr Robert', the white form of *australis*, also 7 ft (2 m), is magnificent with fresh green foliage and large pure white bells, almost startling when in full flower. A selected form, 'Riverslea', is an outstanding Heath producing a marvellous show of rosy-red flowers from late April till early June.

Gaultheria, a genus of ornamental evergreen shrubs grown for their value as ground cover and for shelter, but also for their attractive flowers and fruits.

forrestii is a spreading species from China with conspicuous white-stalked spikes of waxy-white fragrant flowers followed by blue berries, giving a colourful display from the summer months till December.

miqueliana is a neat dwarf shrub from Japan, usually not more than 9 in. (230 mm) high, with apple-green leaves. Its white flowers are conspicuous in June, and the white or pink berries are edible.

procumbens, the Wintergreen or Partridge Berry, is a North American evergreen forming carpets of dark green leaves with bright red berries in autumn and winter.

shallon, the Salal, makes an impenetrable bush or thicket ideal for a shelter belt, and bears sprays of delightful pinkish-white bells followed by large clusters of dark purple berries.

Gaultheria shallon

Kalmia. A genus of most beautiful ever-green shrubs from ten feet tall to tiny.

latifolia, the American Laurel or Calico Bush, is outstanding, with broad glossy green leaves and clusters of rose-pink flowers with a circle of prominent scarlet anthers dotting inside the petals. Flowering in June and July, it is 3 ft (900 mm) high.

polifolia var. *microphylla* is an adorable miniature of *latifolia*, with the prettiest bright-pink saucer flowers in April and May.

Menziesia. A small genus of slow-growing deciduous shrubs suitable for the rock garden, with flowers like those of *Daboecia* but waxy in texture.

ciliicalyx is an exquisite small shrub with oval leaves and clusters of nodding, pitcher-shaped flowers in May, varying in colour from cream to soft purple. It has two varieties that deserve to be better known: *multiflora*, with longer flowers having a purplish corolla; and *purpurea*, enchanting with bright red bells tinged with purple.

Pernettya. Not every good shrub will make a good hedge, but a choice pernettya is one of them. The genus comprises attractive evergreens whose flowers, though small, are so profuse as to be remarkably conspicuous. Likewise their berries, pure white or vividly coloured, are some of the showiest fruits of the plant world. Most of the species are hardy, tolerant of shade but fruiting best in full sun. They should be planted in groups to ensure cross-pollination.

mucronata is everybody's pernettya, a shrub for all seasons, making dense thickets up to 3 ft (900 mm), ground cover if mass-planted, decorative flowers and berries. Myriads of small heath-like

Pernettya mucronata

flowers in May and June are followed by dense clusters of large berries ranging from pure white to mulberry-purple and remaining throughout the winter.

There are some beautiful dwarf varieties: 'Bell's Seedling' with glossy myrtle-like foliage and white flowers followed by large crimson berries; 'Tasmanica', a tiny prostrate shrub with minute pointed leaves on almost microscopic stems. The nodding white bells in May are large for the size of the plant, and are followed by bright red berries.

Among the larger varieties are 'Davis's Hybrids', which vary in the colour of their berries from white to deep purple.

tasmanica is certainly one for the rock garden, a slender fragile little shrub only a few centimetres high and often prostrate. The berries are solitary and usually red, the leaves tiny and leathery.

Phyllodoce. Here we have a genus of hardy dwarf evergreens for the peat bed. They like cool positions or partial shade.

aleutica has 8 in. (200 mm) erect stems forming dense mats and making an unusual picture with its tiny pale-green leaves and heads of chartreuse-green bells in May.

empetriformis is a North American species making spreading mats and producing clusters of pale or deeper pink flowers, sometimes brownish-pink in April and May.

nipponica is a treasure rarely more than 5 in. (125 mm) high and slow-growing. The dark glossy green leaves are white beneath and the white flowers usually appear in April.

Pieris. Has highly ornamental species, evergreen and attractive the whole year round, the flower panicles forming in the autumn and showing red-tinged buds throughout the winter, the flowers typically white and pitcher-shaped.

floribunda, hardy and forming a dense mound 3–6 ft (900 mm–1.8 m) high. The flowers are produced in erect panicles in March and April.

formosa, a magnificent large shrub for mild climates, parent of the variety *forrestii* which is one of the most beautiful of all shrubs, about 8 ft (2.4 m), with

Pieris formosa var. *forrestii*

handsome foliage, the young growths being brilliant red, the large fragrant flowers being borne in long panicles in April. Two striking forms are 'Charles Michael' whose individual flowers are the largest of any form and are produced in large panicles, and 'Jermyns' with young shoots vinous red, the whole inflorescence being of the same rich colour, contrasting boldly with the white flowers.

japonica, the Japanese Bog Rosemary, is a graceful medium-sized shrub with most attractive glossy foliage, coppery when young. Its large waxy flowers are borne in drooping panicles in March and April. It grows about 8 ft (2.4 m) tall. Varieties of this species give us young foliage salmon-pink changing to cream, then white, finally green ('Bert Chandler'); flowers rose in bud opening to pale blush-pink ('Blush'); and there is a silver variegated form making a most attractive shrub called 'Variegata'.

Rhododendron. If the *Ericaceae* family had but one genus, and that *Rhododendron*, it would still yield some of the greatest and most beautiful flowering shrubs, from gorgeous *grande* of football-sized blooms and *giganteum* at 80 ft (24 m) to the tiny creeping *forrestii repens* a few inches high. It is possible to have them in flower from the early days of the year through to late summer, and in a range of colour covering the entire spectrum. When the flowers are over, the young shoots of the species rhododendrons can be almost as beautiful as the flowers themselves: torches of silver, emerald and bronze new leaves springing up in their place. Rhododendrons (apart from Azaleas) are evergreen, and there are more than 800 species, not counting the vast number of hybrids. So here we can only explain the different types, note their countries of origin, and quote a few suitable for the average garden.

The botanists have grouped the species into various series according to their form and geographical range. Himalayan Rhododendrons, for instance, are different from the Chinese, the first tending to produce compact heads of bloom, the Chinese tubular flowers.

Himalaya

Red:

arboreum is a large shrub or small tree, with rich scarlet flowers from January to April, the leaves green above, whitish to brownish-red beneath.

Rhododendron arboreum

barbatum, large but more bushy, extremely hardy, with attractive coloured stems and peeling bark, glowing crimson-scarlet flowers in March.

cinnabarinum, medium-sized to large, bluish foliage, cinnabar-red flowers in May and June.

thomsonii, medium-sized, bark plum-coloured or cinnamon, flowers deep blood-red in April, the fruiting clusters apple-green and bluish.

Yellow:

campylocarpum, small to medium, choice, hardy, clear-yellow flowers in April and May, leaves glossy green above, bluish beneath.

falconeri, with huge domed trusses of waxy flowers in April and May, creamy-yellow blotched with purple, the large leaves with a rust-coloured tomentum beneath.

lanatum, small to medium, leaves brown-felted, bell-flowers in April and May pale yellow with crimson-purple markings.

Pink:

campanulatum, large and lovely, flowers pale rose to lavender-blue in April and May, the unfolding leaves with a suede-like fawn or rusty indumentum.

ciliatum, smallish, peeling bark, trusses of fragrant rose-lilac bells in March and April, the leaves conspicuously fringed with hairs.

hodgsonii, a large shrub or small tree, handsome leaves dark green above, furry grey or fawn beneath, flowers dark magenta in April.

tsangpoense, dwarf to small, aromatic leaves, bluish beneath interspersed with pale green or pink scales which, when looked at through a lens, are like glistening jewels set in white satin, the flowers crushed strawberry to deep crimson or violet in May and June.

Blue:

niveum, the young leaves covered with a white felt turning pale brown beneath, the globular heads of flowers smokey-blue to rich purple.

wallichii, medium to large, flowers lilac with rose spots in April, leaves dark green above and smooth, paler beneath and dotted with powdery tufts of reddish-brown hair.

China

White:

calophytum, hardy, large leaves, large trusses in March and April of white, sometimes pink, flowers, each with a maroon basal blotch.

microleucum, dwarf, densely leafy, clusters of white flowers in April.

Pink:

calostrotum, dwarf, grey-green foliage, large saucer magenta-crimson flowers, May and June.

insigne, exceptionally hardy, slow-growing, leaves glossy green above, silvery beneath assuming a silvery lustre, flowers soft pink with dark markings, May and June.

neriifolium, medium-sized, leaves gleaming white beneath, trusses of fleshy bells from deep rose to scarlet or crimson, April and May.

racemosum, smallish, sprays of pale to bright-pink flowers in March and April.

williamsonianum, bronze aftergrowths, heart-shaped leaves and shell-pink flowers, dwarf and spreading.

Yellow:

citriniflorum, small, leaves with a thick fawn or dark brown indumentum, flowers lemon-yellow sometimes rose-flushed, shaded orange at base.

lutescens, primrose-yellow flowers, February to April, bronze-red young leaves.

Blue:

augustinii, large, one of the finest, quick-growing, lavender-blue to deep violet flowers, April and May.

campylogynum, dwarf, producing rose-purple to mahogany waxy flowers when only a few centimetres high, lustrous green leaves.

russatum, medium-sized, compact, flowers deep blue-purple or violet with a white throat, April and May.

American

America, too, has her native rhododendrons. Among them are:

carolinianum, attractive and free-flowering, medium-sized, soft rose-purple tubular flowers, May and June.

catawbiense, extremely hardy, medium to large, large trusses of bells lilac-purple to pink or white in June. Many hardy hybrids have been bred from *catawbiense*.

chapmanii, smaller, funnel flowers in tight clusters, pink with greenish spots and conspicuous chocolate anthers, April and May.

maximum, the Great Laurel or Rose Bay, large, hardy, funnel flowers in compact trusses, purple-rose to white in July, slightly fragrant.

Hybrids

Some favourites among the countless hybrids raised in Britain are 'Polar Bear' (white), 'Tally-Ho' (scarlet-crimson), 'Blue Bird' and 'Blue Tit', Loderi and its many clones, 'Loder's White', 'Praecox' (lilac-purple), 'Pink Pearl', 'Britannia' (crimson-scarlet), 'Goldsworth Orange', Lady Chamberlain (mandarin-red) and its clones.

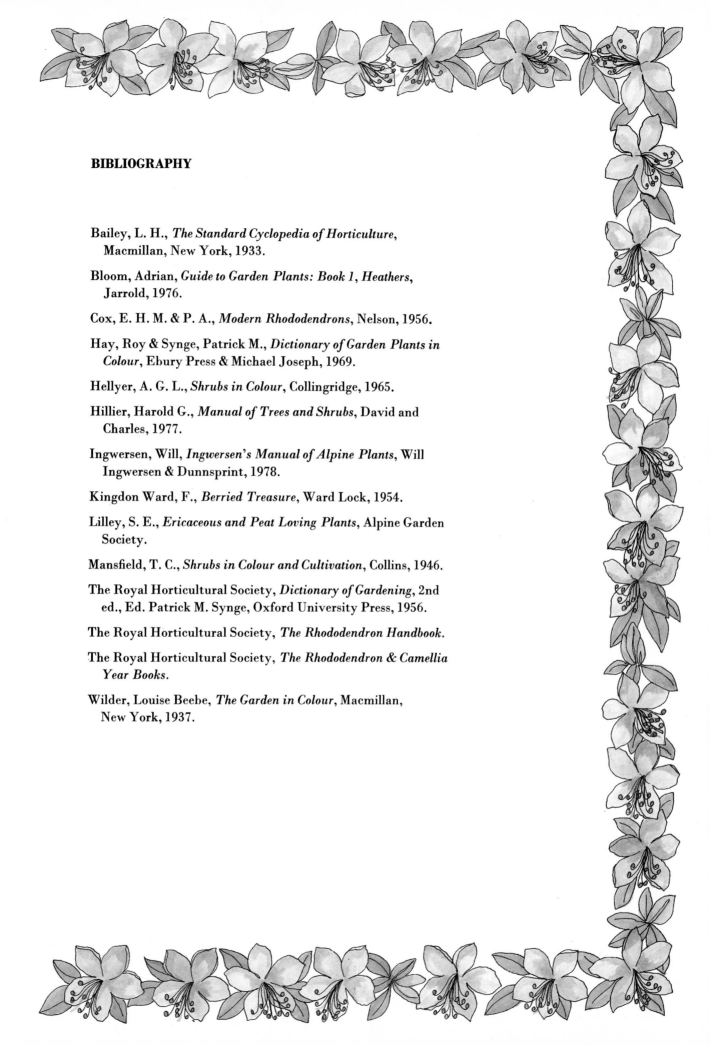

BIBLIOGRAPHY

Bailey, L. H., *The Standard Cyclopedia of Horticulture*, Macmillan, New York, 1933.

Bloom, Adrian, *Guide to Garden Plants: Book 1, Heathers*, Jarrold, 1976.

Cox, E. H. M. & P. A., *Modern Rhododendrons*, Nelson, 1956.

Hay, Roy & Synge, Patrick M., *Dictionary of Garden Plants in Colour*, Ebury Press & Michael Joseph, 1969.

Hellyer, A. G. L., *Shrubs in Colour*, Collingridge, 1965.

Hillier, Harold G., *Manual of Trees and Shrubs*, David and Charles, 1977.

Ingwersen, Will, *Ingwersen's Manual of Alpine Plants*, Will Ingwersen & Dunnsprint, 1978.

Kingdon Ward, F., *Berried Treasure*, Ward Lock, 1954.

Lilley, S. E., *Ericaceous and Peat Loving Plants*, Alpine Garden Society.

Mansfield, T. C., *Shrubs in Colour and Cultivation*, Collins, 1946.

The Royal Horticultural Society, *Dictionary of Gardening*, 2nd ed., Ed. Patrick M. Synge, Oxford University Press, 1956.

The Royal Horticultural Society, *The Rhododendron Handbook*.

The Royal Horticultural Society, *The Rhododendron & Camellia Year Books*.

Wilder, Louise Beebe, *The Garden in Colour*, Macmillan, New York, 1937.

The Iris Family

Iridaceae

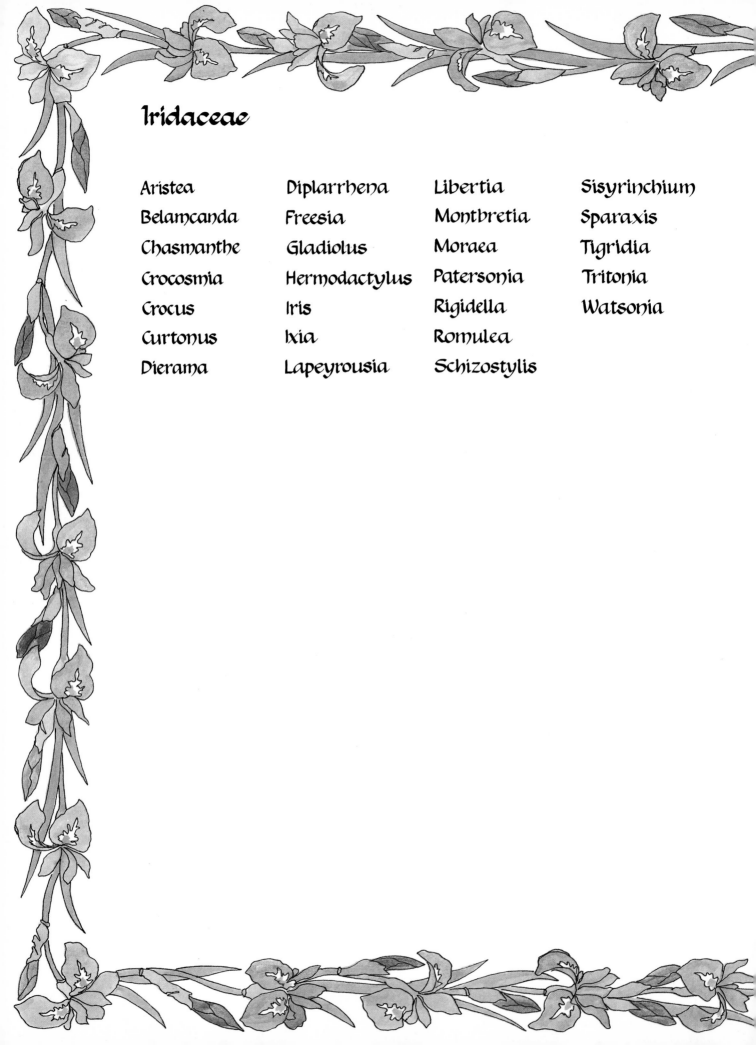

Aristea	Diplarrhena	Libertia	Sisyrinchium
Belamcanda	Freesia	Montbretia	Sparaxis
Chasmanthe	Gladiolus	Moraea	Tigridia
Crocosmia	Hermodactylus	Patersonia	Tritonia
Crocus	Iris	Rigidella	Watsonia
Curtonus	Ixia	Romulea	
Dierama	Lapeyrousia	Schizostylis	

The Iris Family

It was Plato's pupil Theophrastus, philosopher, naturalist and botanist, who named this family after the Greek goddess of the rainbow. The species number nearly 1,000 and they are of such beauty that they are widely cultivated for ornament alone. Not that they do not have their usefulness: the roots of many have been used for such diverse purposes and products as sachet perfume and tooth powder, dropsy and diarrhoea, the iris-green of the painter prepared by treating violet iris flowers with lime, the seeds of another species ground as a substitute for coffee, the dried stigmas of *Crocus sativus*, the Saffron, still used for flavouring and colouring cakes, rice and fish dishes.

The flowers of the family are equally diverse: the long single cups of the Crocus, whose motley of gold, purple, striped lavender, blue and white brings to our borders the first gay colours of the year; summer's carmine stars of *Lapeyrousia;* the small lilies of *Crocosmia* bursting into red and orange flames as they climb up their stem; the graceful wands of Angels' Fishing Rods (*Dierama pulcherrimum*) bending to the weight of pink and wine-red bells; the gorgeous spikes of *Gladiolus* crowding in pastel pinks and peaches and apricots to burgundy, yellows, blues and even green.

And the Iris itself is diverse within its own genus in colour and kind, from stately Bearded Iris to the little scented pink and purple *Iris graminea*, 3 in. (75 mm) high. Because the name is Iris, the flower-colours run through the rainbow—ethereal blues, through rich golds and purple, to lurid thunderstorm bronze.

Borders often cry out for plants that provide a foil for others. The sword-like leaves of *Crocosmia* and *Iris* are a contrast to soft-foliaged plants. In the rock garden even tiny sisyrinchiums can act in this way

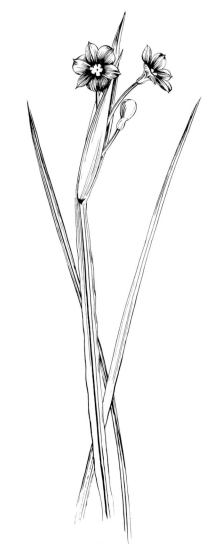

Sisyrinchium bermudiana

among carpeters and cushion alpines. They also provide another dimension.

Those gardening in colder climates who have a greenhouse are specially favoured with the more tender genera. Fresias may struggle outdoors—but thrive under glass, producing their lovely scented sprays of orange, creamy-yellow and lavender blue. Tritonias and Ixias are South Africans with brightly-coloured flowers; and Sparaxis called the Harlequin Flower. Most beautiful of all are the iridescent jewel-like Peacock Moraeas.

CARE AND CULTURE

Colour is the theme of the Iris family. Its members come from the Cape of Good Hope and subtropical America, and from the northern hemisphere particularly round the Mediterranean and into western Asia as far as Afghanistan. These two types of provenance, it can be seen, have produced two definite groups: hardy and tender. But all are worth growing. Some of the genera will be new to most of us: they are a challenge to gardeners to see what they can do with the more unusual.

The family is most nearly related to the *Amaryllidaceae*, but differs in having three stamens instead of six. The leaves come from the rootstock, not from a stem, and are sword-shaped or grassy. The rootstock itself is either a corm or a rhizome, that is a rooting underground stem, although the thick fleshy tubers of the Bearded Iris like to lie along the surface of the ground to absorb the sunshine. All the family are sun-lovers.

Propagating

The two most important genera are the well-known and well-loved Crocus and Iris. Both are easy to grow if you follow a few

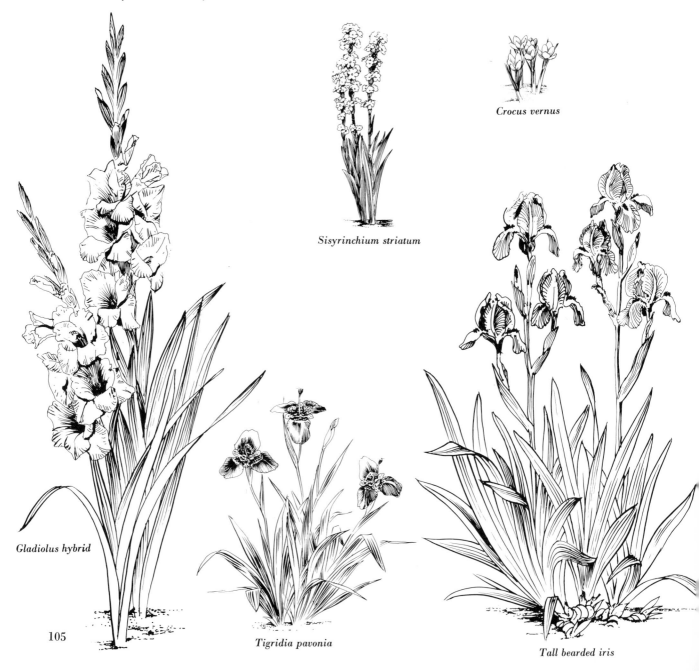

Crocus vernus

Sisyrinchium striatum

Gladiolus hybrid

Tigridia pavonia

Tall bearded iris

105

basic rules. First, the depth at which to plant: for crocuses the corm should be no more than 3 in. (75 mm) below the surface. Crocuses can also be planted in grass, if the grass is cut short at the end of the growing season. Cut a section of turf on three sides and roll it back like a carpet. Stir the soil and scatter a little sand and peat. To each square foot place 6–8 corms in a group. Replace the turf.

A plea to plant species crocuses as well as the commoner large ones! Start with *tomasinianus*, *vernus*, and *chrysanthus*, all of which seed freely. In a few years they will have doubled and trebled themselves. And because they cross-pollinate easily you may find new ones among them. This is one of the gardener's rewards—to breed his own variants.

Crocuses can also be grown in pots for the house. They are a joy in a pretty bowl. When the foliage has died down plant them outdoors where they will get sunshine every day.

It is not generally realised that crocuses give a flowering period of nine months, August to April, depending on the sequence of the species you choose.

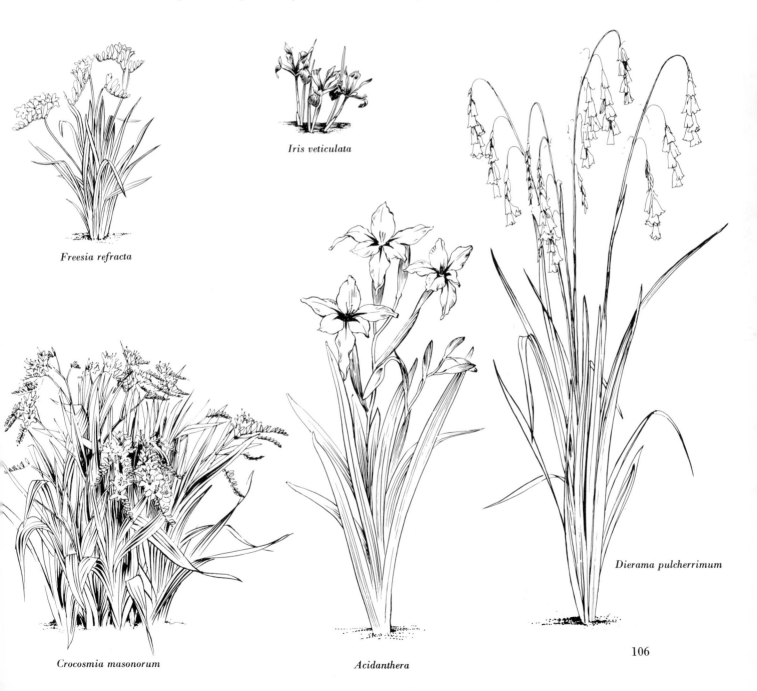

Freesia refracta

Iris veticulata

Crocosmia masonorum

Acidanthera

Dierama pulcherrimum

106

Iris danfordiae

In growing irises one adopts an opposite technique: it is best to choose species and varieties that flower at the same time. A bed or long border of them can be a breath-taking spectacle when they are all in bloom, tall ones at the back, graduating to shorter ones at the front.

There are three flowering seasons. Earliest to bloom is the lovely and fragrant *Iris unguicularis* (*stylosa*) of fragile lavender-blue flowers which brave the winter from December to Easter, followed by the little *reticulata* which in its Oxford and Cambridge blues from February to April matches well with the yellow *danfordiae*. The last-named is reputedly difficult, but this is because next season's flowers grow from newly-formed bulblets. It has to work up a four-year rota before it can be called established. Rhizomatous irises should be divided (with a sharp knife) every four years, late in July after flowering, or in October or March. Sprinkle bone meal round them after replanting.

There is no more elegant flower than the Gladiolus, which again has three seasons, covering early July until late October. It is superb for cutting. Used as a garden flower it will seed itself year after year and increase, too, from cormlets. Most gardeners lift the corms in autumn, planting out again in April. After about eight weeks, when the plant has formed five or six leaves, copious watering and liquid feeding must begin. Feeding should be continued almost until it is time to lift the corms.

Among the tender genera needing shelter or warmth is the single-species *Belamcanda*, the Blackberry Lily or Leopard Flower, whose purple-spotted red blooms are like miniatures of *Tigridia*, the Tiger Plant, which shows its gorgeous spotted flowers for only a few hours before melting away, but is closely followed by others. Ixias and Tritonias are closely related, both with brightly-coloured flowers growing up a spike. Sparaxis has large showy single flowers. The handsome Watsonias are on the borderline of hardiness.

FLOWERS OF THE FAMILY

So we have something for everybody in this beautiful and often fragrant family of flowers.

Crocosmia. The first Montbretias were pretty enough, averaging 1 ft (300 mm) spikes of reddish-yellow flowers rising from sword-like leaves. Now a host of brilliant hybrids has been developed.

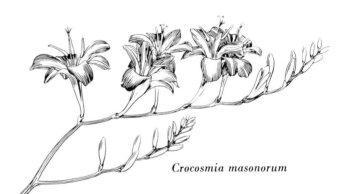

Crocosmia masonorum

masonorum was the forerunner of the new strains, larger in every degree and with vermilion-orange flowers in late summer looking up from the top of the arching stems, instead of poised forward under them. Its height is 3 ft (900 mm).

This plant crossed with *Curtonus paniculatus* has produced a hybrid with flowers twice the size, on sprays $2\frac{1}{2}$ ft (800 mm) tall. Their colour is burnt orange-red, the name 'Ember Glow'. It flowers in July and August. 'Lucifer' is newer but the flowers are incomparably finer and more colourful, brilliant flame-red and the

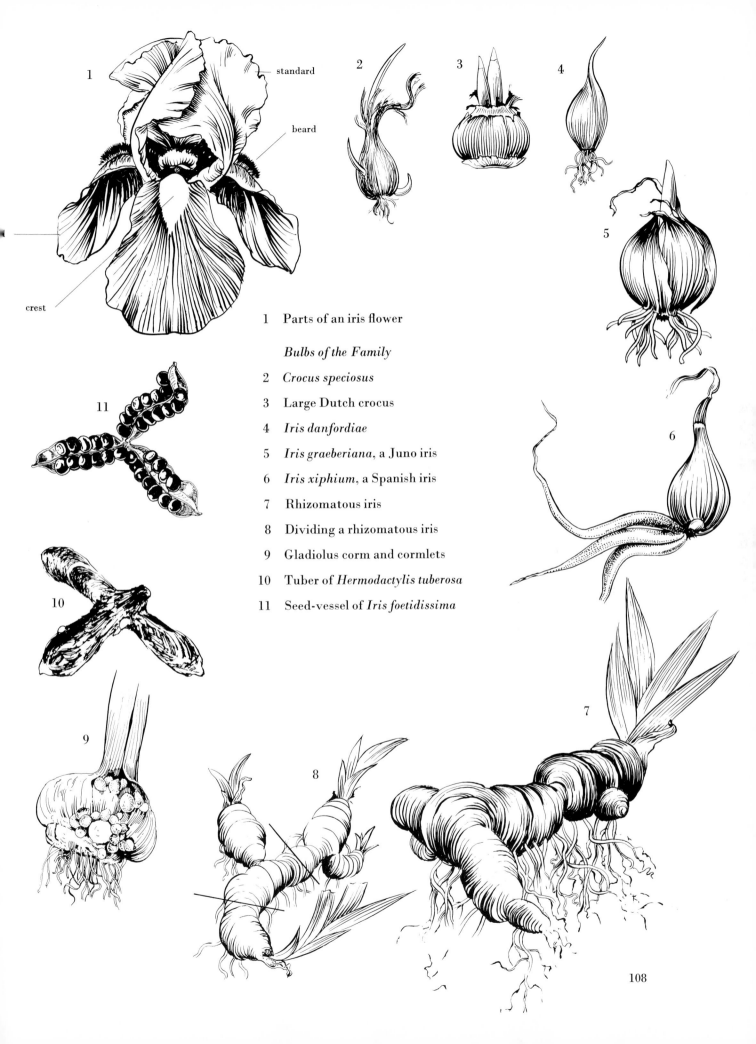

standard

beard

crest

1   Parts of an iris flower

Bulbs of the Family

2   *Crocus speciosus*

3   Large Dutch crocus

4   *Iris danfordiae*

5   *Iris graeberiana*, a Juno iris

6   *Iris xiphium*, a Spanish iris

7   Rhizomatous iris

8   Dividing a rhizomatous iris

9   Gladiolus corm and cormlets

10 Tuber of *Hermodactylis tuberosa*

11 Seed-vessel of *Iris foetidissima*

108

first to bloom, giving a splendid show from late June or early July. Height just over 3 ft (900 mm).

rosea, at 2 ft (600 mm) is smaller than the others, with charming soft-pink flowers from June to August, and always gives the impression of being a rarity. It mingles beautifully with other soft-coloured flowers.

Crocus. Of the hundreds of species and varieties, we can describe only a few, and will do so by dividing them into their three flowering seasons: autumn-flowering (late August to the end of November); winter-flowering (December to mid-February), and spring-flowering (mid-February to April). These will be species crocuses. We will also recommend the best of the garden-raised or large Dutch varieties.

Leafless Autumn-flowering

speciosus, late-August-October, the flowers with their showy stigmas appearing before the leaves. Easy and hardy. By seeding and cormlets will make sheets of blue. Good forms are 'Aitchisonii', the largest, lavender-blue petals 3 in. (75 mm) long, mid-October; 'Artabir', pale lavender-blue with darker markings; 'Cassiope',

Crocus speciosus

bluish-lavender with a creamy-yellow base; 'Oxonian', probably the bluest, mid-October.

byzantinus, September-October. Large outer petals rich bluish-purple, much smaller inner ones pale silvery-mauve, feathery blue stigmas.

kotschyanus, end of August to September. Large rosy-lilac with two bright orange spots inside and yellow throat.

medius, October-November. Large flowers, lilac outside, inside bright purplish-mauve with purple star in the throat, scarlet branched stigmas. Hardy, but also good for the alpine house.

nudiflorus, late-September to November. Handsome with large and long deep-purple petals, sometimes white; orange stigmas. Spreads by underground stolons and should be left undisturbed: one might think they were the roots of Couch Grass.

scharojanii, first week in August. Beautiful deep yellow. Needs more shade and cooler summer conditions than other crocuses.

Autumn-flowering with Leaves

laevigatus, October-March, with one other crocus the longest-blooming. Lilac flowers or white, veined and feathered with crimson-purple on the outer petals. Tiny and sweetly-scented.

longiflorus, October to the end of November. Globular flowers of deep violet with scarlet anthers. Strongly plum-scented.

sativus, Saffron, September-October. Deep purple-red veined with darker purple

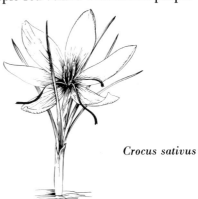

Crocus sativus

in the throat. The large scarlet stigmas are scented and float out from the open flowers. Dried, they are used in cooking as a colouring and flavouring substance, 4,000 being needed to make one ounce.

Winter-flowering

aureus, late-January to mid-February, the original yellow crocus that was cultivated, and parent of the Dutch Yellow Crocus. The flowers are tiny cups of burning orange.

Crocus chrysanthus
'Yellow Hammer'

chrysanthus, mid-January to late-March. The most prolific parent of beautiful varieties and the most reliable of the winter-flowering species. Deep orange-yellow, 2–5 flowers appearing from each of the three sets of sheathing leaves. Prized varieties are 'Blue Pearl', silvery-blue inside with a bronze base and shaded dark blue on the outside; 'Cream Beauty', large globular flowers of a lovely rich cream; 'E. A. Bowles', named in honour of the "Crocus King", with flowers of butter yellow tinted and marked with greyish-brown outside; his 'Yellow Hammer', richest yellow feathered with brown; 'Moonlight' sulphur-yellow shading to pale cream; 'Snow Bunting', scented and glistening white with a golden throat, feathered with purple; and 'Zwanenburg Bronze', deep golden-yellow shaded dark bronze.

imperati, December-March. Large handsome flowers up to 4 in. (100 mm) across, varying in colour and marking, from warm buff to pale straw, and either self-coloured or marked or feathered with deep purple lines.

Crocus sieberi
'Hubert Edelsten'

sieberi, January-March, beautiful globular blooms of bright lilac with an orange throat, tipped and striped with purple-maroon; orange stamens and scarlet stigmas. Superb varieties are 'Hubert Edelsten' with an area of white between the maroon-shaded tips of the petals and the basal markings; 'Bowles's White', one of the best of the all-white crocuses; 'Tricolor' with three distinct bands of colour, "like a lilac egg in a silver and gold egg-cup", as it was once described.

tomasinianus, early February. One of the hardiest, and increasing rapidly from seed and cormlets. Long slender cups of pale lavender-blue shaded silvery-blue. Lovely varieties include 'Taplow Ruby' with outstanding dark ruby-purple flowers; 'Whitewell Purple' of a purple not seen in any other crocus, charming and free-flowering.

Spring-flowering

biflorus, March, the Scottish crocus known as 'Cloth of Silver' for its silvery-mauve feathered flowers with a metallic sheen. Hardy and blooms freely. Some varieties are 'Argenteus', pale lilac feathered with mauve; 'Weldeni Albus', rounded flowers of glistening pure white, very free-blooming.

korolkowii, January to early February. Small, deep yellow, outer petals flushed and feathered with purplish-mahogany, star-shaped when open, revealing glossy deep-yellow interior. Hardy, but also good for the alpine house.

susianus, February-March. Brilliant deep orange, and aptly named the 'Cloth of Gold' crocus. Outer petals and base of inside prominently marked with mahogany. Dwarf, for the rock garden or in drifts.

vernus, March. The flowers come before the leaves. Variable in colour and markings from pure white to deep purple, and has given rise to a large race of garden hybrids sometimes known as Dutch Hybrids. Two recommended are 'Vanguard', early-flowering, ageratum-blue, French-grey outside, good for naturalising or if potted early will flower by Christmas; and 'Vanguard Violet', a beautiful uniform violet-coloured variety for the rock garden or alpine house.

versicolor, February-March. Large, variable from white to purple, unusually feathered inside except in a few white-

Crocus versicolor

grounded forms. A good variety is 'Picturatus', ruby feathers on white, a gem for the rock garden.

Large Dutch Crocus

These flower later than species crocuses and come in purple, amethyst, mauve, lavender, white, yellow, and striped. They should not be planted deeply, just a light covering of soil.

White:

'Jeanne d'Arc', the largest of all the pure whites, vigorous.

'Kathleen Parlow', large globular flowers with golden anthers, fine lasting qualities.

'Peter Pan', of outstanding purity with conspicuous orange stigmas, large flowers in profusion.

Pale lilac-mauve:

'Enchantress', tinged deeper purple towards base, early flowering.

'Little Dorrit', silvery sheen, large globular flowers.

'Pickwick', striped and feathered with deep lilac, enormous golden-yellow stigmas, huge flowers in profusion.

'Queen of the Blues', bold long flowers with purple shading.

'Striped Beauty', glossy purple base, soft lilac stripes.

Deep purple:

'Negro Boy', distinctive shade of glossy blackish-purple.

'Purpureus grandiflorus', large, an old variety still unsurpassed and with a satin sheen.

'Remembrance', one of the best in cultivation, with an abundance of soft purple-blue flowers.

Yellow:

'Dutch Yellow', also called 'Large Yellow', 'Yellow Giant' and 'Dutch Yellow Mammoth', a top favourite, large flowers freely-blooming and long-lasting. Sterile, but reproducing from the cormlets.

Curtonus. A South African genus of a single species, *paniculatus*, with deep orange flowers like a montbretia, on branching zigzag stems up to 4 ft (1.25 m) tall in August and September. It is hardy, and often seen in old herbaceous borders. Formerly called *Antholyza paniculata*, hence its popular name of 'Aunt Eliza'.

Dierama pulcherrimum

Dierama. A genus of 25 species from tropical South Africa. Only one, *pulcherrimum*, is in general cultivation, being hardy and possessing all the virtues of a first-class garden plant. It has a swollen rootstock like a large corm, and fibrous roots. The slender flower-stems hung with dainty bells pink, purple, mauve or white grow up to 5 ft (1.50 m) tall, and arch over at the top like a fishing rod, earning it the name Angels' Fishing Rods. The leaves are narrow, stiff and grasslike. Fine varieties named after birds have been raised in

Northern Ireland: 'Heron', wine-red; 'Kingfisher', pale pinkish-purple; 'Skylark', purplish-violet.

Freesia refracta

Freesia. Of the 20 species of this genus, again only one is generally cultivated, *refracta* var. *Alba*, with white funnel-shaped flowers, also from South Africa. But it has been intensively hybridised, its variety *leichtlinii* of pale yellow flowers and the pink-flowered species *armstrongii* producing a race of exquisitely scented florists' flowers from October to May in almost every known flower-colour, yet all delicately subtle: white, cream and pale yellow, deep yellow and pale orange, pinks and crimsons, blues and mauves. The stems are up to 2 ft (600 mm) tall, often branched. the flowers opening in succession along the branch, which usually becomes bent over to the horizontal, enabling the flowers to face upwards. Corms grown indoors in a warm temperature can be stood outside for the summer in their pots. They must never be allowed to dry out, and in warm weather need watering every day.

Gladiolus. A genus of more than 150 species of which few are in cultivation. They are natives of South Africa and tropical Africa, extending into Asia Minor and southern Europe. The many lovely hybrids of complicated parentage make up for this; but there are three European species hardy in warm places and sometimes spreading and seeding freely. The flowers, funnel-shaped and slightly irregular, are borne on a one-sided spike so that they all face the same way.

Gladiolus byzantinus

byzantinus, Jacob's Ladder. Stems up to $2\frac{1}{2}$ ft (800 mm) with purplish-magenta flowers in June and July.

illyricus, has a slender stem up to $1\frac{1}{2}$ ft (450 mm) with 3–6 loosely spaced flowers of bright magenta-purple in June and July. Though hardy in warmer areas it is not so free-spreading or vigorous.

segetum, resembles *illyricus* but is stouter, almost hardy and flowers earlier, May-June.

Species from the Cape can be grown outdoors if their corms are lifted in the autumn and dried off in winter.

gracilis, the Slender Cornflag, with a wiry stem bearing 2–6 scented flowers in April, blue, pale pink or mauve.

grandis, the Large Brown Afrikander, pale reddish-brown wavy-edged flowers

shaded with yellow but variable, on stems 2 ft (600 mm) tall, with a strong carnation scent in the evening.

tristis, hardiest of the winter-growing Cape species, successfully established in sheltered places in the south and west of England. Sweet-scented flowers in May, sulphur-yellow tinged dull red. Its slightly hardier variety *concolor* is deeper in colour and lacks the red tinge, flowers larger.

Gladiolus callianthus

Gladiolus callianthus is the name now given to the Ethiopian plant long known as *Acidanthera bicolor*, whose vigorous variety *murielae* is more often grown, graceful with its long grassy leaves and white flowers maroon-starred in the throat and sweetly scented. It grows $2\frac{1}{2}$–$3\frac{1}{2}$ ft (800–1100 mm) tall and flowers at the end of September or early October.

The Hybrid Gladioli are divided into three groups, two according to size, from Midget-flowered to Giant-flowered, the third being the early-flowering *nanus* group.

To deal first with the last-named, these have a delicacy otherwise found only in the species and their near hybrids. They flower much earlier than the larger hybrids,

Gladiolus hybrid

Gladioli varieties can also be divided into early-, mid-season – and late-flowering, and by planting some of each a succession of bloom can be ensured from April till mid-October.

Hermodactylis. This used to be classed as an iris, which it closely resembles, but now has been given a genus to itself, the one species being *tuberosus*. In March the single flowers are borne on a 12 in. (300 mm) stem, the falls being purplish-black and the standards olive-green. When closed they resemble the head of a snake, hence the common name of Snake's-head Iris, distinguished from the true iris by its single seed-vessel, that of the iris splitting into three.

usually from April to early June, and with some protection will survive all but the most severe winters. They rarely grow more than 2 ft (600 mm) high.

The next group contains the Miniature- and Small-flowered Hybrids which have become very popular in recent years due to the many new varieties, some with ruffled edges to the flowers. They vary in height from 2–4 ft (600 mm–1.25 m), though height is not necessarily related to the size of the flower. The Butterfly Gladioli are included in this group, as are the Primulinus hybrids, attractive, with hooded upper petal and outer three triangular.

The Large-flowered Hybrids include Medium-flowered, Large-flowered, and Giant-flowered, with florets over 6 in. (150 mm) across. Most of these will attain 4 ft (1.25 m) if well cultivated.

So numerous are the hybrids in each class that it is impossible here to select even a few, for who could say that a salmon-pink with petals lightly overlaid with shrimp-red is more to be desired than a creamy-white with green markings? Suffice it that some at least should have a place in your garden, for their stately beauty and exquisite colours.

Iris. A genus of about 300 species with more hundreds of hybrids. There are many distinctive kinds—frilly-petalled Californians, stiff Dutch, the peculiar bull-headed Oncocyclus—and for easy identification they have been divided into two main groups: those with bulbs, and those with a woody rhizomatous rootstock or tuber.

Group I divides naturally into four categories:

1. Small Bulbous Irises (Early-flowering)

bakeriana, January-March. Lovely pale blue standards, the falls having a deep purple-blue tip with white spots. 6 in. (150 mm).

danfordiae, February, 3–4 in. (75–100 mm) high, golden-yellow speckled with brown, hardy even under snow.

histrioides, January. Brilliant ultramarine flowers 3 in. (75 mm) or so high, coming before the leaves. Also hardy. The form *major* has larger flowers.

Iris reticulata

Dutch iris (*xiphium*)

reticulata, February until April. Dark purple violet-scented flowers like tiny Dutch irises, with an orange flash, on 6 in. (150 mm) stems. Their dark colour is enhanced if grown among lighter-blue varieties such as 'Cantab.' (brightest Cambridge blue) or 'Jeannine' (clear sky-blue), and with 'Purple Gem' (ruby-purple standards, the falls purple-black spotted with white).

2. Juno (mostly flowering later. Distinguished by the large fleshy roots below the bulb)

aucheri (*sindjarensis*), early March. Exquisite lilac blooms, vanilla-scented. 6 in.–1 ft (150–300 mm).

bucharica, end of April. Exquisite lilac blooms vanilla-scented. 6 in. to 1 ft. (150-300 mm).

3. Xiphium (The Dutch, English, and Spanish Hybrid Irises of the florists)

Dutch:
May and June. Stiff petals in a colour-range that includes white, yellow, bronze, blue, mauve and purple. Easy to grow. Height 1–1½ ft (300–450 mm). Among the best are 'Blue Champion' (the largest flower in this section. Clear cornflower-blue); 'Golden Harvest' (the rich yellow iris of the florists); 'Imperator' (the popular indigo-blue); 'Wedgwood' (earliest to bloom. Light blue).

English:
A little later than the Dutch, slightly larger flowers. Colours include light blue, dark blue, mauve, deep purple. Recommended are 'Coombelands' (purplish-blue standards, deep-blue falls); 'King of the Blues' (dark blue with darker flecks); 'Mansfield' (bright wine-purple); 'Mont Blanc' (pure white).

Spanish:
Generally the earliest of the three sections. Among the best are 'Cajanus' (late-flowering, large, rich golden-yellow); 'Canary Bird' (bright canary-yellow, orange blotch on falls, waved margins); 'Hercules' (falls bronzy-brown with golden blotch, standards purplish-blue and bronze).

4. Oncocyclus and Regelio-cyclus

These two groups need summer baking to ensure sufficient ripening, with complete absence of moisture at that season. In spring they should be drenched with buckets of water just as they are starting freely into growth. Oncocyclus contains some of the most beautiful irises, with heavily veined petals such as in *acutiloba*, slate-white with deep chocolate veining up to 12 in. (300 mm) high. A recommended hybrid between Regelia and Oncocyclus is 'Chione', easier to grow, with standards of pale lilac and deeper veining, dark purple blotches on the falls.

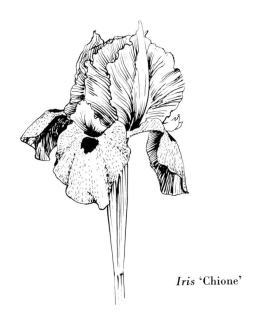

Iris 'Chione'

Group II divides into three categories.

1. Herbaceous Species and Forms

foetidissima, the Gladdon or Stinking Iris, but no garden should be without it. June flowers, smallish, yellowish-green and lilac, heavily veined. Brilliant orange-red seeds lasting throughout the winter. 18 in. (450 mm). The form 'Citrina' has a bigger citron and pale mauve flowers, and much larger seed-pods. 'Variegata' has attractive cream-striped evergreen leaves but seldom flowers.

fulva, from the United States, gorgeous and one of the last irises to flower, in July. Velvety brownish-terracotta. 2 ft (600 mm).

innominata, June. Variable in shades of yellow from pale cream to deep yellow. Up to 8 in. (200 mm), but forms large clumps in lime-free soil.

kaempferi, July. Treasured in its native land, Japan. Happy as a bog plant at pond edges. Bright-green deciduous leaves. Flowers, three short standards, three large drooping falls, usually red-purple. Hybrids from white through palest lavender to dark blue-purple, and red-purple to palest pink, or bicolored, and veined or plain. With its hybrids the richest and largest of all irises. Height 3 ft (900 mm).

pallida, May-June. Pale glaucous leaves, fragrant pale lavender flowers. Height 2–3 ft (600–900 mm). 'Variegata' is outstanding with striped leaves in two forms: 'Argentea', silver-striped; 'Aurea', gold-striped.

sibirica, June. Elegant grassy leaves from tufted roots. Two or three flowers together, bright violet-blue with gold markings. 3–4 ft (900–1200 mm). There are many lovely hybrids.

tectorum, May-June. A dwarf with clear-lilac standards, falls prettily crinkled with darker veining and white crest. 1 ft (300 mm). 'Variegata' has leaves striped with cream.

Iris unguicularis

unguicularis (*stylosa*), December-April. Exquisite lavender flowers; pale, darker, and white forms. For poor dry soil against a sunny wall, 2 ft (600 mm). A must.

2. Bearded Hybrids

These are divided into three classes: Dwarf, Intermediate, and Tall. The Dwarfs, up to 8 in. (200 mm), flower in April and early May. Colours are creamy-yellow, blue, white, purple. They need full sun.

116

Iris 'Amethyst Flame'

The Intermediates are up to 27 in. (680 mm) and bloom from mid-April to June. Among the best are 'Lilli-Bitone' (a bicolor of white standards, deep purplish-red falls); 'Scintilla' (bicolor of white and tawny-brown); 'Small Wonder', (bright sky-blue, orange beard and veining).

The Tall Bearded Irises range between 27 in. (680 mm) and 4 ft (1.25 m) and bloom in early summer, the flowers up to 6 in. (150 mm) across. These have a fantastic colour range, making spectacular displays when grouped together. Among the hundreds of varieties are 'Dancer's Veil' (falls white heavily margined with deep-violet-purple and streaks near the base, standards with a white base, much ruffled at edges); 'Esther Fay' (pale apricot-pink with deep orange-red beard, ruffled edge); 'Helen McGregor' (pale silvery-blue with ruffled edge); 'Rippling Waters' (pale

lilac-purple with orange beard, large flowers with wavy margins to falls and standards); 'Velvet Robe' (deep mahogany-crimson with velvet texture, ruffled edge to falls).

3. Rock Garden Perennials

douglasiana, May. A Californian with stems 6–12 in. (150–300 mm). Extremely variable in colour, mainly purple or bluish-purple. Sun or semi-shade.

lacustris (*cristata* var. *lacustris*), May. Makes a mat of slender rhizomes, falls pale lilac-blue with white and gold markings, standards erect, stems about 1 in. (25 mm).

verna, April-May. From the United States. Lilac-mauve, beardless, but with golden crest to falls. 6 in. (150 mm).

Ixia. The African Corn Lily, is not hardy in most gardens. Mixed hybrids are usually grown now, in pots in the greenhouse, but it is worth quoting two species for favoured places. All are very free-flowering and produce long graceful racemes of colourful blooms on strong wiry stems up to 18 in. (450 mm) high. They are ideal for cutting.

maculata is the hardiest species. April-May. Deepest golden-yellow spotted blackish or purplish on a dense many-flowered spike. Its variety *ochroleuca* has creamy-yellow flowers with a brown ring around the centre.

viridiflora is the species commonly offered by nurserymen. Grown for its striking Prussian blue shading on bright green, star-like flowers. A purple eye completes the brilliant picture. May-June.

Lapeyrousia. Sometimes known as *Anomatheca*, is a genus of South African plants, only one of which is hardy in Britain and North America south of Washington, D.C., although in a light warm soil it will happily naturalize.

Moraea villosa

cruenta, late summer to November, stem up to 12 in. (300 mm) bearing up to 12 carmine-scarlet flowers opening to stars, the lower ones having an indistinct blotch at the base. Like most of the South African introductions, it makes a good plant for pots in a cool greenhouse.

Libertia. Native to Australasia and the South American Andes, so for warmer places.

formosa, from among dark-green swordlike leaves, gracefully recurving, spring white saucer-shaped flowers on a long tapering spike in May. Height 3 ft (900 mm).

ixioides, from New Zealand, is similar but smaller, 2 ft (600 mm). The leaves often turn bright orange-brown in winter, and *grandiflora* is much alike.

Moraea. The Butterfly Iris, also called the Peacock Moraeas because of its brilliant jewel-like and iridescent petals of which there are three large wide-spreading outer ones, rounded at the edge, and three inner ones so small as to be almost rudimentary. For warm places, or the greenhouse.

glaucopis is regularly offered by nurserymen under the erroneous name of *Iris pavonia*. White or very pale blue with a deep peacock-blue spot rimmed like a peacock's eye at the base of each outer petal. 1 ft (300 mm), May-June.

papilionacea, March-May. Only a few inches high. Bright orange-red, yellow or salmon-pink, with a yellow blotch.

villosa, May. Very variable in colour, mauvish-purple with iridescent blue blotch, pale mauve, cream, yellow, orange. The parent of a range of hybrids like tropical butterflies.

Romulea. Though best grown in pans in a cool greenhouse, where they will bloom early in spring, they can also be planted outdoors in short grass in full sun.

bulbocodium. Common in the South of France and in Italy, usually in sand dunes. Small chalice-shaped, bright purple flowers on 6 in. (150 mm) stems, in March and April indoors, a month later outdoors.

118

requienii, from Corsica and Sardinia, hardy, in April bearing large dark-violet flowers on 3 in. (75 mm) stems.

sabulosa, from Natal, one of the best. Bristly leaves and globular cherry-red flowers veined with crimson. Height 5 in. (125 mm), March-April.

Schizostylis. The Kaffir Lily, September-November. Hardy, provided they are grown in a warm sunny place with some shelter.

coccinea, has starry flowers up to 2 in. (50 mm) across, pretty red or pink, borne in a terminal raceme. Also for pots in a cold greenhouse. Height up to 2 ft (600 mm). There are three good varieties.

Sisyrinchium striatum

Sisyrinchium. A large genus of tiny to medium-sized plants, easy and useful. There are many attractive species.

angustifolium, the Blue-eyed Grass from North America, now naturalized in Britain. Tufts of grassy leaves, blue flowers on 6 in. (150 mm) stems in July.

douglasii, early spring, 6–9 in. (150–230 mm) stems bearing pendent wine-coloured bells.

striatum, the Satin Flower, summer. Fans of iris-like leaves and 2 ft (600 mm) spikes of cream or pale-yellow flowers. There is a handsome form with green-and-white variegated leaves.

We have described several genera making good plants for warmer places or the cold greenhouse. Others are given below:

Rigidella. The best-known species is *flammea*, early in summer bearing large umbels of drooping scarlet flowers striped with purple.

Sparaxis, the Wand Flower, of which *grandiflora* has deep-violet or cream flowers on a stem 18 in. (450 mm) tall; *tricolor*, not so tall, orange-red shaded yellow at the centre, long-lasting as cut blooms.

Tigridia. Blooms outdoors in July-September, indoors June, large outer petals forming a deep cup: *curvata*, 12 in. (300 mm), yellow spotted with purple, inner petals brown and heavily spotted; *pavonia*, 18 in. (450 mm), the Peacock Tiger Flower, with outer petals shading to scarlet and with yellow zones.

Tritonia. Has arching spikes of flowers, tangerine-yellow, orange, amber, rich cream or pink.

Watsonia. The Southern Bugle Lily, with fans of leaves, flowers on tall spikes, the species *beatricis* being an evergreen with flowers varying from orange-pink to flame and terracotta in September, 3 ft (900 mm); *pyramidata*, having 5 ft (1.5 m) spikes of clear pink in midsummer.

BIBLIOGRAPHY

Bailey, L. H., *The Standard Cyclopedia of Horticulture*, Macmillan, New York, 1933.

Berrisford, Judith M., *Irises*, Garden Book Club, 1961.

Bowles, E. A., *A Handbook of Crocus and Colchicum*, Bodley Head, 1952.

Dykes, W. R., *The Genus Iris*, Dover Publications, 1976.

Dykes, W. R., *A Handbook of Garden Irises*, Martin Hopkinson, 1924.

Genders, Roy, *Bulbs: a Complete Handbook*, Robert Hale, 1973.

Hay, Roy & Synge, Patrick M., *Dictionary of Garden Plants in Colour*, Ebury Press & Michael Joseph, 1969.

Ingwersen, Will, *Ingwersen's Manual of Alpine Plants*, Will Ingwersen & Dunnsprint, 1978.

Synge, Patrick M., *Collins Guide to Bulbs*, Collins, 1961.

The Royal Horticultural Society, *Dictionary of Gardening*, 2nd ed., Ed. Patrick M. Synge, Oxford University Press, 1956.

Thomas, Graham Stuart, *Perennial Garden Plants*, Dent, 1976.

Wilder, Louise Beebe, *The Garden in Colour*, Macmillan New York, 1937.

The Lily Family

Liliaceae

Agapanthus
Allium
Anthericum
Aphyllanthus
Asphodeline
Asphodelus
Brodiaea
Bulbine
Bulbinella
Bulbocodium
Calochortus
Camassia
Cardiocrinum
Chionodoxa
Clintonia
Colchicum

Convallaria
Dianella
Disporum
Endymion
Eremurus
Erythronium
Fritillaria
Galtonia
Hemerocallis
Herpolirion
Hosta
Kniphofia
Lilium
Liriope
Milligania
Muscari

Nomocharis
Oakesiella
Ophiopogon
Ornithogalum
Paradisia
Paris
Philesia
Phormium
Polygonatum
Puschkinia
Rohdea
Scilla
Scoliopus
Smilacina
Speirantha
Sternbergia

Tricyrtis
Trillium
Triteleia
Tulipa
Uvularia
Veratrum
Yucca
Zigadenus

The Lily Family

Consider the lilies . . . There are a lot of them, about 2,000 species arranged in some 200 genera and inhabiting both the temperate and tropical regions of the world.

Most are herbaceous perennials, some are annuals, a few are shrubs or even trees. They grow from rootstocks or bulbs and the veins of their leaves are parallel, running the length of the leaf and not branching from a mid-rib. Botanically the flowers are called 'perfect', meaning that they are complete with all the flower-parts. Aesthetically in beauty and fragrance those we call lilies are surely as perfect as a flower can be.

The members of the family greet us from the first days of the year when the little *Chionodoxa*, Glory of the Snow, spreads its blue carpet for Spring to walk upon. More blue comes with scilla and the Grape Hyacinths, followed by the blue, pink and white bells of endymion. Then in May arrives the battalion of tulips of very colour and kind: the stately Darwins, exotic Parrots, and Fringed, Feathered and Flamed; with the Lily of the Valley, Sir Walter Scott's "Sweet May lilies" that "richest odours shed down the valley's shady bed".

Summer is with us when the lilies themselves open their trumpets, heralding the arrival in August of *Lilium auratum*, the Golden-rayed Mountain Lily of Japan, acclaimed Queen of Lilies.

Meanwhile other lilies have been coming into flower: the noble Crown Imperial that sheds its tears at Easter, and the smaller fritillaries of chequerboard cups; the exquisite Ornithogalums of jade and silvery-grey and pure white stars; Wake Robin Trilliums and the gorgeous Yuccas with their astounding creamy heads.

September brings the freakish Toad Lilies into flower. *Hemerocallis*, the Day

Convallaria majalis

Lilies, orange, yellow and pink, have delighted us, their leaves have faded into gold. Now the flaming pokers of *Kniphofia* carry the torch for autumn.

October, and the blue heads of the agapanthus still hold, but the lily year is almost over. It has been with us for eight months, displaying an unforgettable pageant of beauty but, wonderfully, one that will return to us year after year.

124

CARE AND CULTURE

First we consider the most important member of the family, *Lilium*. There are about 80 species, natives of the temperate regions of the northern hemisphere including the temperate heights of the Nilgiri Hills.

Nearly all are hardy, and most will succeed in any light sandy or loamy soil. Add peat or leaf-mould, particularly to please the American species. All like cool for their roots, and this is best provided by growing them among other plants, where their trumpets, golden or white, pink and speckled, will be highlighted against a darker background—of shrubs, for instance, or tall border plants like delphiniums. Then, even if the border is in full sunshine, this is all right: most lilies come from sunny regions. A few, such as *henryi*, *hansonii*, *auratum* and *washingtonianum*, fail or their flowers suffer bleaching or fading. For them, shade from the mid-day sun.

So too for *canadense*, surely the most graceful with its candelabrum of pale orange flowers on arching and dipping pedicels; but give the martagons from Greece the full flood of sunshine so that their pink flames burn the more brilliant. The Tiger Lilies from Japan like a lime-free soil. Humboldt's Turk's-cap, primarily a woodland plant, grows well on lime.

Lilies are difficult to grow, we have been told. But they are easy, except for the few capricious ones like the pale pink trumpet *japonicum*. Understand their needs, and lilies will be yours.

Alliums benefit roses, it is said, if grown near them: they reduce black spot. In some countries where roses are grown for making perfume, garlic is grown with them. We can choose ornamental species such as *moly*, and enjoy its large brilliant-yellow blooms, or the purple-headed *schoenoprasum* (chives) as an edging.

In the forest clearings of the Rockies and

Lilium 'Black Dragon'

Kniphofia 'Royal Standard'

Trillium grandifolium

Hosta fortunei

the Blue Mountains camassias grow in drifts, concentrating the blue of their spikes. In Britain we can emulate this by letting them colonise like our own bluebells.

Indeed, many of the lily family should be grown in a mass. This is their natural habit. Those who have seen a field of the Snake's-head Fritillary must at first glimpse have held their breath in wonder. When E. H. Wilson was plant-hunting in China he walked through valley after valley, each filled with a different lily. So by separating bulbils and bulblets, scales and offsets, we too can make carpets of lily-flowers—colchicums in a few yards of grass, under trees if the soil is not too dry increase the fascinating trilliums, with all parts of their flower in threes. A woodland companion might be a colony of *Erythronium*, the Dog-tooth Violet of England, America's Trout Lily.

And everywhere we can grow hostas— for their bold foliage and spikes of lilac, violet or white flowers, adding a dramatic touch with one of the new phormiums of blue or scarlet leaves.

We might try experimenting with something we have never grown before. Liriope? Worth growing for its pretty foliage in December and January. Galtonia? This Giant Summer Hyacinth, with white bells on 4 ft (1.2 m) stems, is a lovely subject for the herbaceous border. For a cool position in the rock garden an oddity from Japan, the ophiopogon which has tufts of almost black leaves.

Not half enough attention is given by the home gardener to species tulips. Delight in the gorgeous and exotic hybrids, but learn about the Horned Tulip of the Pyrenees with its narrow twisted petals of yellow and red. See how the Lady Tulip opens to show its pink and white stripes. Plant the Water Lily Tulip in a sheltered nook of the rock garden, to give colour before the end of February; and, beneath young trees, the scented *florentina* of Italy.

Colchium autumnale

Chionodoxa luciliae

Fritillaria meleagris

Tulipa kaufmanniana

Erythronium dens canis

Darwin tulip 'La Tulipe noire'

126

Propagating

It is interesting that if we know which side of the world each species of lily comes from, we shall know how to plant them. They fall into two groups: those producing roots from the base of the bulb only, as in *candidum*, the Madonna Lily, and most of the European and American species; and the others including nearly all the Eastern Asiatic species, rooting from the base of the bulb and later from the stem above the bulb. This difference dictates the depth to which the bulbs should be planted: those rooting from the base only succeed well at a depth of 4–6 in. (100–150 mm), the stem-rooting at 8–10 in. (200–250 mm), to allow for the development of the stem roots. In heavy soil do not plant so deeply, but top-dress to help root development. There are exceptions: *candidum* is better planted with the top of the bulb only just covered. Always sprinkle a layer of clean sharp sand at the bottom of the hole.

Both lily and tulip bulbs need careful handling. Lily bulbs are not protected by a tunic or covering and the scales are easily broken. These store up nutrition, so it is important they do not become shrivelled. Do not remove the bulbs from their packing until you are ready to plant them. Similarly, with tulip bulbs, which should be planted with a wide trowel so that no air pocket is left beneath the bulb.

The month for planting is according to the species or variety. Unlike lilies, which hate to be disturbed, if tulip bulbs are allowed to remain in the ground year after year without division they will deteriorate. Species tulips are probably best lifted every year, dried off, and replanted in the autumn.

Most plants like plenty of room for their roots. Agapanthus is an exception. It will grow happily in a tub until its roots are snaking about the surface. Even then it does not ask to be disturbed, for it likes being pot-bound.

There is no difficulty with the other members of the family. Those with root-stocks, like Day Lilies and hostas, can easily be propagated by division.

Lilium candidum

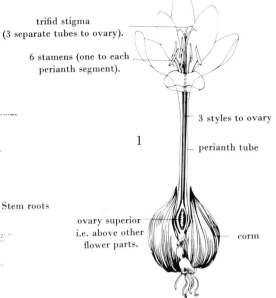

trifid stigma
(3 separate tubes to ovary).

6 stamens (one to each
perianth segment).

3 styles to ovary

perianth tube

1

ovary superior
i.e. above other
flower parts.

corm

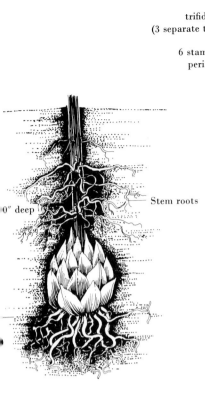

0" deep

Stem roots

6" deep

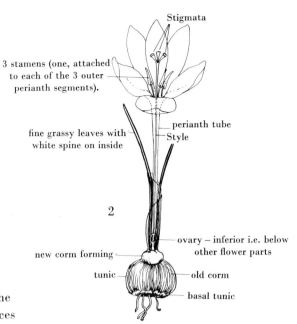

Stigmata

3 stamens (one, attached
to each of the 3 outer
perianth segments).

perianth tube
Style

fine grassy leaves with
white spine on inside

2

ovary – inferior i.e. below
other flower parts

new corm forming

tunic

old corm

basal tunic

Colchicums and crocuses look much the
same, but it is easy to tell the differences
between them.

1 Colchicum (Lily family), 6 stamens and
with ovary superior (*above* the other
flower-parts)

2 Crocus (Iris family), 3 stamens and
with ovary inferior (*below* the other
flower-parts)

3 Floral diagram of a scilla (Lily family)

4 Leaf of a hosta showing the parallel
veins typical of all lilies.

Root Systems

5 Rhizomatous root of Solomon's Seal

6 Bulb of tulip

7 Bulbs of Dog-tooth Violet

8 Bulbs of Snake's-head Fritillary

9 Basal-rooting lily

10 Stem-rooting lily (which also has
basal roots)

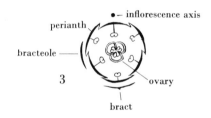

● – inflorescence axis

perianth

bracteole

3

ovary

bract

4

8

7

6

5

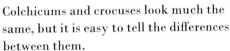

128

FLOWERS OF THE FAMILY

Agapanthus. The Blue African Lily always makes an impact with its huge round heads rising from among dark green strap-shaped leaves. In colder districts it should be grown in big pots or tubs, wintering indoors.

praecox (*umbellatus*) with heads of trumpet-shaped flowers, rich blue, growing to 4 ft (1.25 m), flowering late summer into early autumn. Two subspecies are *orientalis*, shorter, and *praecox praecox*, the largest and tallest. 'Maximus Albus' and 'Albatross' are two large white Californian varieties.

The Headbourne Hybrids are renowned: 'Luly', a magnificent light blue 2½ ft (800 mm); 'Loch Hope', a valuable late-flowerer with large heads, 4 ft (1.25 mm); the tiny dark blue 'Lilliput', and 'Cherry Holley' producing secondary flowers after the main crop, very dark blue, 2½ ft (800 mm).

Agapanthus praecox
(*umbellatus*)

Allium. Besides the onion, garlic and chives, the genus has many ornamental plants, some quite small, others highly decorative and good for winter flora.

beesianum, small flowers in heads of a beautiful blue rising from grassy leaves, 18 in. (450 mm) in late spring.

cernuum, rich amethyst or deep lilac-pink flowers borne in pretty drooping heads followed by exquisite seed-heads, 18 in. (450 mm).

giganteum, superb and stately with heads of tiny flowers of a rich warm lilac, 4–5 ft (1.25–1.5 m), in summer.

pulchellum, rich amethyst-purple flowers in summer, nodding in bud, after pollination turning upwards. Height 2 ft (600 mm). 'Album' is a beautiful white form.

senescens, with a dwarf tuft of curly grey leaves making a ground cover, the heads of the lilac flowers like a giant thrift. Height 1 ft (300 mm), late summer.

unifolium, flowers of old-rose in early summer. Height 2 ft (600 mm).

Anthericum. St Bernard's Lily of alpine meadows, *liliago*, is the species generally grown, for its racemes of charming lily-like flowers in June or early July. Height up to 2 ft (600 mm). It has good seed-spikes.

ramosum, tiny white flowers in summer borne in dainty much-divided spikes like a gypsophila. Height 3 ft (900 mm).

Asphodeline. A small genus with one member providing a handsome plant for the summer border: *lutea*, the Asphodel or King's Spear, with spikes 3 ft (900 mm) tall rising from a fountain of long narrow glaucous leaves. The yellow flowers pop out indiscriminately up and down and round the spike, followed by big green berries.

Brodiaea. A large genus of Western North American plants growing from corms, popular in California for naturalising but not yet understood in Britain. They should be planted in a group at least, and divided every few years. Good for heavy soil.

bridgesii, lilac-mauve, blue or reddish-lilac flowers in June, star-like when open, in small umbels on stems 8–12 in. (200–300 mm).

Brodiaea ida-maia

ida-maia, the Californian Firecracker, with drooping long tubed flowers, bright crimson-red topped with bright yellow and yellow-green in tight umbels of up to 15 flowers on the 3 ft (900 mm) stem in June.

laxa, probably the finest species. Like a small agapanthus, flowering June-July on stems up to 3 ft (900 mm). The best forms have deep violet-blue or white flowers on long pedicels in large umbels up to 1 ft (300 mm) across.

Camassia. E. A. Bowles used camassias effectively in his alpine meadow, but they produce better spikes in the garden border. Plant the bulbs 9 in. (250 mm) deep. One of the finest species is *leichtlinii* of long slender spires of starry flowers in early

summer, varying from whitish to deep blue, sometimes light yellow. Height 3–4 ft (900 mm– 1.25 m). The form 'Plena' has starry rosettes of creamy-yellow.

Chionodoxa. The wild plant flowers among the melting snows, hence its name Glory of the Snow. The leaves are grassy, the flowers up to a dozen on a scape, starry and blue shading to white. The only species commonly grown is the 6 in. (150 mm) *luciliae* flowering February-April. There are pink and white forms.

Colchicum. The best-known species is commonly called the Autumn Crocus, but there are spring-flowering and winter-flowering kinds as well, and although like a crocus in appearance the colchicum differs in almost every detail, as the drawings show. They are easy to grow, but allowance must be made for their very large leaves which die back in June and should not be removed until they wither.

Colchicum autumnale

autumnale, sometimes called Naked Boys or Naked Ladies, the pinkish-purple flowers blooming without the leaves. There are fine purple and white doubles.

byzantinum, one of the largest and most free-flowering of the autumn colchicums, producing up to 20 pale rosy-lilac flowers.

speciosum, probably the finest of the genus, with large tulip-like flowers in September and October, varying in colour from pale rosy-lilac to deep reddish-purple. The white variety, 'Album', is one of the finest white garden flowers.

Some superb hybrids and forms have been raised, inheriting the good constitution of *speciosum*. Recommended are 'Atrorubens', 'Disraeli', 'Huxley' and 'The Giant'.

Winter-flowering

These species are tessellated, the petals of their large flowers covered with a chequerboard pattern in dark and light rosy-mauve. They flower in November and December and are less vigorous but so beautiful that they are worth the challenge.

Colchicum bowlesianum

bowlesianum, egg-shaped flowers, very large, the broad petals pointed, rosy-lilac unevenly chequered with darker purplish-violet, flowering in November.

variegatum, later flowering, usually in December, the chequering more distinct and the petals tapering to long points. This could be a plant for the alpine house.

Spring-flowering

Some of these are charming little plants with flowers considerably smaller. This section also contains the only yellow-flowering species.

catacuzenium, pale rosy-lilac and globular, the petals about 1 in. (25 mm) long and half as wide, the flowers borne in a large cluster practically on the ground, March-April.

luteum, medium-sized bright yellow flowers with narrow petals, 2–3 to a spathe in February. Good for the alpine house.

Convallaria. A genus of a single species, *majalis*, the Lily of the Valley, famed for its perfume. It has rhizomatous roots from which arise a pair of beautiful spathe-like leaves and sprays of dangling white bells. It flowers early in May, the variety 'Fontins Giant' with larger bells 3–4 weeks later. The form *rosea* has bells of palest pink, and there is a double white form *flore-plena*.

Eremurus. The Foxtail Lilies are among the most magnificent of all perennials, sending up from clumps of strap-shaped leaves that die away in the summer tapering columns of starry flowers up to 9 ft (2.75 m) tall. The long stamens give them the fuzzy appearance of a fox's brush.

bungei, a dwarf about 1 ft (300 mm) high with bright yellow spikes in June. It has various yellow varieties.

131

elwesii, up to 6 or 9 ft (1.75–2.75 m)
with pink spikes in May.

himalaicus, up to 2 ft (600 mm) with
starry white flowers.

robusta, 8 or 9 ft (2.5–2.75 m) with
peach-coloured flowers and wide bright
green leaves.

Erythronium. Small plants generally called
the Dog-tooth Violet, with leaves prettily
mottled, single flowers with petals either
reflexed like a cyclamen, or upturned at
the tips. They are at home in broken
sunshine, and, like all lilies, are best grown
in groups, and in soil that is not too dry.

americanum, single pale or deep-golden
flowers in April flushed dull red on the
outside at the base of the petals, red-
speckled inside. The thick narrowly oval
leaves have liver-coloured blotches.

californicum, one of the best for English
gardens. Flowers creamy-white, the wide-
spreading petals with tips reflexed, at the
base of each a faint ring of orange or
orange-brown beady markings, the leaves
dark green and heavily mottled.

Erythronium dens-canis

dens-canis, the European Dog-tooth
Violet, varying from white through pale
pink to deep pinkish-mauve, always with a
ring of orange-red markings at the base,
the blue-green leaves heavily marbled.
March-April.

hendersonii, vigorous and easy to grow,
heavy mottling of the dark leaves divided
by lighter green lines. Large flowers several
to a stem, their anthers and stalks pale
mauve. April.

Fritillaria. A genus divided into two
groups: European and Asiatic species, and
American, the second with only a few
exceptions difficult and unsatisfactory in
English gardens.

The flowers are unique: six petals
arranged in two whorls forming a bell, the
petals often chequered, with a conspicuous
nectary at the base like a dark maroon or
green dot. The colours of the flowers make
them distinctive.

acmopetala, translucent bronzy-green
bells with recurved pointed tips, shading
to yellowish-green at the base, nectaries
green. 1–3 flowers on 6 in. (150 mm) stem.

camschatcenis, long livid wine-purple
flowers 1–3 on a stem 6–18 in. (150–450 mm)
high. Good for the scree or rock garden.

imperialis, the Crown Imperial, the giant
of the genus, with huge bells in a cluster
at the top of a bare stalk up to 4 ft
(1.25 m) tall, surmounted by a tuft of
green leaves. Plants with yellow bells are
borne on green stems, those with red bells
on purplish stems.

meleagris, the European Snake's Head,
the flower usually solitary, purple with
white chequering or white with green veins.
The form *contorta* has the bell contracted
and the petals joined in the lower part,
making a narrow flower about 2 in.
(50 mm) long.

waved and with tips reflexed, June-August, 4 ft (1.25 m) tall. Some variants have double flowers which of course do not shrivel so quickly. A pink form from China is *rosea* with narrow recurving petals.

A dwarf strain is being developed, particularly in the United States.

Hosta. In Grandma's day they were Funkias, and are still Plantain Lilies. They are chiefly grown for their foliage, and thrive under a north wall. Most come from Japan.

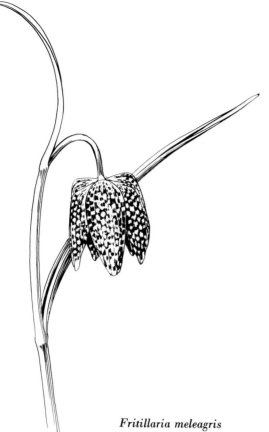

Fritillaria meleagris

verticillata, elegant with wide bells of pale creamy-green slightly chequered inside, the upper leaves glaucous and curling like tendrils.

Hemerocallis. The Day Lilies muster about a dozen species of funnel-shaped yellow to reddish-orange flowers in an irregular cluster at the top of a tall stem. The flowers last only a day but are numerous and open successively.

aurantiaca, 8–15 flowers in the cluster, orange, often with a purplish flush, in June and July. The variety *major* has up to 24 orange flowers lacking the purplish flush.

fulva, vigorous, forming a clump, 10–14 orange brick-red flowers with an apricot line on each petal, wide funnel-shaped,

Hosta fortunei

decorata, low-growing, the dark-green ribbed leaves margined with cream. The spikes carry rich deep-lilac bells beautifully marked inside. Height 2 ft (600 mm), flowering in early summer.

fortunei makes a clump of sage-green leaves with waved edges, the pale lilac flowers rising above them. The form 'Albopicta' is a spectacular spring foliage-plant with scrolled leaves opening to display bright butter-yellow blades edged with pale green, fading to primrose. The light-lavender trumpets are borne on graceful stalks. Height 2½ ft (800 mm).

sieboldiana, with the largest and most sumptuous leaves of all the hostas, sometimes 1 ft (300 mm) wide and more than a foot long, deep grey-green, bluish or glaucous. The flowers, white with a lilac flush, only just stand above them. The variety *elegans* has dense heads of lilac-white trumpets.

Kniphofia. The Red Hot Pokers or Torch Lilies are the tall spikes of flowers in flame-yellows and reds. Most of those grown nowadays are hybrids.

    'Dwarf' kinds attain about 3 ft (900 mm) and flower from June to September. Choice are 'Maid of Orleans' (ivory or primrose-white); 'Goldelse' (yellow); 'Bressingham Flame' (deep orange); 'Bressingham Torch' (flame-orange); 'Green Jade' (primrose-yellow with pale green); 'Snow Maiden' (cream and coral).

    The tall hybrids, up to 4 ft (1.25 m), flower from early summer to autumn. Recommended are 'Atlanta' (orange-red, earliest to flower, May); 'Royal Standard' (scarlet buds opening to yellow); 'Wrexham Buttercup' (bright clear yellow).

Lilium. The Royal Horticultural Society and the North American Lily Society have classified species lilies and their varieties into nine Divisions. To aid the gardener we have divided our choice into two groups: basal-rooting (European and American) and stem-rooting (Eastern Asiatic).

European and American

canadense, a most graceful lily with whorls of reflexed yellow bells from June to August hanging from arching pedicels on a stem 4–6 ft (1.25–1.75 m) tall.

candidum, the Madonna Lily, best-loved of all. The stem, up to 6 ft (1.75 m) tall carries a clustered head of glistening white flowers with golden anthers, chalice-like and fragrant.

Lilium 'Shuksan' (Bellingham Hybrid)

humboldtii, a vigorous Turk's-cap of brilliant reddish-orange freckled with maroon, 10–12 on a stem up to 6 ft (1.75 m) tall. Variable in colour and markings, a wonderful parent from which the Bellingham Hybrids were developed in America by Luther Burbank. Their basic colour is a rather hot orange, though 'Royal Favourite' is deep lemon-yellow. 'Shuksan', with heavily spotted yellow-orange flowers, is one of the best.

martagon, the common Turk's-cap of Europe, with 10–30 flowers varying from light pinkish-purple to wine-purple, June-July, height 3–4 ft (900 mm–1.25 m). From its variability Mrs Robert O. Backhouse of Hereford, England, created the Backhouse Hybrids, their colours yellow or tawny-orange flushed with pink. Two are 'Brocade' (butter-yellow); and 'Mrs R. O. Backhouse' (pink shading inwards to rich gold spotted with purple).

Some selected hybrids flowering June and July are × *testaceum*, recurved apricot waxy flowers with large red anthers, 6–12 on the stem; 'Nightingale', hanging Turk's-caps, pale lilac with a splash of orange in the middle of the petals and heavily spotted; 'Marhan', a rich orange Martagon freckled all over, with big red anthers; 'Cinnabar', upright flowers of deep crimson numerous on 2–3 ft (600–900 mm) stems.

Eastern Asiatic

auratum, the Golden-rayed Lily of Japan, with purplish-green stems 5–8 ft (1.5–2.5 m)

Lilium auratum

tall carrying eight or more large waxy white flowers with a golden ray down the centre of the petals, freckled with crimson and delightfully scented, flowering August-September.

henryi, a rich-orange Turk's-cap with strongly recurved petals, up to 50 flowers on a stem 5–6 ft (1.5–1.75 m) tall, in August. A parent of the great race of Aurelian Hybrids with broad-petalled trumpets in various shades.

regale, the Regal Lily, well-named for its majestic height, 5–6 ft (1.5–1.75 m) stems bearing 20 or more magnificent trumpets pure waxy white shaded yellow in the throat, wine-red on the reverse, superbly scented and vigorous. Summer-flowering.

speciosum, a 'florist's' lily of long white trumpets heavily spotted with crimson, the tips of the petals slightly recurved, borne 4–12 on a 3 ft (900 mm) stem clothed in glossy dark-green leaves. Of the many varieties *album* is most widely grown for cutting with broad petals waved at the margins and a pale green band radiating from the centre; 'Cinderella', flushed peach-pink shading out to blush-pink at the petal-tips; 'Lucie Wilson', soft rose-pink flowers edged with white and freckled with red in the throat; 'Grand Commander', glowing crimson flowers edged with white.

Choice hybrids in this group are 'Destiny', early-flowering, with upright lilies of purest lemon-yellow freckled around the centre, outstanding scarlet anthers; 'Enchantment', large cup-shaped upright flowers of blazing nasturtium-red; 'Discovery', a Turk's-cap of soft pink tipped with a more intense shade and with deep-crimson spots; 'Black Dragon', a magnificent trumpet pure white inside with mahogany anthers, rich mahogany outside margined with white; and 'Journey's End', huge purple-crimson

Lilium 'Black Dragon'

flowers often 9 in. (225 mm) across, flat
with recurving tips and freckled with
deep maroon.

Muscari. The name refers to the musky
scent of the flowers. The long tubular
leaves appear in autumn, the flowers March
to May, small rounded spikes of densely
packed beads.

botryoides, the Grape Hyacinth,
resembling tiny black grapes, with a grape-
like bloom. Height 6 in. (150 mm). The
form *album* has bells of pure white.

comosum, the scented Tassel Hyacinth,
with purple flowers at the top of the
cluster sterile and growing upwards,
green fertile flowers below hanging
downwards, giving the tassel-like
appearance. Height 16 in. (400 mm), May
and June.

tubergenianum, the Oxford and
Cambridge Grape Hyacinth, with buds
deep turquoise-blue, when open sky-blue
at the top of the spike, navy-blue below.
Height 8 in. (200 mm). The broad leaves
lie flat on the ground.

Ornithogalum. Exquisite bulbous plants,
but they become rampant. Best for
naturalising in grass.

nutans, spikes of open bells silvery-
white inside, striped jade outside. Height
1 ft (300 mm), April-May.

thyrsoides, the Chincherinchee from
South Africa, with dense spikes 12–15 in.
(300–350 mm) high carrying white cup-
shaped flowers with long yellow stamens,
June-September. Very long-lasting when
cut.

umbellatum, the Star of Bethlehem, a
few inches high but with large umbels of
white stars in May.

Phormium. Two garden species strike a
dramatic note with their exotic sword-like
leaves.

cookianum, the Mountain Flax, is
suitable for the smaller garden, with light-
green compact leaves, yellow flowers;
two new varieties are 'Cream Delight', with
a creamy band in the centre of the green-
margined leaves, and *tricolor* has bright
green leaves, striped with white and
margined with red.

tenax, the New Zealand Flax, stiff
grey-green leaves, dull red flowers borne
on plum-blue stems, height 5–7 ft
(1.5–2.25 m).
    Exciting new forms include 'Bronze
Baby', 2 ft (600 mm) high with deep
coppery-bronze leaves; 'Dazzler', slightly
taller, forming a clump of arching leaves
reddish-brown overlaid with luminous
carmine bands; 'Sundowner', about 3 ft
(900 mm), wide leaves with a greyish-
purple midriff and creamy-pink outer
bands.

Polygonatum. An old favourite is
Solomon's Seal with its long arching stems
of lily-leaves hiding creamy bells.

Polygonatum multiflorum

canaliculatum, a giant up to 5 ft (1.3 m), with superb rounded leaves, the flowers in large clusters.

hookeri, a tiny species only 4 in. (100 mm) high, with pale lilac flowers.

multiflorum, the usual Solomon's Seal, has two interesting varieties: 'Flore Pleno' with double flowers like a ballet dancer's tutu; and 'Variegatum', its foliage striped creamy-white.

Scilla. The Squills are ideal bulbs for the rock garden and for naturalising, providing dainty spikes of flowers in a range of colours, January to May.

bifolia, narrow bronze-green leaves, and turquoise-blue flowers on a 9 in. (225 mm) stem, March-April. Forms are *album*, white; *rosea*, soft shell-pink; *praecox*, earlier-flowering; and *taurica*, deepest violet.

sibirica, the best-known species for its prussian-blue flowers.

tubergeniana, several spikes to each bulb, the flowers of softest grey-blue with darker stripes down each petal. Height 4 in. (100 mm).

Trillium. The Wood Lilies are for naturalising under deciduous trees where they will get shade and leaf mould. The three-petalled flowers appear in April and May.

cernuum, the Nodding Wood Lily, flowers white or pinkish, drooping and hiding themselves under the luxuriant leaves. The recurving petals are divided by green sepals, with maroon centre and anthers. Up to 1 ft (300 mm).

Trillium grandiflorum

grandiflorum, Wake Robin, the finest and largest species at 2 ft (600 mm) tall, the flowers up to 3 in. (75 mm) across, pure white fading to pinkish-purple, *roseum* a particularly pinkish form.

rivale, the Brook Trillium, pink and white marbled flowers, a tiny gem for the peat bed.

undulatum, white petals conspicuously striped or blotched with purple or crimson at the base. The margins of both the petals and leaves waved.

Tulipa. As with other big groups of plants, tulips have been classified into distinctive divisions. We will describe some of the best species and list a good selection of hybrids.

Species

batalinii, a small tulip with pointed petals, creamy-yellow, 6–10 in. (150–250 mm) high.

clusiana, the Lady Tulip, one of the most graceful, white with a crimson streak on the outside of the petals, the inner petals having a purplish-crimson blotch. The narrow leaves are often edged with red.

fosteriana, very large flowers up to 10 in. (250 mm) across, bright vermilion-scarlet outside, glowing crimson-scarlet inside, with a purplish-black basal blotch. Height 1–1½ ft (300-450 mm), flowering towards mid-April.

humilis, a 6 in. (150 mm) dwarf, variable in shocking-pinks and magentas, opening to a flat star with a yellow centre. Very early-flowering, often in February.

kaufmanniana, the Water Lily Tulip resembling a *Nymphaea* when open, with narrow reflexing petals of creamy-white shaded carmine-pink on the outside, with a yellow base. Flowering end of February until mid-April, height 4–8 in. (100–200 mm). Among the attractive hybrid varieties are 'Alfred Cortot' (beautifully mottled leaves, glowing scarlet flowers with a black base); 'Ancilla', dwarf, (pure white inside, shaded rose-pink outside); 'Josef Kafka' (foliage striped with purple, flowers deep golden-yellow heavily shaded scarlet).

orphanidea, medium-sized flowers on stems up to 15 in. (375 mm), buff-orange with buff streaks, pinkish-purple at the base, but very variable.

Tulipa kaufmanniana

sprengeri, the latest to bloom, generally towards the end of May, globular mahogany-red flowers, leaves a shining green. It naturalises and tolerates semi-shade. Stem up to 18 in. (450 mm). Giant forms are sometimes up to 2½ ft (800 mm).

Hybrids

Early-flowering:
Sweetly scented and blooming from the middle to end of April: 'Bellona', large bell-shaped flowers, golden-yellow, 15 in. (375 mm); 'Brilliant Star', dazzling orange-scarlet; 'Diana', pure white, sturdy; 'First Lady', deep violet; 'Mr van der Hoef', an exquisite golden-yellow double; 'Peach Blossom', double, brilliant pink.

Darwins:
The most popular class of May-flowering tulips, up to 2 ft (600 mm). 'Anjou' is pale canary-yellow inside and edging petals, pale buttercup-yellow outside; 'Clara Butt', an old favourite, bright rosy-pink; 'Queen of Bartigons', rich salmon-pink; 'Eclipse', deep scarlet-crimson with deep violet base inside; 'La Tulipe Noire', deep maroon, almost black.

'Mrs John Scheepers'   'Kreizerskroon'

'Queen of Bartigons'

'Mariette'

'Fantasy'

Flowering slightly earlier:
'Apeldoorn', bright scarlet with a pale
mauve sheen outside, base black, bordered
with yellow; 'General Eisenhower',
orange-red with a yellow base;
'Gudoshnik', creamy-yellow, splashed and
flecked with rose-red.

Lily-flowered:

Long pointed petals reflexing as
they open, flowering beginning to
mid-May:
'Mariette', deep China-rose, long-lasting
with very large flowers; 'Queen of Sheba',
very large, glowing rusty-red with orange-
red; 'White Triumphator', an elegant white
flower.

Cottage:
Late-flowering with egg-shaped blooms.
'Mrs John Scheepers', large deep yellow;
'Rosy Wings', clear pink with a white base.

There are also Parrot Tulips, with jagged
petals, generally having very large flowers

tending to be top-heavy, though effective as
cut flowers; Fringed Tulips which can be
exquisite; and Multiflowering Tulips giving
3–6 blooms from each bulb.

With all these to choose from we can
make our borders brilliant with colour
from February to May.

Yucca. These form massive clumps of
evergreen sword-like leaves, from among
which rise dense spikes of creamy bells,
fragrant in the evening. Two species are
of great garden value.

filamentosa blooms in summer, and is up
to 5 ft (1.5 m) tall. Called Adam's Needle,
the greyish-green needle-pointed leaves
are upright and have thread-like hairs along
their margins.

gloriosa, flowers intermittently every
few years in autumn from among great
rosettes of recurved foliage.

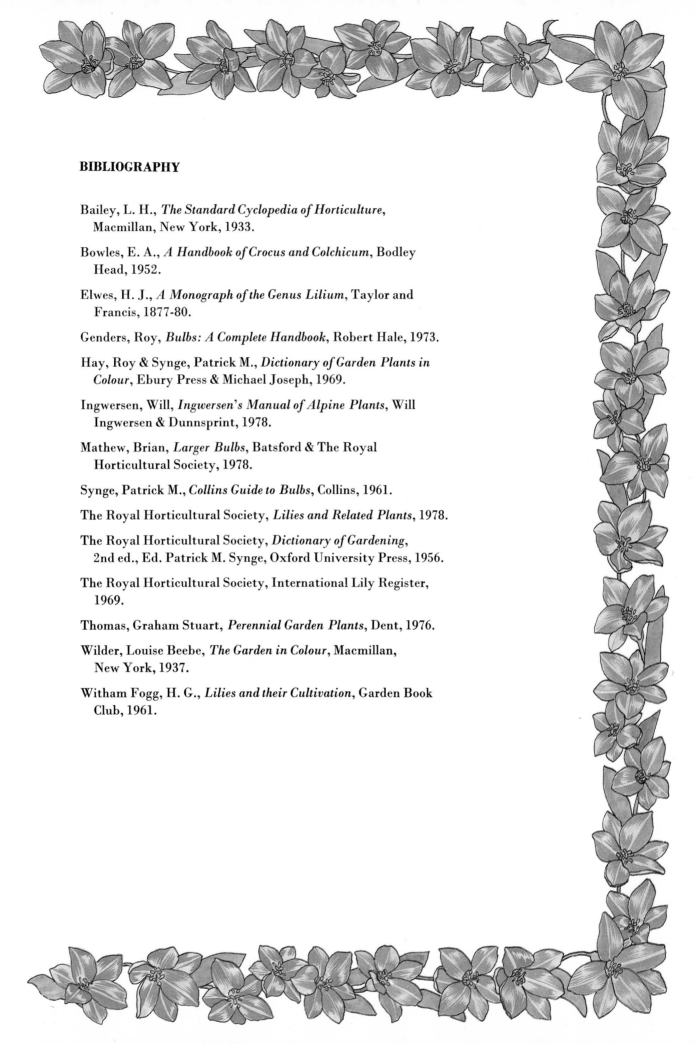

BIBLIOGRAPHY

Bailey, L. H., *The Standard Cyclopedia of Horticulture*, Macmillan, New York, 1933.

Bowles, E. A., *A Handbook of Crocus and Colchicum*, Bodley Head, 1952.

Elwes, H. J., *A Monograph of the Genus Lilium*, Taylor and Francis, 1877-80.

Genders, Roy, *Bulbs: A Complete Handbook*, Robert Hale, 1973.

Hay, Roy & Synge, Patrick M., *Dictionary of Garden Plants in Colour*, Ebury Press & Michael Joseph, 1969.

Ingwersen, Will, *Ingwersen's Manual of Alpine Plants*, Will Ingwersen & Dunnsprint, 1978.

Mathew, Brian, *Larger Bulbs*, Batsford & The Royal Horticultural Society, 1978.

Synge, Patrick M., *Collins Guide to Bulbs*, Collins, 1961.

The Royal Horticultural Society, *Lilies and Related Plants*, 1978.

The Royal Horticultural Society, *Dictionary of Gardening*, 2nd ed., Ed. Patrick M. Synge, Oxford University Press, 1956.

The Royal Horticultural Society, International Lily Register, 1969.

Thomas, Graham Stuart, *Perennial Garden Plants*, Dent, 1976.

Wilder, Louise Beebe, *The Garden in Colour*, Macmillan, New York, 1937.

Witham Fogg, H. G., *Lilies and their Cultivation*, Garden Book Club, 1961.

Pally Carswell
The Orchid Family

Orchidaceae

Aerides	Chysis	Lycaste	Paphiopedilum
Angraecum	Cirrhopetalum	Masdevallia	Phaius
Anguloa	Cyprepedium	Maxillaria	Phalaenopsis
Brassavola	Dactylorhiza	Miltonia	Renanthera
Brassia	Encyclia	Mormodes	Trichopilia
Bulbophyllum	Gymnadenia	Oncidium	Vanda
Catasetum	Laelia	Ophrys	Vanilla

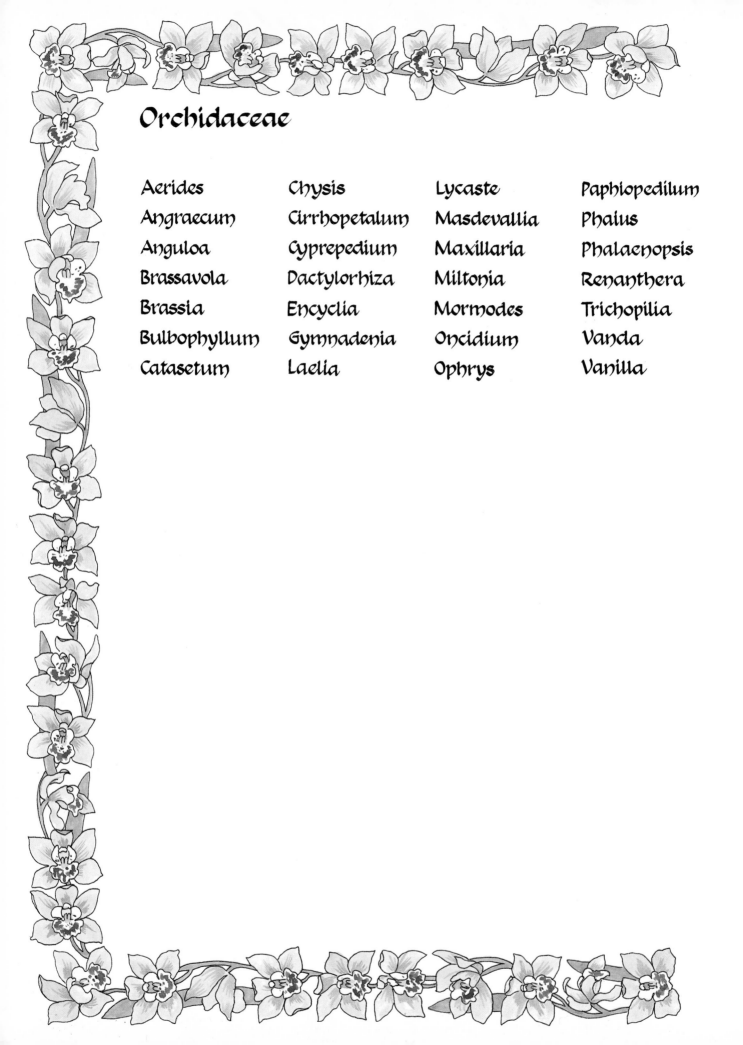

The Orchid Family

Jacob Breynius, the seventeenth-century German botanist, said "Nature has formed orchid flowers in such a way that unless they make us laugh they surely excite our greatest admiration."

They excited the admiration of Charles Darwin, who tested his theory of natural selection through plants. Orchids fascinated him, and he found that in no other plant are pistils, stamens and petals so perfectly formed to secure cross-pollination by the aid of one particular insect or another.

For the orchid is different from any other flower. Its construction is a most sophisticated piece of floral engineering.

Yet it was not this ingenuity which at first captured Darwin's attention. On the *Beagle* voyage it was their fantastic beauty that overwhelmed him.

Orchids, then, have the power of arresting our notice. Large and small, they have star quality. We are awed by them, we may be repelled by some of them, but finally we must fall under their spell.

They are an enormous family, second only to the daisies, over 17,000 species in more than 800 genera, yet somehow we can recognise an orchid at a glance. They are becoming popular with the ordinary home gardener, for when summer is over he can enjoy the long season of orchids that flower in winter. Cymbidiums, cattleyas, dendrobiums and coelogynes form the basis of beginners' collections, to say nothing of their hybrids and varieties. Think of going into your own greenhouse and being able to cut sprays of the exquisite *Cymbidium* 'Oriental Legend', or of *Odontoglossum crispum* with its snowflake petals holding a 'bee', or for a special occasion making a corsage of *Cattleya* 'Fabulous', like a beautiful purple owl with its two big yellow 'eyes' in a large round 'head' and even a 'beak'.

There are outdoor orchids for a cool climate, beauties like *Orchis spectabilis* of opulent violet, purple, and white flowers; showy cypripediums, the Lady's Slipper of pinks and rich red-browns and yellows; the fragrant *Gymnadenia conopsea* of small purple flowers, and others.

So orchid-growing can extend your gardening world with a taste of the tropics, as no other plant can do.

Cattleya 'Fabulous'

CARE AND CULTURE

Orchid-growing is no longer veiled by the mystique it used to have: methods of culture have been much simplified, and even the recommended baskets of teak can be replaced as containers by old nylon stockings. Nor are orchids now beyond the reach of the ordinary pocket: even some of the world's finest can be bought at reasonable prices, thanks to meristem culture—mass propagating of one individual plant to produce many identical plantlets.

Orchids in their native homes are of two kinds: terrestrial, the ground-dwellers rooting in and feeding from the soil; and epiphytal, perching on the branches of trees or dead trunks and deriving their nourishment from moisture in the air and humus in the crevices of the bark, by means of specially adapted aerial roots. They are not parasites, nor is any other kind of orchid.

Terrestrial orchids include the species of the temperate regions and most of the largest and most stately orchids of the tropics. Epiphytes inhabit the tropics and subtropics and exhibit the most varied forms. This gives us the direct clue to their culture, and growers have classified them in three categories according to the temperature they need: Warm, Intermediate, and Cool, for which the initials **W., I.,** and **C.** will be used in the descriptions.

Among the tropical orchids needing warmth are the angraecums with fantastic long nectaries; the fragrant Swan Orchids (*Cycnoches*), and *Phalaenopsis* species from the Philippines with their sprays and spikes of creamy-white, greeny-white, and pink, the most rewarding of Warm orchids, producing their flowers throughout the year and lasting in perfection for many weeks. To grow any of these the temperature must not fall below 65° F (18° C) day or night, summer or winter.

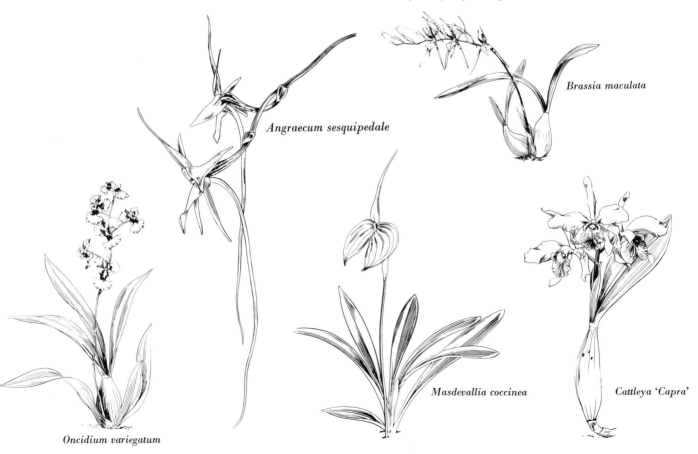

Angraecum sesquipedale

Brassia maculata

Oncidium variegatum

Masdevallia coccinea

Cattleya 'Capra'

145

The Intermediate orchids give us paphiopedilums from Thailand, brassavolas from Mexico, and exquisite frilly-petalled cattleyas and their thousands of hybrids. The temperature should not fall below 55° F (13° C).

Included among the Cool orchids are some of the most beautiful of all. Chief among them are the cymbidiums with their sprays of apple-green or pink, white or golden flowers; glorious odontoglossoms of almost endless variations of colours and markings; many of the lovely dendrobiums; and, for quaintness, masdevallias with windblown tails of petals. All these require a minimum of 50° F (10° C).

Fresh air is necessary to all orchids, but draughts are dangerous. In the Warm House air is best admitted through bottom ventilators, so that it is warmed by the heating pipes before reaching the orchids. To counteract the drying influence of the heating-pipes the floor, walls and staging should be damped by syringing two or three times a day. The greater the heat inside or outside from the sunshine, the greater the amount of moisture is necessary. In hot weather syringe or spray the plants themselves once or twice a day, using soft water of the same temperature as the house.

Although all orchids appreciate light they are unable to stand the direct rays of the sun. Lath blinds are the answer.

Many need a rest when the season's growth is completed. During this period they need little or no water.

When growing orchids, try to simulate their natural habitat. Epiphytes look well when perched on a branch made from a piece of rolled-up wire netting stuffed with sphagnum moss, and the moss when sprayed gives off needed moisture. Bulbous orchids, which are the ones originating in hot climates, are usually grown in baskets or on rafts. The compost used should be orchid compost which contains a mycorrhizal fungus that lives symbiot-

Cymbidium Iouianum

Odontoglossum Grande

Dendrobium nobile 'Stella Hallmark'

Paphiopedilum philippinense

ically with the acids and feeds them with nutrients.

Among the surprising number of orchids that can be grown outdoors are the sub-tribe cypripediums like *spectabile*, *reginae* and *acaule*; *Dactylorhiza foliosa* for a moist part of the garden; and some lovely species of *Orchis*, with many Italian forms of this genus. They like a good rich compost to grow in.

There are of course the 'wild' orchids (all orchids are 'wild' in their native home) and these can be grown from seed rather than transplanting what may be a protected species.

Propagating

Most orchids are propagated from back bulbs, properly called pseudobulbs, that have flowered. These are usually leafless. They should be carefully detached and planted immediately.

Orchids that do not have bulbs but rootstocks should be propagated by division.

Climbing orchids such as vandas can be propagated quite simply by cutting off the upper half of the plant below some of the aerial roots. They can also be rooted by cutting a ring in the stem below some aerial roots and surrounding the ring with sphagnum moss, keeping it moist. When what are called adventitious roots have formed, you should cut the stem cleanly below the ring and pot the new plant.

Orchids can, of course, be grown from seed, either bought or from your own growing, mating two flowers of the same species to reproduce the plant, or one species with another species (though some will not accept the other) to create a hybrid. The first step is pollination.

For thousands of years natural selection has been modifying the orchid, adapting it to a single purpose—foolproof cross-pollination by an insect. Old organs have

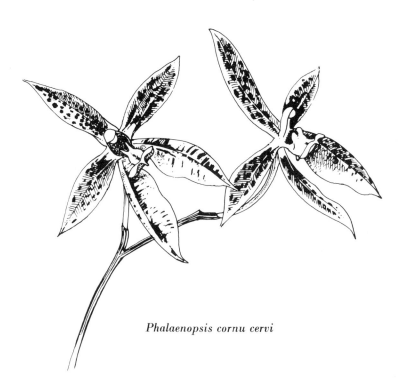

Phalaenopsis cornu cervi

been replaced by new, and a special vocabulary deals with them, since most are possessed by no other flower—though in fact they are merely so modified that we do not recognise them: the *column*, for instance, is the compacted stamens and pistils.

Again, the pollen is different from that of other flowers. Instead of being a loose powder it is glued together in little parcels called pollinia which the bee or other insect is obliged to detach, carry away and deposit on the stigma of another flower.

How the bee does it and how the different orchids with their wonderful battery of mechanisms make the bee release the pollen (first ensnaring the insect, imprisoning it or even drugging it until pollination is ready to take place) is a marvellous study. The orchid-grower must understand the process if—with a long sharp pencil-point—he is to play the bee with his odontoglossums or other marvellous inhabitants of the orchid world.

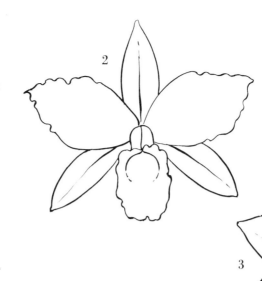

sepal

petal

petal

umn

sepal

sepal

lip, or labellum

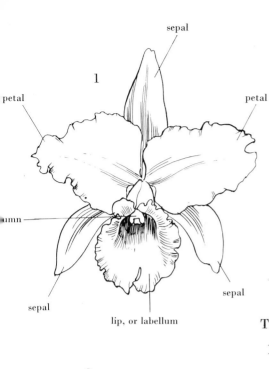
9

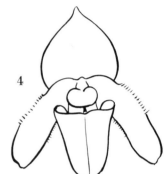
3

4

The Orchid Family

1   Structure of an orchid flower

Shapes of different orchids

2   Dendrobium

3   Cymbidium

4   Paphiopedalum

5   Phalaenopsis

6   Odontoglossum

7   Lycaste

8   Pleione

9   Cattleya

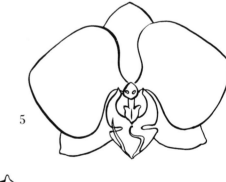
5

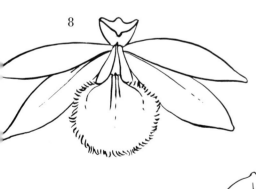
8

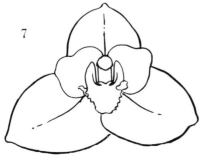
7

6

FLOWERS OF THE FAMILY

From this vast family we select genera with species more easily grown by the beginner, with a few special ones showing to what limits the sophisticated orchid can go in colour and form, and to what heights the home gardener can aspire. The emphasis is on those for Cool conditions followed by Intermediates.

Angraecum. Most of this large epiphytic genus are all white, creamy-white, greenish-white and snow-white, the flowers having long nectaries and growing either singly on the stem or in sprays.

distichum, a miniature, which has single whitish flowers from the axils of very short bright-green leaves. Summer. **W.**

infundibulare is a curious-looking flower like a white sea shell, the base of the lip being contracted into a broad funnel 4 in. (100 mm) or more long, which becomes a long spur. Fragrant. Summer. **W.**

Angraecum sesquipedale

sesquipedale, the finest species, and one of the most remarkable of all orchids, with a nectary 11½ in. (290 mm) long, it requires a Sphinx moth with a proboscis of the same length to pollinate it. The flower, up to 8 in. (200 mm) across, is like a great six-pointed star, with three ivory-white petals and, behind them, three ivory-white sepals. Spring. **W.**

Brassavola. Epiphytes with pseudobulbs carrying a single leathery leaf. The flowers are large, single or in racemes, the sepals and petals so narrow and green as to look like leaves.

cucullata, the Ghost Orchid. The creamy-white sepals and petals are like ribbons, the mid-lobe of the lip being long and narrow with pure white side-lobes rounded and fringed, encircling the base of the white column, a unique feature. Autumn. Rest. **C.**

digbyana, with large single fragrant flowers of a delicate pale green, the lip large and frilly. Flowering at various times. Needs decided rest. **I.**

An exquisite variety is 'David Sander' with petals and sepals a delicate pale pink, long and pointed. The lip, pale blue and fringed, forms a scarf round the centre of the flower and extends forward.

Brassia. A genus of easily cultivated epiphytes. They have long tail-like sepals and petals, giving them the name Spider Orchids, and some are pleasantly scented. A long rest should not be given, as many of the species are seldom really dormant.

caudata, producing numerous drooping spikes 18 in. (460 mm) long with 6–12 flowers, the sepals and petals yellow and barred with brown, the lip broad and yellow spotted with greenish-brown. Summer. **C.**

maculata, one of the most showy and popular of brassias, the fragrant pale greenish flowers being irregularly barred and spotted with brown, the lip white and spotted brown and purple. Spring, early summer. **C.**

bowringinia has large heads of rich rosy-purple flowers, 12–15 on a short stalk, the throat with a large white spot surrounded by a zone of bright maroon bordered with deep purple. Autumn. Rest. **I.**

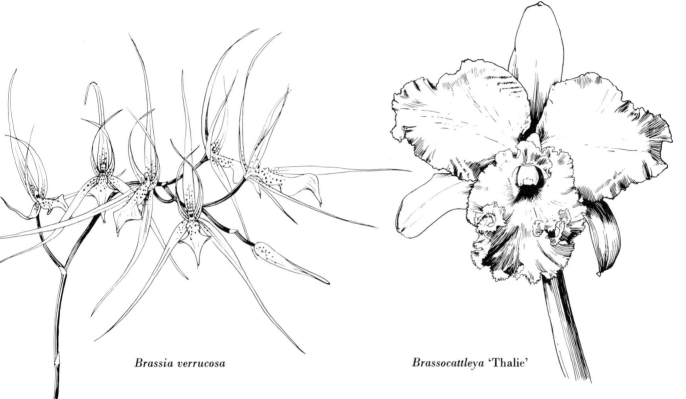

Brassia verrucosa

Brassocattleya 'Thalie'

verrucosa, arching sprays, each carrying 10–15 large fragrant flowers, greenish blotched blackish-purple, the lip white with many small green warts. Early summer. **C.**

Cattleya. Best-known and showiest of all orchids, yet easy to cultivate. This epiphytal genus has about 40 species and innumerable natural hybrids. With man-made intergeneric hybrids and varieties, flowers are provided all the year. The pseudobulbs are either club-shaped and carry a single leaf, or cylindrical and stem-like with two leaves.

citrina—the one that is different, a single deliciously fragrant flower, yellow with the front lobe of the waxy frilled lip bordered with white, arising from between the 2 or 3 leaves and hanging downwards. Early to late summer. Rest. **I.**

The form *gigantea* is larger and intensely coloured.

harrisoniana is a noble, free-flowering species with beautiful blooms of pale lilac-rose, the lip tinged with yellow. Late summer. Rest. **I.**

labiata has spikes of 3–7 large flowers of deep rose, the petals very broad and beautifully waved, the large hooded lip of an intense deep velvety crimson. It is very variable and therefore of great value to hybridists. Typical hybrids are *candida*, pure white with a crimson lip; *coerulea*, pale lilac with a slate-blue lip; *pallida*, light pink with a fringed crimson lip. Summer to autumn. Rest. **I.**

Cattleyas have also been bred with other orchids to produce various intergeneric hybrids such as brassocattleya, epicattleya and laeliocattleya. The last-named has a gorgeous variety in 'Bonanza', with fringed petals of a rich brick-red. A Brassocattleya is the lovely *cliftonii* 'Magnifica' with pink-lilac flowers, the throat shaded with yellow, the soft-crimson lip fringed and exquisitely waved and bordered with the same pink-lilac.

There are hundreds of other cultivars. 'Bow Bells' is probably the best-known white Cattleya.

Cirrhopetalum. These epiphytes are not large-flowered, but are remarkable for their forms. Many have petals ending in a tassel or a tuft of hair-like filaments. The sepals are much enlarged and so twisted as to be completely upside down, the under-surface having become the upper, and what were the outer margins becoming the inner. They are of rambling habit and need a great deal of light.

auratum, with straw-coloured flowers stained and striped with crimson and gold, making a circular umbel. Spring. **C.**

medusae (*Bulbophyllum medusae*), the flowers in compact heads, pale straw-coloured dotted with pink on an erect scape, two of the three sepals lengthened into long threads, the whole resembling a mop of tangled hair. Summer. **C.**

vaginatum, with small white flowers in round clusters and resembling a miniature *medusae*. Summer. **C.**

Coelogyne. There are more than 150 kinds of these popular epiphytes with their racemes of predominantly white flowers opening simultaneously or in succession.

cristate has hanging racemes of crispy white scented flowers with a yellow streak in the throat. Spring. Rest. **C.**

This species and its forms make fine house-plants. The variety *maxima* is perhaps the whitest of all orchids.

elata, with upright spikes holding many white flowers, the lip prettily marked in yellow and orange. A large robust grower. Spring. Rest. **C.**

Cymbidium. Their adaptability to grow in almost any surroundings has made these orchids not only the most popular in cultivation, but also ideal for beginners. Added to this, their beautiful sprays of flowers are long-lasting. They are epiphytal, rarely terrestrial, and bloom any time from December to April in the northern hemisphere.

devonianum, sprays of closely-packed miniature flowers, olive-green overlaid with purple lines. Spring. **C.**

Bulbarrow is a wonderful type bred from it, the variety 'Friar Tuck' perfect in shape with its uniformly olive sepals and petals like wings flying out from the rich maroon of its lip. Spring. **W.**

lowianum is a handsome species from Burma, with long arching sprays of apple-green flowers, still supreme even among its hybrids. In the variety *concolor* the blotch on the lip is orange-yellow. Spring. **C.**

tracyanum, a fine old species from India with long spikes of very fragrant flowers, the petals lined with red and the creamy lip spotted. Autumn. **C.**

Today most people grow hybrids rather than species, and some wonderful types

Cymbidium lowianum

producing them in a cascade. The form *jenkinsii* is a real miniature. Spring. Rest. **C.**

amethystoglossom from the Philippines is a charming and dainty species producing hanging clusters of white flowers tipped with amethyst. Winter. Rest. **I.**

nobile, one of the oldest species in cultivation, easy to obtain, easy to grow and inexpensive. It has spikes of large pinkish-purple flowers with a white lip velvety-maroon in the throat. Spring. Rest. **C.**

In the host of hybrids, the colour-range includes rich lavenders, reds, whites and yellows.

Dendrobium nobile

have been bred from cymbidiums, for instance Tapestry 'Long Beach', one of the finest red cymbidiums of all time; Ormoulu, another superb type, the outstanding feature being a startling red blotch on the lip which is of the same golden colour as the rest of the flower; 'Monterey Hills', a lovely variety from the type Parfait, creamy-white faintly flushed with pink on the lower sepals, the lip speckled with maroon.

Dendrobium. A large and widely popular epiphytal genus for all three temperatures—Warm, Intermediate and Cool. They must have plenty of light and humidity. Some are exceptionally beautiful. All are long-lasting as cut flowers.

aggregatum is a small plant with fragrant golden flowers, its variety 'Papaya'

secundum, an extremely pretty species, which blooms profusely. The small flowers, rosy-pink with an orange lip, are densely packed on sprays. Spring and summer. Rest. **I.**

spectabile, one of the most curious plants in cultivation. It is from New Guinea, home of many extraordinary orchids. The fragrant flowers, growing on stalks protruding untidily from a stem, are patterned in brown and pinkish white and are crumpled and twisted. Spring. Rest. **W.**

williamsonii produces a profusion of greeny-white flowers, fragrant and long-lasting. The lip is fringed and hairy, the throat splashed with orange. Spring. Rest. **C.**

Dendrobium hybrids are moth-like, or are in drooping clusters. Colours include rosy-mauve, deep vivid purple and bluey-mauve, while the type American Beauty has in the variety 'Roya', a most beautiful carmine flower with an explosion of black in the throat.

Encyclia. A genus until recently included among the cattleyas and epidendrums. They are extremely pretty epiphytes, all easy to grow, some in a cool greenhouse or indoors, others needing more warmth.

citrina is rather like a daffodil growing downwards but with its trumpet-lip frilled and tipped with white. Spring. Rest. **C.**

Cochleata, the Cockleshell Orchid, is remarkable for its ribbon-like pale green petals and sepals. The upright lip, shaped like a shell, is lined and marked with dark purple. It will remain in flower for months. Summer.

C. mariae is a truly delightful species of small size with flowers extremely large by comparison. The lip makes a frilly trumpet of a beautiful pale blue, and is framed by vivid green petals and sepals. The throat is splashed with the same bright green. Summer. Rest. **C.**

nemorale has tall spikes with attractive spidery pink flowers. The more solid lip is white freckled and blotched with deeper pink. Spring. Rest. **I.**

Epidendrum. This genus has both epiphytal and terrestrial orchids, most of them easy to grow.

pseudepidendrum grows to $3\frac{1}{2}$ ft (1 m) and has large apple-green flowers with a lip of brilliant orange or orange-red in clusters of 3–5. Summer. **I.**

radicans has erect reed-like leafy stems up to 4 ft (1.2 m). The bright red to orange flowers are in clusters on slender stems and bloom continuously. There are many colourful hybrids. **C.**

stamfordianum, with tall spikes carrying many tiny yellow flowers spotted with dark red. Spring. **C.**

Laelia. Closely related to cattleyas, these attractive epiphytes range from Mexico to South America. The petals and sepals are narrower, not frilled, and stand around the lip, which is frilled.

anceps, one of the finest, has large rose-violet flowers with a crimson-purple lip yellow in the throat. It is suitable for outdoor planting in frost-free areas. Autumn and winter. Rest. **C.**

Laelia anceps

cinnabarina has 10–15 flowers on a long scape, the narrow sepals and petals cinnabar-red, the leaves and pseudobulbs flushed with purple. Spring and summer. Rest. **C.**

pumila is a pretty little miniature only 6 in. (150 mm) high, ideal for those who live in small rooms. The flowers are rose-purple, the throat having yellowish ridges. There are many hybrids. **I.**

purpurata, by contrast, is tall with large heads of white flowers, sometimes tinted with rose, the bell-shaped lip rich crimson-purple. Spring and early summer. **I.**

Lycaste. A genus of curious epiphytal orchids from tropical America. They produce large soft foliage which lasts for a single season and is then discarded by the plant. The flowers are produced freely on a single stem from the base of the bulb.

aromatica, in half-open bud, is rather like a tulip. The yellow sepals open flat, the golden petals and lip standing round the column. Very fragrant. Winter. Rest. **C.**

deppei has green sepals spotted with reddish-brown standing in a wide triangle, the white petals within very small, the lip bright yellow spotted with red. Early spring. Rest. **C.** Its hybrid Virgo is similar but with wider shorter sepals suffused with pink, two beautiful wide white petals, and a short fringed lip spotted with crimson.

skinneri virginalis reaches 30 in. (740 mm) in winter when it produces a single 5–7 in. (130–180 mm) white or pink bloom, the lip spotted rose to red. No definite rest. **C.**

Masdevallia. A genus which has over 150 species, all colourful and of extraordinary shapes. The lip, usually prominent in other orchids, is insignificant, and so are the two lateral petals. The sepals, on the other hand, are grossly exaggerated in size and often adorned with long tails.

elephanticeps has the sepals joined at their base, giving the flower a trumpet shape, but then elongated into three long tails somewhat resembling the trunk and tusks of an elephant. The diminutive lip is almost black and is hairy. It is loosely hinged and can be moved by the slightest touch, a mechanism to trap a pollinating insect. Flowering time various. **C.**

Masdevallia veitchiana

veitchiana is the most striking of the species, the three sepals of brilliant coral making a jib-sail tapering to points, and held on a slender stem. It propagates readily and is the parent of many superb hybrids. Various. **C.**

Miltonia. These epiphytes are called Pansy Orchids because their flat-faced open flowers resemble pansies in shape and markings. The species bruise easily, and their tougher hybrids are grown in preference and are popular.

clowesii from Brazil has spikes of chestnut-brown flowers barred and tipped with yellow. The lip is fiddle-shaped and half white, half purple. Autumn. **I.**

vexillaria has soft greyish-green foliage and upright stems bearing up to a dozen flowers on each, usually in a shade of pink to red with a darker lip. Early summer. **I.**

Of the many beautiful hybrids, 'Emotion' is one of the finest, white with the two upper petals blotched with carmine, the lower petal with yellow, the 'pansy' look provided by the striking carmine honey-guides. Hamburg × Self is a very prolific deep red of perfect shape. Hamburg × Deousa has rich red-purple flowers with contrasting lips.

Odontoglossom. This name covers one of the largest and most varied tribes in the orchid family. They are popular because of their easy culture and free-flowering habit. The flowers, fascinatingly different from each other, have earned such names as 'Spider' and 'Dancing Dolls'.

crispum has flowers most commonly pale rose with exquisite fringed edges, but often flushed pink and freckled with brown or reddish-brown. Spring or summer. **C.**

grande, the Tiger Orchid of the USA, the Clown Orchid in Britain, has magnificent yellow flowers barred with reddish-brown. Autumn. Rest. **C.**

nobile has up to 100 blooms on each stem. The flowers, faintly fragrant, vary in colour from white to flushed pink with the lip spotted and streaked in rose and crimson. Spring. **C.**

Odontoglossum grande

rossii is a little charmer with short sprays of white flowers, the sepals dotted with mushroom-pink. The white frilled lip makes the perfect finishing touch. Winter. **C.**

Odontoglossums have been bred with other genera to make a wonderful range of intergeneric hybrids under the names Odontocidium, Odontioda, Odontonia, Miltassia, Vuylstekeara and Wilsonara. The results are hardiness, vigour and increased flowering, making rewarding plants for the home gardener.

Oncidium. A large and varied genus full of surprises. The flowers are of subtle beauty in their colouring of yellows and browns, sometimes charming pinks.

crispum has crimped petals and sepals of a lustrous pink-brown like shot silk. The lip is dashed with yellow at the base. Various. **C.**

155

Oncidium crispum

Paphiopedilums remain the most important genus within the group. They are the widely grown and very popular Slipper Orchids, earning this name from the shape of the lip which is like a moccasin.

acmodontum, a species with mottled leaves and the most exquisitely coloured flower, the dorsal sepal pale blue flushed at the base with pale mauve and streaked with maroon, the two lateral petals soft crimson shading into green at the base, the slipper being of the same beautiful green. Winter. **I.**

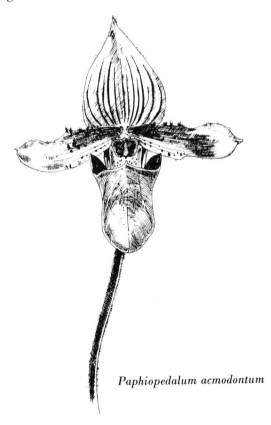

Paphiopedalum acmodontum

leucochilum, fantastically long spikes carrying many beautifully coloured flowers, yellow-green with light brown markings. The contrasting lip is white. Spring. **C.**

microchilum has hundreds of brightly-coloured dainty flowers on a tall branching spike, the colour mainly red-brown with the same colours marked on the white lip. Summer. Rest. **I.**

pusillum is a miniature continually in bloom, the flowers bright yellow barred with reddish-brown. It does well indoors in artificial light.

Paphiopedilum. This curious branch of the orchid family belongs to a tribe which bears its name but has three other members: cypripediums which are herb-like plants growing as terrestrials—and Selenipediums and Phragmipediums, neither of which are generally grown.

appletonianum, a very dainty species with neat handsomely mottled foliage, the flowers single or two on a tall slender stem. It is a symphony of green and mauve shading and is free-flowering, making a most attractive indoor plant, even when not in bloom. Spring. **I.**

fairieanum—"chic" is the word for it, a pink slipper against bandbox stripes on petals and sepals, mauve and green. Autumn. **C.**

insigne is arresting and easy to grow, even on a window-sill. The slipper and petals are coppery-brown tipped with yellow, the dorsal sepal densely striped and spotted. Winter. **C.**

philippinense, like a bird in flight, with two elongated maroon petals winging from the centre. The white sepal is striped with maroon and the slipper pale green. Spring. **W.**

Phalaenopsis. The Moth Orchids, a name aptly describing their winged petals. They are all for the Warm house. Individual flowers last for two months or more, and the succession of blooms on a single plant may provide flowers for more than half the year.

amabilis has large pure-white flowers with purple on the lip, five or six, on a long spike which is sometimes branching. Winter. Its hybrid Latone is larger and more mop-like, with exquisite flowers, eight to a spike. Autumn. **W.**

leuddemanniana has single flowers, fragrant and long-lived, varying in size and colour but usually with brown, purple and yellow variously streaked and blotched. There are many beautiful hybrids. **W.**

equestris (*rosea*) is an extremely pretty species with small pink flowers on dainty sprays. The lip is carmine. Various. **W.**

Pleione. A genus which has beautiful terrestrial orchids easily grown in the alpine house or indoors. During the summer they may be stood outside in a shady place and kept well-watered. They are immensely popular, growing and spreading very quickly. The flowers look rather like a short-stemmed daffodil with a frilly trumpet.

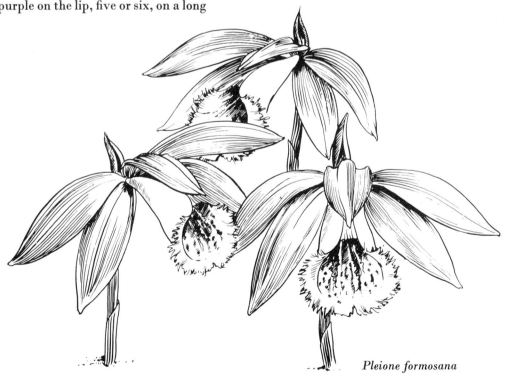

Pleione formosana

formosana has lilac and pink flowers, the lip freckled with orange inside. Some very beautiful hybrids have been produced with deeper colouring, and there is a charming white variety. Spring. **C.**

limprichtii, superb with bright purple-violet flowers, the white lip streaked with reddish-violet. Spring. **C.**

Vanda. The species and hybrids fall into two groups, by leaf types. Those with pencil-like leaves need full sun in order to flower and are suited only for tropical temperatures. Vandas with strap-shaped leaves need less light.

coerulea, the Blue Orchid of Assam which became a craze. Its flowers are many to the spray and in the wild are like the flutterings of thousands of azure butterflies. Late summer or autumn. **I.**

cristata has flowers of a light refreshing green with a prominent white lip heavily lined with red. They are long-lasting. Spring. **C.**

A wonderful deep-blue hybrid is Rothschildiana, among the finest, but it requires Warm-house culture with high humidity. The variety 'Jessie' is a magnificent purple netted with darker mauve.

Hardy Orchids

We close our orchid catalogue with a hardy group for growing outdoors, even in a British climate! The smaller ones are lovely in the rock garden.

Bletilla. A small Eastern genus easy to grow and liking semi-shade.

striata has beautiful carmine-pink flowers and is valuable for cutting. There is an attractive white form.

Cypripedium. The Lady's Slipper Orchids or Moccasin Flowers belong to the Paphiopedalum tribe. Some species are hardy in a cool climate and in a cool peaty soil in partial shade. Several species are available, either as seed or plants—they should not of course be dug up in the wild.

acaule, a North American species with a solitary greenish flower. The rosy lip is blotched with purple.

calceolus is a European species. The flower is reddish-brown or maroon, with a pale yellow lip.

Cypripedium calceolus

japonicum, a most attractive Japanese species in green and white, the lip tinged with crimson. The leaves spread like a fan.

reginae, a strong-growing species from the Northern United States. It likes a position such as the shady edge of a rhododendron bed. The flowers, 1–3 together, are pink and white.

Dactylorhiza. Stately orchids that grow up to 2½ ft (750 mm) tall. They like ordinary fertile soil with some humus and bloom in early summer.

elata (*Orchis elata*) has dense spikes of rosy-purple flowers, with sometimes a white form. It is a vigorous grower.

foliosa (*Orchis foliosa, O. maderensis*), bright reddish-purple flowers in long dense spikes up to 8 in. (200 mm).

Orchis. This genus gives us attractive and sometimes curious orchids for northern and European gardens. They are difficult to obtain, but it is worth trying to get them from a specialist.

maculata, the Spotted Orchis, has dense conical spikes of pale lilac-pink or white heavily spotted. It is a lovely little plant for the rock garden, though difficult to establish.

spectabilis is the Showy Orchid with dark glossy leaves and opulent violet-purple and white flowers—a really spectacular plant for a shady part of the garden.

Orchis spectabilis

BIBLIOGRAPHY

Allan, Mea, *Darwin and his Flowers: the Key to Natural Selection*, Faber, 1977.

Bailey, L. H., *The Standard Cyclopedia of Horticulture*, Macmillan, New York, 1933.

Blowers, J. W., *Orchids*, Blandford Press, 1962.

Blowers, J. W., *Pictorial Orchid Growing*, Maidstone, 1966.

Darwin, Charles, *The various contrivances by which orchids are fertilised by insects*, John Murray, 1877.

Northen, Rebecca, *Home Orchid Growing*, Van Nostrand, 1950.

Rittershausen, Brian & Wilma, *Orchids*, Blandford Press, 1979.

Sander, David, *Orchids and their Cultivation*, Blandford Press, 1969.

The American Orchid Society, *Bulletin* (monthly).

The Orchid Review (monthly).

The Orchid Society of Great Britain, *Journal* (quarterly).

The Royal Horticultural Society, *Dictionary of Gardening*, 2nd ed., Ed. Patrick M. Synge, Oxford University Press, 1956.

White, Edward A., *American Orchid Culture*, 3rd ed., McClelland, 1947.

Wilder, Louise Beebe, *The Garden in Colour*, Macmillan, New York, 1937.

The Rose Family

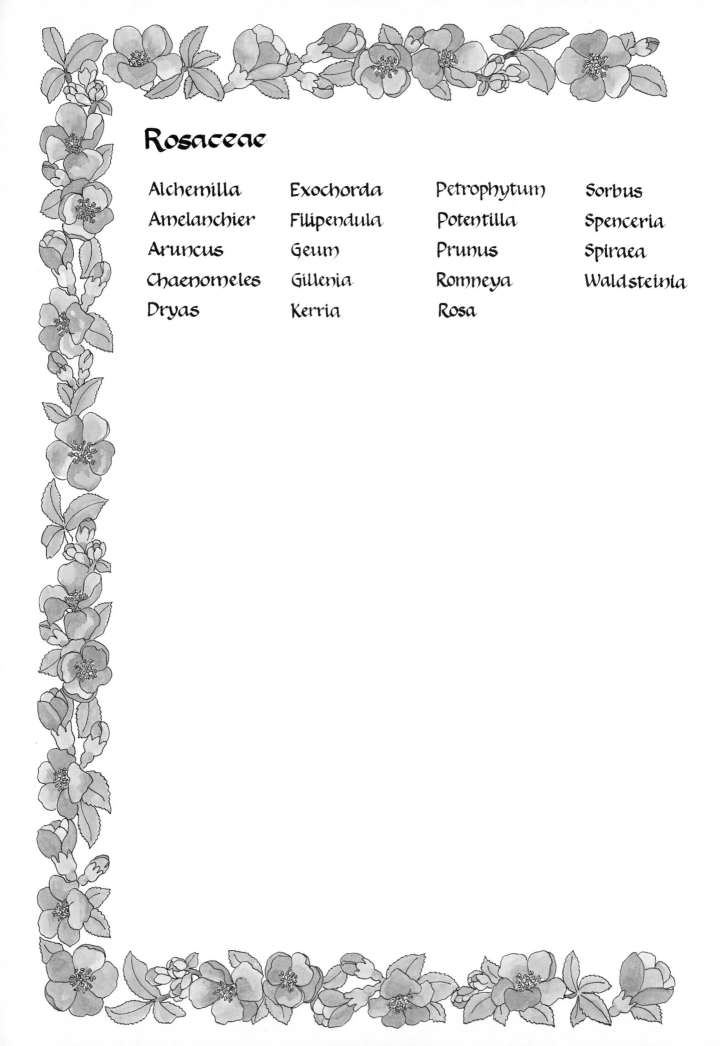

Rosaceae

Alchemilla	Exochorda	Petrophytum	Sorbus
Amelanchier	Filipendula	Potentilla	Spenceria
Aruncus	Geum	Prunus	Spiraea
Chaenomeles	Gillenia	Romneya	Waldsteinia
Dryas	Kerria	Rosa	

The Rose Family

It is thought that the rose is a very English flower, but of the 125 species recognised by the rosarians 95 are Asiatic, 18 American, the rest chiefly natives of Europe or North-west Africa.

The pedigree is long, for roses have been loved since time immemorial: about 450 BC Heroditus observed that the roses growing near the gardens of Midas had sixty petals and were the most fragrant in the world. His description seemed to fit the old Cabbage Rose which has about a hundred petals, as its name *Rosa centifolia* tells us, and it was long believed that it was the oldest of the roses. Evidence, however, has proved the Cabbage Rose to be a sixteenth-century creation by Dutch hybridists. We have to look to four wild species—the Red Rose, the Phoenician Rose, the Musk Rose and the Dog Rose—for the origin of our garden roses, ancient and modern.

From these have been evolved all the roses we know: the sweet-smelling Shrub Roses, the Hybrid Teas and Perpetuals, the Moss Roses, the China Roses, the poly-Pompons and Noisettes. From Climbing to Fairy, they are of every size, and all delight us. More poems must have been written about the rose than about any other flower.

There are, of course, other members of the *Rosaceae* family, and we grow many of them without realising, perhaps, that they have anything to do with roses. Look at the flower of a potentilla, a geum and a single rose like 'Mermaid'. You will see that the stamens are arranged in whorls. But this might apply at first glance to the buttercup family. There is a distinction. In the buttercups the seed-vessel is above the petals and sepals; in the rose the seed-vessel sits on top *surrounded* by the sepals, petals and stamens.

Our hawthorn hedges are roses, as are some of our most delicious fruits— plums, apples, cherries, pears, apricots, peaches. Among the soft fruits— blackberries, dewberries and raspberries, to say nothing of the quince and strawberry. We grow them as trees—the amelanchier, the rowan and other *Sorbus;* as beautiful shrubs, and as rock plants.

Certainly as we walk round our gardens it is "roses, roses all the way".

Rosa moschata

164

CARE AND CULTURE

There are about 2,000 species in the family, in about 90 genera—including *Rosa* itself, the roses.

The family comprises perennial plants, shrubs and trees, often thorny, sometimes climbing. None is an annual, and none requires hot-house treatment. They come from many parts of the world, and any of us can grow any of them in almost any place. All are tolerant of almost any soil.

Some, it is said, do better in one kind of soil than another. Roses, for instance, prefer a clay soil. But I have seen perfect beds of them in a sandy soil with no hint of clay. The secret of success is double-digging when preparing the bed, and mixing in some good garden compost and a liberal sprinkling of bone meal. If the subsoil is clay, fork into it hydrated lime. Light and gravelly soils benefit from the addition of chopped-up turves, granulated peat and other organic material.

Old rose beds must have the same attention when replacing dead roses with new ones, for a rose bed that has grown roses for 10 years or more may be 'rose sick', although some of the old plants will go on growing because their root systems command a wide area. The old soil should be removed to a depth of 12 in. (300 mm) and 18 in. (450 mm) square, and new soil put in.

No garden is complete without roses. It is surely the first flower that comes to mind when planning a new garden, and there must be a thousand ways of growing them. We can make beds of them, concentrating on one particular rose or type of rose, or

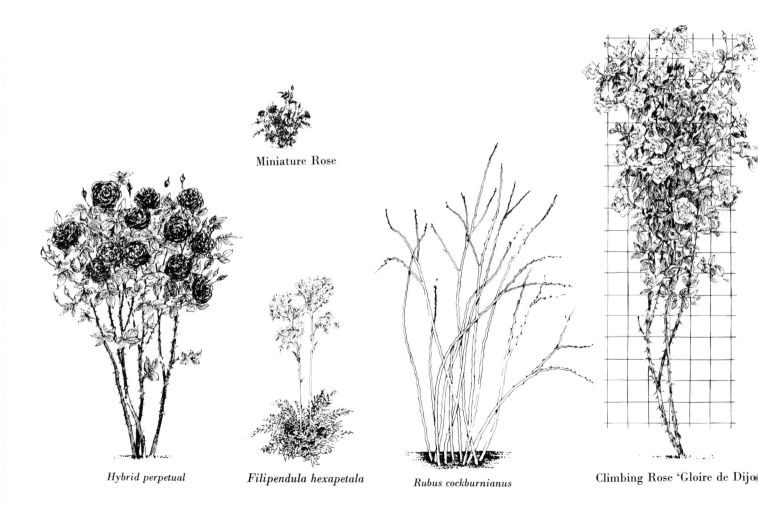

Miniature Rose

Hybrid perpetual *Filipendula hexapetala* *Rubus cockburnianus* Climbing Rose 'Gloire de Dijo

165

mix their colours, or graduate them from shell-pink, say, to darker pink and finally to velvety damask. We can grow them up pillars or a trellis, make ceilings of them in a pergola, arches of them, or screens. We can blanket ugly walls with them and peg them down for ground-cover. We can even make boy-proof hedges of them. What other flower is so useful and adaptable, and which at the same time gives us such perfection in colour, form and fragrance?

Roses seem happier when planted quite close together. Without indulging in whimsy, they seem to like touching each other, as African Violets certainly do, and of course when their leaves intermingle they create a ceiling of foliage that acts as a weed-smotherer. This helps to banish the hoe, a vile instrument anywhere but the kitchen garden, for it breaks the precious surface roots which are the ones that feed moisture to plants.

Roses and the other members of the family make a summer garden, although the leaves of the Snowy Mespilus (*Amelanchier*), for instance, provide wonderful autumn colour, their red fruits adding a bonus. Similarly with the Rugosa roses: their large round or lantern-shaped hips make scarlet brightness among the autumn gold of the leaves.

While we cannot deal here with trees— even the delectable Sato Zakura of Japan, those ornamental flowering cherries with enchanting names like Sekiyama and Ito-kukuri—we can find their diminutive cousins a place in the rock garden: the ground-hugging *Prunus prostrata* with its

Potentilla fruticosa

Alchemilla mollis

Damask rose

Rosa rugosa 'Frau Dagmar Hastrup'

Floribunda Rose

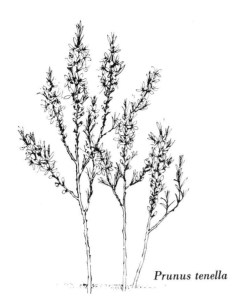

Prunus tenella

bright pink flowers, and the dwarf almond which now goes by the name *Prunus tenella*.

Somehere in the garden we must have the glittering 'whitewashed' stems of *Rubus cockburnianus*, and among the alpines the tiny marauding bramble that creeps about sowing white flowers. We must have some easy-to-grow potentillas, particularly yellows and the new flames and scarlets. They too have small relatives which like to live among rocks and which, if sheltered, are never out of flower.

Among other shrubs we have *Kerria japonica* whose golden buttons, single or double, are welcome in early summer. The spiraeas give us an enormous range of more than 30, not counting wonderful hybrids like Bridal Wreath of graceful twiggy branches snowed over with flowers. Very like them are the splendid sorbarias with their plumes of creamy-white flowers and long pinnate leaves.

Filipendula and *Aruncus* are for the herbaceous beds, or even standing alone as eye-catchers, the first providing in *purpurea* mounds of attractive foliage mantled with glistening pink heads; *Aruncus*, the Goat's Beard, with its broad ferny leaves making an elegant hummock overtopped at midsummer by great cream plumes of tiny starry flowers.

Propagating

It is easy to propagate any woody members of the family from cuttings, making the usual heel by tearing off a small side shoot that has not flowered. Layering is another way of increasing your stock, by pegging down a new supple branchlet and covering the peg with soil, not letting it dry out.

Few people think of increasing a favourite rose by taking cuttings, but this can be done, and these roses will never throw suckers because, of course, they have not been grown as grafts. Yellow varieties do not strike so well as red and pink ones. Choose well-ripened shoots of first summer's growth, about 10 in. (260 mm) long in November and make a clean cut immediately below the lowest eye. The upper end of the cutting should be trimmed above an eye with a slanting cut, leaving two or three leaves. A better and more successful method is 'budding', but this is more complicated. Ramblers succeed well because they are more vigorous.

You may look one day at a leggy shrub and wonder if you should consign it to the bonfire. Prune it instead, for this gives new life to a shrub. Plants do not think, (though they do have a plant brain), nor do they have emotions, but it is a fact that they react to pruning by bursts of new growth, as if in defiance. Too-woody branches heavily pruned will bring the shrub back to vigorous youth. Always prune after flowering, and never into artificial shapes such as a neat globe.

Pruning roses can be a terrifying prospect. There are three golden rules: cut out all spindly stems; always cut to an outward bud, cutting above the bud, cleanly, and slanting outwards; keep the centre of the bush free.

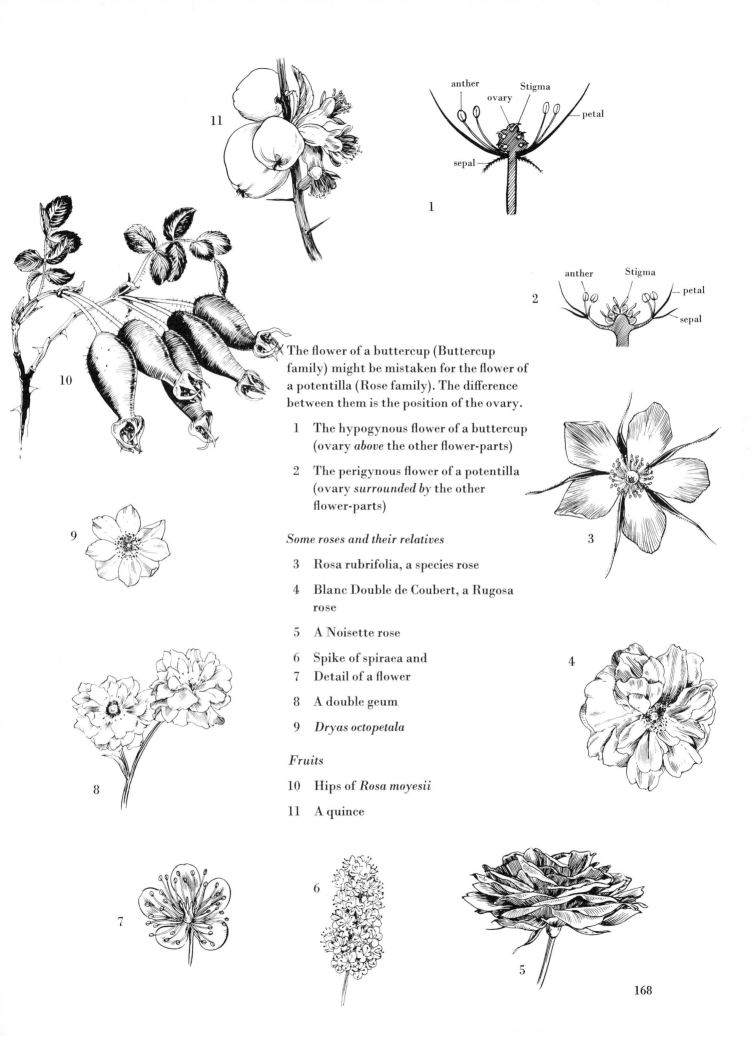

11

anther   Stigma
ovary
petal

sepal

1

anther   Stigma
petal

sepal

2

10

The flower of a buttercup (Buttercup family) might be mistaken for the flower of a potentilla (Rose family). The difference between them is the position of the ovary.

1   The hypogynous flower of a buttercup (ovary *above* the other flower-parts)

2   The perigynous flower of a potentilla (ovary *surrounded by* the other flower-parts)

Some roses and their relatives

3   Rosa rubrifolia, a species rose

4   Blanc Double de Coubert, a Rugosa rose

5   A Noisette rose

6   Spike of spiraea and

7   Detail of a flower

8   A double geum

9   *Dryas octopetala*

Fruits

10   Hips of *Rosa moyesii*

11   A quince

3

9

8

4

7

6

5

168

FLOWERS OF THE FAMILY

Acaena. A large genus of small plants, mainly carpeters and natives of New Zealand, South America and Polynesia. The attraction is their foliage, silvery-grey, rusty-brown, steel-blue. Use them for ground-cover, rock garden or walls.

adscendens, tiny crimped grey-green leaves on pink arching stems, reddish burrs in summer. Height 6 in. (150 mm).

glaucophylla, beautiful steel-blue cut foliage rapidly making a carpet, 3 in. (75 mm).

novae-zealandiae, a lovely variety is 'Pulchella', making a dense mat of rich crimson-purple foliage, 2 in. (50 mm).

Alchemilla. Again the foliage is often decorative, glistening silver underneath the palmate and saw-edged leaves.

alpina the short-stemmed corymbs of greenish flowers are unimportant compared with the pretty leaves, green above and silver-edged, silver on the undersides. For a chink in a wall or in the rock garden.

mollis, the Lady's Mantle, the best-known species, with downy rounded leaves and

Alchemilla mollis

feathery sprays of tiny greeny-yellow stars, long-lasting. Not only are the undersides silver, but the cupped leaves turn raindrops to quicksilver. Up to 18 in. (450 mm).

Amelanchier. Snowy Mespilus, June Berry and Shadblow are its names, a genus of wonderful hardy shrubs or small trees, beautiful for their young and autumn leaves, flowers and fruit.

asiatica, an elegant large shrub flowering in May and intermittently over a long period. The fruits are like blackcurrants.

laevis, a large shrub or small tree, sometimes confused with *canadensis*, a picture of striking beauty in April or May when the profusion of white flowers are in bloom among pink leaves. The fruits are purple-black and sweet. The leaves turn rich red in autumn.

ovalis, a shrub 5–9 ft (1.75–2.7 m) tall with downy shoots and spikes of large white flowers in May followed by red fruits turning blue-black.

Aruncus. A single herbaceous species closely related to *Spiraea* and *Filipendula*. Its broad ferny leaves and airy cream plumes of tiny starry flowers make handsome plants, particularly the males which are usually the most feathery but do not of course have the ornamental seed-heads of the female plants, which are useful for drying.

dioicus (*sylvester*), the Goat's Beard, grows up to 7 ft (2.1 m) tall. The variety *astilboides* with white flowers is an exact miniature at 2 ft (600 mm). 'Kneiffii' is slightly taller at 3 ft (900 mm) with leaves so finely divided as to be like threads.

Chaenomeles. The Flowering Quince is the delightful wall shrub once known as *Cydonia* or 'Japonica'.

169

japonica, Maule's Quince, is spreading and
spiny, growing up to 3 ft (900 mm) but
with a spread of 8 or 9 ft (2.5–2.7 m). The
flowers are like apple blossom but orange-
scarlet and come in April. The apple-shaped
fruits make an excellent jelly. The variety
alpina is dwarfer.

speciosa (*lagenaria*) is the well-known
early-flowering 'Japonica', and the parent
of very many beautiful varieties with
flowers white to deep crimson but
dominantly red: 'Brilliant' (clear scarlet,
large); 'Falconnet Charlet' (double salmon-
pink); 'Moerloosii' (thick clusters of
delicate pink and white); 'Nivalis' (large
pure-white); 'Knap Hill Scarlet' (bright
orange-scarlet flowers profusely borne
throughout spring and early summer).

All these can be used not only as wall
shrubs but also grown free-standing. When
grown as bushes no pruning is needed.

Chaenomeles speciosa

Cotoneaster. This genus includes some of
the most indispensable of the hardy
ornamental shrubs. They vary from
prostrate creepers to small trees, and give
brilliant autumn colour in leaf and fruit.

adpressus, a dwarf wide-spreading shrub,
a gem for the rock garden with bright red
fruits and small leaves turning scarlet in
autumn.

bullatus is one of the finest species in
cultivation, with large handsome
corrugated leaves colouring richly, and
clusters of large bright-red fruits. The form
floribundus is most beautiful with more
abundant flowers and fruits.

conspicuus, medium-sized and graceful
with arching branches. White flowers cover
the plant in early summer, followed by
equally numerous red fruits. 'Decorus' is a
low-growing form excellent for covering
banks. 'Highlight' makes a spectacular
mound of arching shoots with masses of
white flowers in May, followed by orange-
red berries.

dammeri is quite prostrate and has long
trailing shoots studded in autumn with
sealing-wax red berries. It is ideal for
banks or for ground-cover beneath other
shrubs.

horizontalis, well-named the Herring-bone
or Fishbone Cotoneaster, is low-growing
and spreading, invaluable for north or east
walls and giving rich autumn colour in
berry and leaf.

Dryas. A small genus of ground-hugging
sub-shrubs with tiny oak-like evergreen
leaves, the flowers comparatively large.

drummondii has bell-shaped nodding
yellow flowers seldom expanding fully and
carried singly on erect stems, 4–6 in.
(100–150 mm).

Dryas octopetala

Filipendula hexapetala

octopetala, the Mountain Avens, trails its bright green leaves to form a mat, producing large white flowers on short stems in May.

Exochorda has some beautiful May-blooming shrubs with long arching branches festooned with paper-white flowers.

giraldii, the Pearl Bush, is deciduous and grows up to 10 ft (3 m) tall. The branches tend to curve downwards and near the ends are covered with white pearly buds opening to shell-like flowers up to 2 in. (50 mm) across.

racemosa, the best-known species, is large and rather spreading. It is not suitable for a shallow chalk soil—unlike *korolkowii*, which is one of the best for chalky soils.

Filipendula. The Meadow Sweets, which used to be called *Spiraea*. They all have flat feathery heads of minute flowers on leafy stems sometimes up to 8 ft (2.5 m). All are hardy perennials, the leaves pinnate or palmate, and all except the species *hexapetala* like a moist soil, and therefore make good plants for the sides of ponds or brooks.

hexapetala, the Dropwort, has carrot-like foliage, the heads of white flowers on

branching stems reaching 2 ft (600 mm). 'Flore Pleno' is a double form, and the variety 'Grandiflora' has larger flowers.

palmata has handsome leaves and broad heads of light pink. 'Elegantissima' and 'Rosea' are fine varieties, all attaining 4 ft (1.2 m). There is a pretty dwarf form 18 in. (450 mm) high, 'Digitata Nana'.

ulmaria 'Aurea', a superior form of the Meadow Sweet or Queen of the Meadow, most attractive in spring when it produces its beautifully divided and veined leaves. These are vivid golden-green, in some lights pure yellow, becoming creamy-yellow in summer. The flowers are insignificant and should be removed before seeding, otherwise green-leafed seedlings will take over. It likes a deep moist soil, partial shade in hot districts.

Geum. These smallish perennials are always useful for providing patches of bold colour in summer. They have fairly recently been greatly improved, sparse stemmy plants now replaced by dense clumps and more prolific flowers.
× *borisii* makes hummocks of bright green leaves, hairy and rounded, useful as ground-cover. The single cupped flowers are warm pure orange. Height 1 ft (300 mm).

chiloense is the parent of two popular strains easily raised from seed: 'Lady Stratheden' with double flowers of pure warm yellow, and 'Mrs Bradshaw', a flaming brick-red double. Between them in colour are 'Princess Juliana', 'Fire Opal' and 'Dolly North', all of which should be increased by division of the clumps in early spring.

Potentilla. These are low-growing shrubs, some most attractive dwarfs for the rock garden, many flowering a second time. They have showy cupped flowers of heart-shaped petals.

alba is a valuable ground-cover plant producing mats of leaves divided into leaflets which are silver-haired beneath. The flowers are charming, white with a yellow eye. They will go on blooming all year if given some protection in a nook of the rock garden.

eriocarpa is another spreader for the rock garden, making mats of grey-green leaves with many short-stemmed yellow flowers all summer.

fruticosa, an indispensable small shrub for sun or light shade, flowering for months on end. It has been an ideal subject for the hybridists, and many varieties and forms have been introduced with bigger white flowers, rich yellows, pinks and reds, even a stunning orange, though this last has so far proved fugitive in colour and should be given light shade to prevent it from fading.

hyparctica, a small neat plant for trough and sink gardens, making hummocks of softly hairy grey leaves and large yellow flowers on short stems.

nitida is an exquisite plant from the high screes of the European Alps, forming flat mats of silver foliage with almost stemless pink flowers. 'Rubra' has flowers more richly coloured, 'Lissadell' particularly so. There are also forms with white or almost white flowers.

Prunus. Apart from those trees giving us cherries, almonds, plums and other fruits, many of which are splendidly ornamental, this great genus gives us some useful shrubs.

× *cistena* is a hybrid plum with purple leaves which grows only a few feet high and can be pruned to make a dwarf hedge.

glandulosa, usually referred to as an almond, but more nearly allied to the cherries, has two popular forms: the early-flowering *albiplena*, 4–5 ft (1.2–1.5 m) tall, its slender stems crowded with double white flowers in April; and the form known as *sinensis* or *roseo-plena* with double pink flowers.

Potentilla fruticosa

Prunus lusitanica

lusitanica, the evergreen Portugal Laurel, is used for hedges and windbreaks, and sometimes to make topiary specimens or leafy umbrellas.

mume is the Japanese Apricot, a vigorous bush with pink flowers in March and April. Good garden forms have deeper rose or carmine flowers.

prostrata is a compact rock-hugging shrub with woody stems which twine into intricate tangles. Before the leaves develop, small bright pink flowers appear.

subhirtella var. *autumnalis* is so slow-growing a tree as to remain shrub-size for years. In America it is bush-like. This is the winter-flowering cherry which delights us with two flowerings—in October onwards, when the semi-double clusters are white, turning pink, and again in April.

Pyracantha. The Firethorn will make any wall look attractive, with bunches of creamy-white flowers in June and brilliant berries in autumn. These evergreen shrubs can also be grown in the open but are rather prickly plants. If used against a wall they need pruning immediately after flowering to keep them in shape, care being taken not to remove the trusses of young berries.
coccinea lalandii is the most popular variety, with large orange-red berries. There is also a yellow-berried variety, *aurea*.

Rosa. A bewildering array of beauty faces us when we come to consider roses. Which to plant in our garden? The Hybrid Teas that fill the catalogues? Shrub roses for their scent? Old roses? New roses? What about floribundas and climbers and ramblers?

To help you choose, we have arranged the different kinds in easy categories under three main headings: Species Roses; Modern Roses; and Shrub Roses.

Species Roses

These are the parents of all other roses. They have a special beauty in their leaves, often fern-like; in their fragrance (the leaves of some are fragrant, too); with a bonus of large colourful hips shining like brilliant gems among the golden leaves of autumn.

We give a selection of some of the best for flowering and scent. Not included in this section are species like *centifolia* and *gallica* which have been so extensively hybridised that they form groups of their own. They are to be found in the Shrub Roses section under such headings as "*Rosa damascena*—The Damask Rose".

Rosa banksiae

banksiae, the Banksian Rose, thrives best on a warm wall. The white double rosette flowers are deliciously fragrant of violets. The double 'Lutea' is the famous Yellow Banksian.

bracteata, the Macartney Rose, with rambling stems. The lemon-scented flowers are white with golden anthers, the hips round and orange-red.

canina, the Dog Rose, familiar in hedge-rows, is the probable parent of × *alba*, the White Rose of York. The flowers, usually semi-double, are richly scented, cultivated for making Attar of Roses. 'Andersonii' is of the Tudor Rose type, with clear rose-pink flowers over a long period.

chinensis, the China or Monthly Rose, is the parent of the old Tea Rose and Fairy Rose.

cinnamomea, deep lilac-pink flowers, but variable, spicily fragrant. The hips are small and red.

ecae, a dainty shrub with small buttercup-yellow flowers carried all along the branches from late May and through June.

farreri, spreading branches of ferny leaves and pale pink or white flowers followed by bright coral-red hips when the autumn foliage has turned purple and crimson. Its form *persetosa* is the Threepenny-bit Rose, with smaller leaves and flowers coral-red in bud opening soft pink.

fedtschenkoana is medium-sized with attractive sea-green leaves. The white flowers go on throughout the summer, and are replaced by bristly orange-red pear-shaped hips.

filipos, rambling or climbing, forms curtains of fragrant white flowers over a

Rosa moyesii

suitable support in late June. This is the parent of the famous 'Kiftsgate', whose panicles may have as many as a hundred sweetly-scented flowers. It is almost as spectacular when bearing its small red hips.

lutea (*foetida*) is the parent of the Austrian Briars of copper-coloured flowers.

moyesii, one of the most beautiful single roses, rich cherry-red with a boss of yellow stamens in June and July, followed by flagon-shaped bright crimson hips. It is happy growing up into trees.

multibracteata, of medium size and very graceful, with fragrant ferny leaves and bright rose-lilac flowers over a long period.

pimpinellifolia (*spinosissima*), the Scots or Burnet Rose, a small suckering shrub with very bristly and prickly stems. The small white or pale pink flowers are borne along the stems in May and June, followed by round black hips. The variety 'Lutea' has buttercup-yellow flowers and bright green leaves.

rubiginosa, the Sweet Briar or Eglantine, medium-sized with densely prickly stems and deliciously aromatic leaves. The clear pink flowers stud the arching branches during summer, and the bright-red oval hips last well into the winter. It makes a vigorous hedge and is a parent of wonderful hybrids.

rubrifolia is ornamental with its reddish-violet stems and beautiful blue foliage with single pink flowers and oval red hips.

villosa, the Apple Rose, has bluish-green downy leaves fragrant when crushed, the carmine buds opening to clear-pink flowers followed, in the early autumn, by large apple-shaped crimson hips. 'Duplex' has semi-double flowers.

xanthina has the daintiest of ferny leaves and golden-yellow semi-double flowers. It is the parent of the well-known 'Canary Bird'.

174

Modern Roses

This section is divided into Hybrid Teas (H.T.'s) which can be both bush and standard roses; Floribundas; Climbers and Ramblers; Garnettes; Miniature Roses.

Hybrid Teas

The choice is vast. We select a few, arranging them under their colours.

Red:
Ernest H. Morse, brilliant unfading turkey-red, disease resistant.
Papa Meilland, glorious red with shading of black velvet, richly scented.
Wendy Cussons, light rosy-red, trouble-free.

White:
Pascali, shapely and full.
Virgo, purest paper-white.
White Wings, exquisite single.

Pink:
La France, bright silvery-rose, fragrant.
Shot Silk, pink shaded gold, fragrant.
Prima Ballerina, fragrant rich rosy-pink.

Yellow:
King's Ransom, rich yellow.
Sutter's Gold, buds flushed red opening to clear yellow, scented.
McGredy's Yellow, primrose-yellow.

Coppery:
Whisky Mac, golden-amber, sweetly scented.
Diorama, golden-orange, vivid in autumn.
Lady Hillingdon, deep apricot-yellow, tea-scented, foliage deep red.

Mauve:
Blue Moon, clear lavender, richly scented.
Great News, rich plum-purple with silver reverse, scented.

Floribundas

These have their flowers in large clusters and are a most important group because of their toughness and prolific and persistent bloom.

Hybrid Tea Rose 'La France'

Floribunda Rose 'Anne Poulsen'

Red:
Dusky Maiden, single, velvety-crimson with a black sheen.
Anne Poulsen, brilliant scarlet-crimson, almost luminous, semi-double, scented.
Frensham, deep blood-red, wonderful for difficult places or conditions, very tall.

White:
Iceberg, exquisite long buds flushed shell-pink opening to coolest greenish-white and going on into winter.
Dimples, creamy-white with golden centre.

Pink:
Dearest, double, charming noisette shape, salmon-pink and scented.
Blessings, dawn-pink, resistant to disease.
Whisper, soft-pink and white blooms in profusion.

Yellow:
Allgold, really deep-yellow double flowers.
Chinatown, deepest gold shading out cream.

Coppery:
Copper Pot, attractive and sweet-scented.
Woburn Abbey, clearest tangerine.

Mauve:
Africa Star, richest mauve in masses.
Lilac Charm, single with a boss of golden stamens.

Climbers and Ramblers

Climbing roses are those flowering on the old wood (up to three years). Ramblers flower on the previous year's growth. Some in both categories are once-flowering; others recurrent-flowering.

Albéric Barbier, rambler, once-flowering. Almost evergreen, buds pure yellow opening to large double blooms of rich creamy-white, scented. Excellent for screening.

Albertine, rambler, once-flowering. Copper-pink buds opening to large rich salmon-pink flowers. Highly scented.

Altissimo, climber, recurrent. Almost single flowers of pure velvety-red, dark foliage.

Climbing Rose 'Gloire de Dijon'

Gloire de Dijon, climber, recurrent. The favourite old tea-rose, very double and fragrant.

Leverkusen, climber, recurrent. Dark shiny foliage, shoots tinged with gold, deep tawny-gold flowers in clusters, lemon-scented.

Madame Alfred Carrière, climber, recurrent. Fragrant white noisette, very free-flowering.

Mermaid, climber, recurrent. Huge yellow saucers holding a boss of golden stamens.

Paul's Scarlet Climber, rambler, once-flowering. Brilliant scarlet flowers in huge clusters.

Zéphirine Drouhin, climber, recurrent. The thornless rose. Deep pink flowers, sweet old-fashioned scent.

Garnettes

These are famous for their long-lasting blooms which open like a lovely camellia. They are hardy and vigorous floribundas, about 2½ ft (750 mm) high. The original was the Red Garnette. Varieties are Deep Pink, Carol (pink), Pink Frills, Rose, Salmon Pink, and Scarlet. These are the true Garnettes.

Garnette Rose 'Carol'

There are also hybrids, differing in shape and somewhat larger in flower: White, Yellow (scented), Sonora (apricot), Junior Miss (pastel pink), Zorina (salmon-orange), Bridal Pink, White Junior Miss.

Miniature Rose 'Perle de Montserrat'

Miniature Roses

People with a love for toys and dolls fall under the spell of these tiny roses, smallest of which is 4 in. (100 mm) high. The average height is 9–12 in. (230–300 mm).

They come as little bushes, as standards up to 18 in. (460 mm) high, and even as climbers. Most varieties are available as pot plants throughout the year, but they should be planted outside after flowering.

Baby Darling, salmon-orange, double.
Cinderella, shell-pinkish white.
Dwarf King, dark red.
Perle de Montserrat, pink stained with carmine.
Mr Bluebird, lavender-blue, semi-double, scented.
Pour Toi, white with tint of green.
Yellow Doll, lemon-yellow.

SHRUB ROSES

These are the roses full of scent and charm. They are becoming increasingly popular because they need less attention, little pruning, and are generally hardier and less prone to disease.

They divide into about a dozen groups, each with its own character and history, and lend themselves to an informal type of gardening nearer to Nature than the planned bed of H.T.'s. They are, besides, exquisite for picking. The following is a selection from these groups.

Rose alba
One of the oldest roses, grown in England since the Middle Ages. They are mostly robust shrubs with bluish leaves, pale flowers, and exquisite scent, flowering June and July. Hardly any pruning is needed.

Rosa alba semi-plena, the White Rose of York. Smothered with golden-centred flowers.

Great Maiden's Blush, flesh-pink opening paler.
Queen of Denmark, warm rich pink.

Bourbon Roses
These were the result of an accidental cross between a China Rose and a Damask, one giving perpetual-flowering, the other the glorious scent.
Honorine de Brabant, pale rosy-mauve with darker stripes.
Louise Odier, richest pink, warm and glowing.

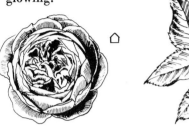

Rosa centifolia–The Cabbage Rose
Known in England in the sixteenth century, they are richly scented with full globular blooms nodding on curved stems.

Fantin Latour, large clusters of fresh pale-pink flowers opening flat.

The Old Cabbage Rose, deep glowing rose-pink.
Robert le Diable, rich purple with slate-blue and ashen shading, splashed with carmine.

Rose centifolia Muscosa–The Moss Rose
The first rose of this type was a sport of the Cabbage Rose in the eighteenth century, taking its name from the mossy sepals and flower-stalk, its outstanding feature. The flowers have a rich fruity scent.

Alfred de Dalmas (Mousseline), delicate flowers throughout summer and early autumn. Moss short, brownish-green.

Blanche Moreau, paper-white flowers sometimes striped, thick dark red moss.
William Lobb, the 'Old Velvet Moss', fuchsia-purple shot with lilac.

Rosa Damascena–The Damask Rose
Legend says that the Crusaders brought these roses from Damascus. They are richly scented, tall and hardy.

Marie Louise, enormous brilliant pink flowers in profusion.

Quatre Saisons, the famous autumn-flowering Damask of the Romans, soft pink flowers.

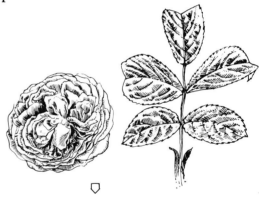

Rosa gallica–The French Rose
Distinguished by its dwarf compact growth, thick dark-green leaves, and smallness of its few thorns.

Belle de Creçy, a harmony of purple, lilac, silver-grey and soft rose.

Charles de Mills, full flowers, velvety plum-crimson.

HYBRIDS

Rosa moschata–The Musk Rose
These are clustered roses deliciously tea- and musk-scented, flowering into October.

Buff Beauty, double rich-creamy flowers.
Golden-tinged foliage.
Felicia, large full flowers, salmon-pink
opening to shell-pink.

Hybrid Perpetuals
The gloriously scented Victorian roses
which introduced autumn-blooming.
Climbers, they can be used on walls,
fences, pergolas and pillars.

Frau Karl Druschki, the classic white rose
of magnificent blooms.
Paul Neyron, rosy flowers like a peony,
suffused with lilac, silver reverse.

Rosa rugosa
Hardy compact shrubs with distinctive
foliage, good for poor soils, some perpetual-
flowering, scented. The singles with
brilliant hips.

Blanc Double de Coubert, snowy semi-
double flowers, buff and green centres.
Roseraie de l'Hay, clear apple-green
foliage, large wine-purple flowers.

Modern Shrub Roses

Constance Spry, centifolia type, clear pink
and richly scented.

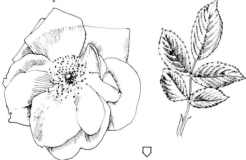

Frühlingsgold, *spinosissima* hybrid.
Masses of fresh creamy saucers with golden
centres.

Kassel, Hybrid Musk parentage, dusky
orange-red double flowers in large clusters.

Rubus. Ornamental brambles have
attractive flowers and foliage. Some of the
species have striking white stems in winter.

arcticus, a creeping species with tufts of
small three-lobed leaves and short stems
each carrying a large pink flower.

calycinoides is the white-flowered prostrate
species.

cockburnianus (*giraldianus*), the best of
the 'whitewashed' brambles.

Tridel, a beautiful hybrid with peeling
thornless shoots up to 10 ft (3 m) and
glistening white flowers along the arching
branches.

Spiraea. A variable and useful genus of
hardy flowering shrubs, many of them
graceful and with pleasing foliage.

× *arguta*, the popular 'Bridal Wreath' or
'Foam of May'. It is medium-sized, the
leaves coming early and the pure white
flowers clustering all along the branches.

× *bumalda*, a dwarf shrub with deep pink
flowers in terminal panicles throughout the
summer. The leaves are often variegated
with pink and cream. The variety 'Anthony
Waterer' has bright crimson flowers and
variegated foliage.

japonica, small and erect, with heads of
pink flowers from midsummer onwards.
The variety 'Alpina' ('Nana') is a superb
dwarf forming a dense compact mound,
spectacular in flower. 'Macrophylla' is the
best for autumn leaf colour.

Waldsteinia. This for the rock garden, or
to make ground-cover for shady places.
There are two species, *geoides* and *ternata*,
both carpeters with heads of golden
flowers.

179

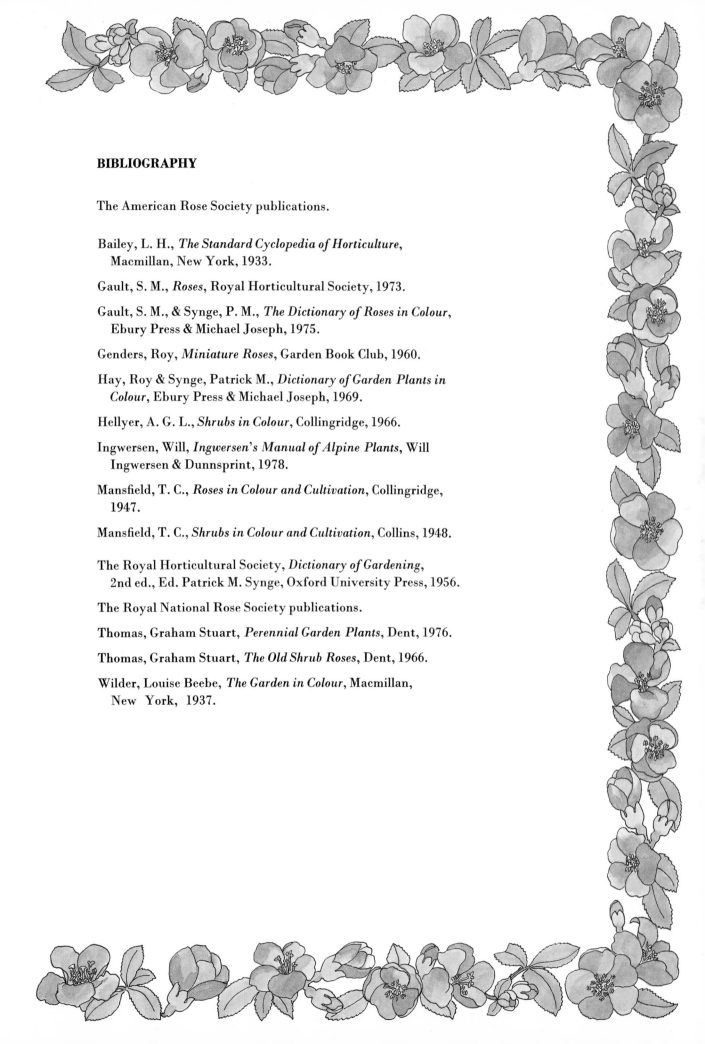

BIBLIOGRAPHY

The American Rose Society publications.

Bailey, L. H., *The Standard Cyclopedia of Horticulture*,
Macmillan, New York, 1933.

Gault, S. M., *Roses*, Royal Horticultural Society, 1973.

Gault, S. M., & Synge, P. M., *The Dictionary of Roses in Colour*,
Ebury Press & Michael Joseph, 1975.

Genders, Roy, *Miniature Roses*, Garden Book Club, 1960.

Hay, Roy & Synge, Patrick M., *Dictionary of Garden Plants in
Colour*, Ebury Press & Michael Joseph, 1969.

Hellyer, A. G. L., *Shrubs in Colour*, Collingridge, 1966.

Ingwersen, Will, *Ingwersen's Manual of Alpine Plants*, Will
Ingwersen & Dunnsprint, 1978.

Mansfield, T. C., *Roses in Colour and Cultivation*, Collingridge,
1947.

Mansfield, T. C., *Shrubs in Colour and Cultivation*, Collins, 1948.

The Royal Horticultural Society, *Dictionary of Gardening*,
2nd ed., Ed. Patrick M. Synge, Oxford University Press, 1956.

The Royal National Rose Society publications.

Thomas, Graham Stuart, *Perennial Garden Plants*, Dent, 1976.

Thomas, Graham Stuart, *The Old Shrub Roses*, Dent, 1966.

Wilder, Louise Beebe, *The Garden in Colour*, Macmillan,
New York, 1937.

The Snapdragon or Figwort Family

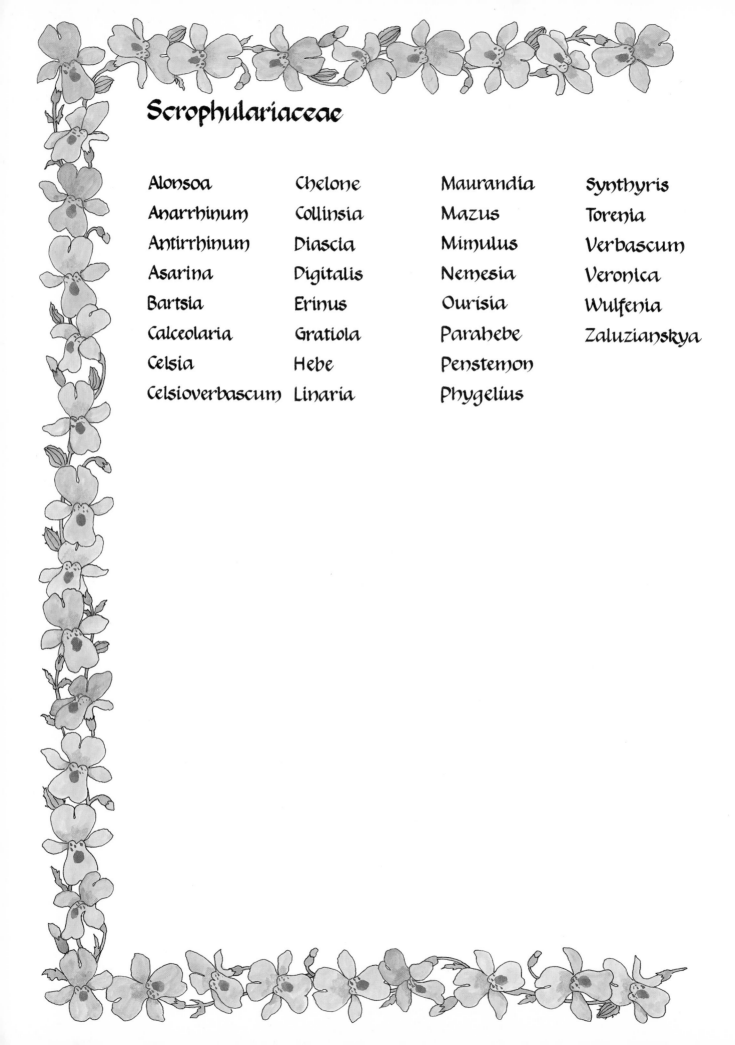

Scrophulariaceae

Alonsoa	Chelone	Maurandia	Synthyris
Anarrhinum	Collinsia	Mazus	Torenia
Antirrhinum	Diascia	Mimulus	Verbascum
Asarina	Digitalis	Nemesia	Veronica
Bartsia	Erinus	Ourisia	Wulfenia
Calceolaria	Gratiola	Parahebe	Zaluzianskya
Celsia	Hebe	Penstemon	
Celsioverbascum	Linaria	Phygelius	

The Snapdragon or Figwort Family

At first glance this family has little to offer us. Few of the names in the list of genera are familiar, though we recognise the foxglove in *Digitalis*, the speedwell in *Veronica*, and of course the snapdragon itself in *Antirrhinum*. But when we learn that there are such plants to be grown as Chinese Houses, the Wishbone Flower, and Turtlehead, our gardening world reaches to a new horizon.

In fact, the Snapdragon or Figwort family has some delightful members. Who would be without those valuable shrubs the hebes, with such a wealth of variety to give us, from tiny huddled bushes for the rock garden to opulent shrubs that can vie with any other in beauty? There are many pretty annuals: the scarlet Mask Flower, the useful nemesias in all their bright colours; and that old favourite the penstemon which will obligingly last for years if the winters are mild enough.

Such different flowers! They are certainly very varied, as we see when we compare the tall spike of a mullein with a quaint pouched calceolaria; the lowly speedwell making a patch of blue eyes, with the speckled mimulus of pouting lip. They all belong to the same family—but where is the link that makes them akin?

We see that we can at least divide the plants into two kinds of flowers. One, the veronica for example, has its petals arranged symmetrically; so that if we took a knife and quartered the flower, each quarter would be the same as the other three. The other kind is irregular in shape, the petals forming a tube (as in the penstemon), and in some a hood and a lip (as in the snapdragon). In their case if we took a knife and quartered a flower, we would have two quarters alike and two different.

Antirrhinum majus

Identification, however, is quite distinct and is something that does not happen in any other family: all have two long and two short stamens. You sometimes have to look carefully inside the flower for the short ones, but they are there.

Although we cannot expect from them the exotic beauty of orchids, or the velvet scent of roses, the family contributes much to our gardens in useful and showy plants providing months of bright colour wherever they are planted.

CARE AND CULTURE

The family, a large one, is widely scattered across the world from the Arctic to the tropics, although they are mainly to be found in the temperate regions. There are about 200 genera containing 3,000 species. Some of the veronicas have wandered beyond the tropics and far into the southern hemisphere, and of these a few are found only in Australia, and very many only in New Zealand.

Most of the 200 species of *Calceolaria* are natives of Chile and Peru, some growing as far north as Mexico. They are splendid plants for bedding and for winter flowering in a cool greenhouse. A tiny charmer for the rock garden is *darwinii*, and although its home is the Strait of Magellan it must be sheltered from cutting winds. The Monkey Flower (*Mimulus*) has travelled from north-western Mexico to Alaska. This is a streamside plant or at least preferring moist cool conditions, and there are several species suitable for rock gardens. The flower gets its name from its resemblance to the face of a monkey. It has some lovely colours among the yellows and coppers, with some crimson or deep pink, the lips attractively freckled.

The maurandias are little-known climbing plants which really are tender perennials, but they may be grown as half-hardy annuals and planted outdoors in early June to climb up a trellis or other support. They can also be used as winter-flowering climbers in a cool greenhouse. The showy trumpet-shaped flowers are white, rose, purple and blue. Another half-hardy annual deserving to be more widely grown is the Twinspur (*Diascia*) whose flowers are like a nemesia with two spurs or pouches. These also make excellent pot plants for the cool greenhouse. Their colours are coral and terracotta-pink.

Gone are the days when we knew the foxglove merely as a wildflower with spikes of pink or white. The hybridists have been busy, and you can now have them in cream, primrose, carmine and purple. Grow foxgloves, too, for their virtue as good companions, encouraging neighbouring

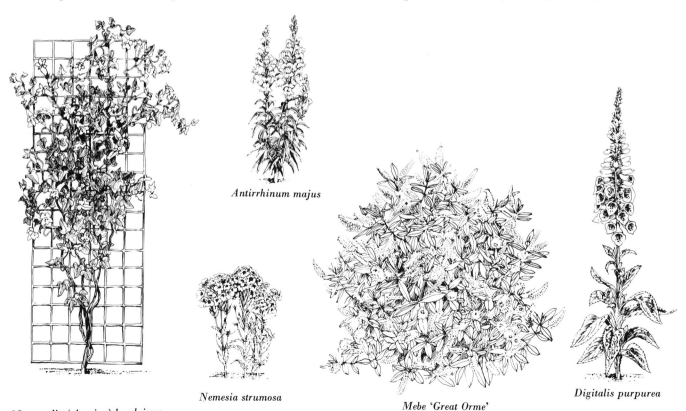

Antirrhinum majus

Nemesia strumosa

Mebe 'Great Orme'

Digitalis purpurea

Maurandia (Asarina) barclaiana

185

plants and stimulating their hardiness.

The hebes and veronicas have been, and still are, much confused, but as a rough and ready guide the hebes are mainly a group of Australasian shrubs with leathery leaves for withstanding drought conditions, their flowers in poker-like spikes; while the veronicas—not only from New Zealand but also from Europe and Asia—are generally quite small and have softer foliage, though in some species waxy and evergreen, their starry flowers carried on short spikes, sprays or racemes.

It is to David Douglas, the intrepid young plant hunter sent to Canada and California by the Horticultural Society (later "The Royal Horticultural Society"), that the gardening world is indebted for nineteen species of penstemons. The tubular flowers, which are of lovely colours from pinks through to purples, are borne on long spikes. The plants throw up a succession of these, and in mild places they are evergreen and may last well into the winter. Elegant and wonderfully decorative, they are rivalled only by the Cape Fuchsia (*Phygelius*) with its candelabra of dangling bright scarlet flowers, shrubs of a warm climate but thriving in sunshine and even on a north-facing wall.

Snapdragons are beloved by children for the fun of pressing the back of the flower to make it open its jaws. Not long ago all snapdragons had these soft velvet jaws, but new ones have come on the floral stage in tall hybrid varieties with double flowers and frilled petals, semi-doubles, ruffled, semi-dwarfs with azalea-like flowers, and bell-flowered varieties looking like freesias, all in a marvellous range of colours from soft salmon-pink to brilliant flame-scarlet, lavender, orange, bronze, as well as the old familiar yellows, pinks and white. With new miniature varieties one can make a floral carpet. These are neat and compact and all the colours bloom together. There are also rust-resistant varieties intermediate in height, and others resistant to rain and bad weather. We could hardly ask for more variety or better value from one single kind of plant.

Ourisia elegans

Celsia acaulis

Mimulus luteus

Nemesia sufforii

Linnaria maroccania

Veronica nummularia

Those for whom rock gardening holds an especial appeal can revel in the Snapdragon family. There are numerous carpeting veronicas, mostly with blue flowers, and such treasures as the ourisias of elfin-like pure white flowers or brilliant scarlet trumpets; for dry walls and sunny places *Erinus*, called the Fairy Foxglove; and what one might call the 'Fairy Snapdragon'—since *Asarina* used to have the name *Antirrhinum*, a trailing plant for banks and walls, in sun or shade, with big creamy-yellow snapdragons all summer and autumn. Another miniature snapdragon is the Toadflax (*Linaria*) of ivy leaves, a lovely little plant which wanders about mingling its purple flowers with those of other inhabitants.

The large hebes are splendid shrubs growing up to 5 ft (1.5 m) and taller, always causing comment for the beauty of their spikes densely packed with tiny flowers and made fluffy by their long stamens, spikes that may begin the prettiest pink and turn purple as the flowers mature. They are all evergreen, some with beautiful variegated leaves, and give a long flowering season. They make good seaside plants, and there are hebe shrublets for the front of the border or here and there in the rock garden, casting just enough light shade for those rock plants which do not like the full sun.

Propagating

Most of this family are easy to grow. Antirrhinums, calceolarias and nemesias should be sown in boxes under glass in February and March and transplanted when a few inches high. Foxgloves can be sown where they are to grow, and the annuals unless they are half-hardy.

Any of the shrubby plants, even to the tiniest veronicas if they are woody, and including the penstemons, can be increased by cuttings. If severe winter weather is

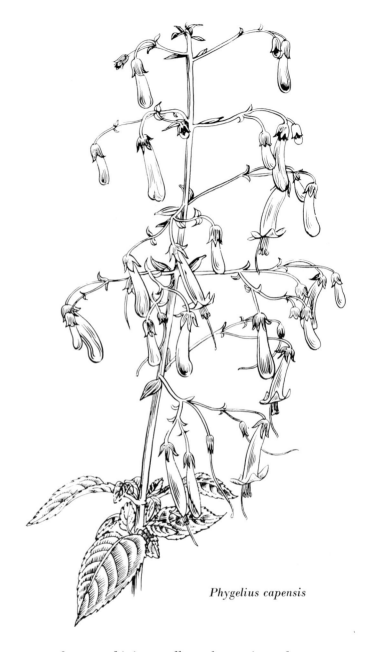

Phygelius capensis

threatened it is as well to take cuttings of precious hebes. Some of the hebes hybridise readily, so seedlings may show considerable variation from their parents. This can be a fascinating exercise if one wants to try raising a new variety.

Phygelius can also be increased by cuttings, but the seed must be sown in a slight hotbed in spring.

187

1

2

3

vertical cross-section of Veronica

Irregular and regular flowers of the family

1   Antirrhinum

2   Mimulus

3   Calceolaria

4   Veronica

5   Penstemon

4

How flowers are arranged

6   on a raceme or spike (Mullein)

7   on a cyme (Figwort)

Dissections of mimulus and Veronica
flowers

vertical cross-section of Mimulus

5

7

6

FLOWERS OF THE FAMILY

Alonsoa. The Mask Flower, a group of showy plants perennial in their native Chile and Peru, but in Britain and temperate North America should be treated as half-hardy annuals. They are excellent for sunny beds and borders and make splendid pot plants for a cool greenhouse.

linearis is bushy, with narrow toothed leaves and scarlet irregular flowers on graceful stems 1–1½ ft (300–450 mm) high. Its variety *gracilis* (*pumila*) is even more graceful and is smaller. Both flower from summer into early autumn.

warscewiczii is the one most commonly seen in gardens. It has masses of bright orange-scarlet flowers, again from summer to early autumn, growing up to 1½ ft (450 mm). A dwarf form is *compacta*, and one with soft pink flowers and a scarlet centre *mutisii*, while *mutisii compacta* has flowers of a charming chamois-rose.

Antirrhinum. The lovely colourful snap-dragons we know descend from a common ancestor, the species *majus* from the Mediterranean region. This used to be grown as a biennial or perennial, but nowadays is cultivated almost entirely as a half-hardy annual. This change has encouraged the development of larger flowers and a much wider colour-range, and so great is the number of varieties today that they have been divided into three groups: tall, intermediate, and dwarf.

Tall (2–3 ft, 600–900 mm)

'Bright Butterflies', trumpet-shaped penstemon-like flowers in shades of crimson, deep rose, pink, apricot, yellow, bronze and white. They are excellent for cutting.

'Frontier Mixture', sturdy and free-flowering, each plant producing a dozen or more equally tall spikes of crimson, scarlet, orange, rose, lavender, yellow or white.

'Topper', long shapely spikes packed with large flowers in beautiful shades of rose, lavender, orange and yellow, also white. These are what every antirrhinum-lover dreams of having—rust-resistant plants.

There are also double hybrids, bringing in a unique flower-form that eliminates the snapdragon jaws, as do the single Butterfly Hybrids, but compensates with attractive frills and flounces.

'Madame Butterfly', the first truly double antirrhinum, her flowers like double azaleas massed on the stems. They provide a riot of colour.

'Madame Butterfly'

189

'Double Supreme', with flowers ruffled and frilled in shades of pink, cerise, yellow and cream, each plant bearing six or seven sturdy spikes.

'Bellflowered Super Pink' has spikes of freesia-like flowers, soft salmon-pink with a yellow centre.

'Tetraploid Mixed' has large flowers, very ruffled and veined, of orange, yellow, bronze, pink, crimson, and white.

Intermediate (15–18 in., 380–450 mm)

Some exquisite flowers come in this group, excellent for the fronts of borders and for mass display.

'Black Prince' is gorgeous with deep crimson flowers and dark foliage.

'Rembrandt' is most unusual with orange-scarlet flowers tipped with gold on the lower petals.

'Golden Eclipse' is a clear canary-yellow.

In this intermediate group there are also reliable varieties which are, to some extent, resistant to antirrhinum rust. These come in a mixed colour blend or in their own individual colours.

'Coral', spikes of bright coral-pink on compact plants.

'Crimson', dark velvety crimson and deep green foliage.

'Orange', beautiful spikes of light orange flowers flushed with pink.

'Scarlet', bright scarlet flowers above dark foliage. A compact plant.

'Yellow', fine sturdy spikes of canary-yellow on neat-growing plants.

In a series called Coronette are vigorous plants producing a central spike of large individual flowers surrounded by a cluster of 8–12 equally large spikes which all

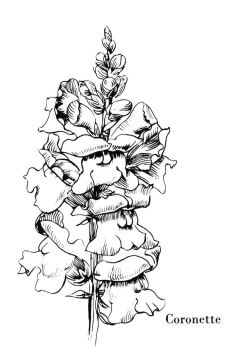

Coronette

bloom together. They also are resistant to rust, and to rain and bad weather. They come in a range of brilliant colours.

Dwarf (6–12 in., 150–300 mm)

'Little Darling', trumpet-shaped flowers like penstemons, early and free-flowering in gay colours.

'Sweetheart', like double azaleas on neat spikes and flowering throughout the summer. It is rust-resistant.

'Tom Thumb Floral Carpet', beautiful ball-shaped plants covered with masses of flowers in a very wide colour-range.

'Magic Carpet', a strain of trailing dwarfs in many attractive colours.

There are also species antirrhinums suitable for the rock garden.

hispanicum is a Spanish species making foot-high bushes carrying loose sprays of flowers which may be white, pink or purple, with a yellow throat. The sub-species *glutinosum* is a neat compact plant with soft yellow flowers and narrow red stripes on the throat.

molle from the Pyrenees makes dwarf woody bushlets with slightly sticky stems and leaves, and sprays of white and yellow flowers.

sempervirens is a prostrate plant with a tangle of woody stems. Its white flowers are striped with lilac, and the throat is yellow.

Asarina. A genus of a single species, is the Spanish vernacular name for an antirrhinum, and until recently it was classed as one.

procumbens, a delightful trailing plant for banks and walls in sun or shade. It has sticky stems and softly-hairy grey-green leaves, and the large white snapdragon flowers in spring and summer are tinted with yellow and red. Its height is only 2 in. (50 mm).

Calceolaria. The Slipperwort—an allusion to the flower's pouched lower lip, from *calcelus*, a little slipper. These flowers are not so popular as they used to be, but there are some species and varieties well worth growing. They provide brilliant yellows, bronzes and crimsons.

acutifolia makes creeping mats of light green leaves from which appear large single yellow flowers on 2 in. (50 mm) stems in early summer. Plant in a moist shady spot.

amplexicaulis is a very handsome plant growing up to 30 in. (760 mm). It sends up a number of suckers which give a constant succession of soft lemon flowers from late May till quite late in the autumn.

darwinii, an amusing little plant forming a colony of tiny skirted dwarfs, the single flowers standing upright on the scape. It can be fugitive and is an exciting challenge to the alpinist. Its height is a mere 2–3 in. (50–75 mm), and it flowers in summer.

Calceolaria darwinii

fothergillii, a lovely plant for the alpine house or peaty scree in part shade. The leaves are small downy rosettes from which spring a profusion of pretty red and yellow flowers in spring and summer on stems 6 in. (150 mm) high.

integrifolia is a 4 ft (1.2 m) evergreen sub-shrub, valuable for its long flowering, mid-summer to mid-autumn. The yellow flowers are in dense clusters.

× *multiflora* is the name covering the modern large-flowered hybrids of brilliant yellows, reds, bronzy-browns and pinks. 'Grandiflora' is the ultimate in selection, and 'Nana' are the dwarfs. These are treated as half-hardy annuals and as greenhouse perennials.

Celsia. Includes some attractive shrubby and hardy perennials and biennials.

acaulis is a rosette plant for the scree bed, with thick puckered leaves and almost stemless bright yellow flowers. There are numerous hybrids. All are summer-flowering.

Celsia acaulis

cretica, biennial, 4–6 ft (1.2–1.8 m), has yellow flowers in June with rust-coloured spots on the upper lip. It is good for producing seedlings.

Chelone. The Turtlehead is a genus of four species of perennials producing showy two-lipped flowers on spikes in summer.

lyonii is 3–4 ft (900 mm–1.2 m) high with rosy-purple flowers in clusters on the spikes.

obliqua grows up to 2 ft (600 mm) high and has deep rose flowers.

Collinsia. Innocence or Chinese Houses, is a genus of easily-grown and very pretty hardy annuals flowering in summer. They do not object to partial shade.

bicolor, a showy Californian species, has clusters of white flowers marked with rose, lilac or purple. It grows 12–15 in. (300–380 mm) high. The variety 'Salmon Queen' is in an attractive shade of pink.

grandifiora, of the same height, has fascinating flowers, the lower lip deep blue, the upper lip varying from white to purple.

Diascia. The Twinspur, is a small genus of South African summer-flowering annuals and perennials. Outdoors they like a sunny spot, and they make excellent pot plants.

barberae is a half-hardy annual about 18 in. (450 mm) high with two curved spurs on the soft coral and pink flowers.

coradata makes mats of dark glossy leaves and produces a succession of spurred pink flowers.
'Rugy Field' is a superb new hybrid from the above two species, completely hardy with spikes of rich salmon-pink flowers of a most intriguing shape, summer into the autumn.

Digitalis purpurea

Digitalis. It is not only to the tall hybrid foxgloves we look for their decorative spikes, but also to ones of much shorter stature, and to the species which have much to offer. Foxgloves of some kind should be in everybody's garden.

davisiana comes from Turkey and has 18 in. (450 mm) stems carrying sprays of bronze-yellow flowers.

dubia, a tiny perennial of soft purple-pink flowers on stems 6–9 in. (150–225 mm) high, rising from rosettes of downy leaves.

grandiflora (*ambigua*) is a perennial fox-glove forming a clump and with pleasing flowers of soft creamy-yellow. It is ideal for the small garden, as it grows to only 2 ft (600 mm). Evergreen, it is tolerant of sun or part shade.

× *mertonensis*, a beautiful hybrid with large flowers strangely tinted with rosy-mauve and shot with coppery-buff. It breeds true from seed and is evergreen. Height 2 ft (600 mm).

Erinus. The Fairy Foxglove is a small genus of alpine plants for crevices and crannies, hardy when self-sown.

alpinus, 5–6 in. (125–150 mm) high, has small clusters of flowers which may be lavender-pink, white or carmine-red from spring to late summer.

Hebe. A genus of many beautiful evergreen shrubs flowering more or less continuously from July to October. Choose the hardier ones if your garden is not sheltered.

× *andersonii* is a splendid hybrid with violet flowers fading to white. It is most striking in the form which has leaves variegated with creamy-white. The height for both is 4–6 ft (1.2–1.8 m), flowering August-September.

brachysiphon, a shrub of bushy rounded shape up to 7 ft (2.1 m) tall with box-like foliage and short spikes of white flowers in July. This is one of the hardiest species.

cupressoides, normally a small shrub but occasionally reaching 6 ft (1.8 m) and distinctive for its long slender green or grey branches, the scale-like leaves mimicking a cupressus. The small pale-blue flowers are produced freely in June and July.

epacridea is another mimic, its trailing stems looking like a prostrate conifer. It has short sprays of white flowers in summer.

hulkeana is one of the more tender kinds and usually needs the protection of a south- or west-facing wall. It is probably the most beautiful species of *Hebe* in cultivation, with glossy green leaves and large sprays of delicate lavender-blue flowers in May and June. Height 3–4 ft (900 mm–1.2 m).

pinguifolia is dwarf to prostrate with small grey-blue shell-like leaves and white flowers. It makes a bush up to 18 in. (450 mm) high. The variety 'Pagei' is dwarfer with silvery-blue leaves, forming low mats covered with sheets of white flowers in early summer.

salicifolia is hardy and grows up to 10 ft (3 m) high. It has willow-like leaves and long slender spikes of white flowers. There are a great many forms and hybrids.

speciosa is a small shrub, dense and rounded with handsome leathery leaves and dark reddish-purple flowers. It also has innumerable colourful hybrids and cultivars, many suitable only for seaside gardens.

Hybridists have developed even the naturally beautiful hebes, giving them a new appeal in form and flower.

Named Varieties

'Great Orme', exquisite tapering racemes of pink going to lavender as the flowers mature. A most beautiful shrub up to 3 ft (1 m), reasonably hardy.

'Midsummer Beauty', a handsome small shrub with conspicuous reddish undersides to the leaves. The flowers in long lavender

Hebe 'Great Orme'

racemes go on throughout the summer.
Quite hardy.

'Mrs E. Tennant', a comparitively hardy
small shrub with light violet flowers in
1 ft (300 mm) long racemes from July into
the early autumn.

'Sapphire', with remarkably dense racemes
of rosy-violet tipped with white, free-
flowering.

Linaria. A large genus with some delightful
plants, sun-loving and all bearing tiny
snapdragon flowers.

alpina, a tiny perennial with whorls of
blue-grey leaves on trailing stems, and
orange and violet flowers all summer. It is
short-lived, so let it seed to ensure survival.

dalmatica (*grandiflora*) has graceful freely-
branching stems with small bluish leaves,
one or more branches being continuously in
flower with its clear bright yellow
snapdragons from June onwards. Height
3 ft (900 mm).

Linaria maroccana

maroccana has short spikes of tiny violet-
purple snapdragons with yellow markings
on stems 9–15 in. (200–400 mm) high.
There are hybrids in separate colours (the
'Excelsior' strain, 12–15 in., 300–450 mm),
and a good mixed strain ('Fairy Bouquet',
9 in., 225 mm) of large flowers in the
colours carmine, crimson, orange, purple,
and white.

purpurea, the Purple Toadflax, long spikes of tiny blue-purple or pink snapdragons, with whorls of narrow greyish leaves. Useful and pretty but a terrible seeder.

tristis 'Lurida' is from North Africa and is best grown in the alpine house. Its flowers, borne in loose racemes, are weirdly attractive in their colouration of yellowish-grey, veined on the lip and spur with red-purple and having two large velvety patches of dark purple on the mouth. Summer-flowering, its height is 3 in. (75 mm).

Maurandia. A Mexican genus of free-flowering plants climbing by coiling and twisting their leaves and flower-stalks. Outdoors they flower from July till October; under glass, in winter.

barclaiana, the most popular species, is small-leaved with showy violet-purple flowers like a snapdragon with an open throat. It grows about 10 ft (3 m) in a season. Forms are in a great range of colours, rose and white being two favourites, and they also come in mixed colours.

Mazus. This genus gives us a collection of small creeping or prostrate plants with flowers like a mimulus, good for growing between paving stones and as cover for small bulbs. They flower in spring and early summer.

pumilio spreads mats of tiny dark green leaves studded with lilac flowers.

radicans comes from moist mountain meadows in New Zealand and asks for

Maurandia barclaiana

195

similar conditions. The prostrate pads of bronzed leaves are patterned with pure white flowers marked with a violet blotch in the centre.

reptans is a vigorous spreader, making tufts of fresh green leaves and purple-blue flowers blotched with yellow and white.

Mimulus. Musk, is a genus of about 70 annuals and perennials, most of them showy and easily grown. The herbaceous species like rather moist places such as a damp border or the margins of streams. The few shrubby species do best in pots in the cool greenhouse.

glutinosa is an evergreen shrub up to 5 ft (1.5 m) high with pretty orange, salmon or pale buff flowers, the petals so lobed and notched as to be frilled. Being a tender species, this is one for warmer areas, or for summer planting outdoors against a warm wall, if it can be wintered under glass. Two brilliant varieties are *aurantiacus*, bright orange-red, and *puniceus*, crimson-scarlet.

guttatus (*luteus*), the Monkey Musk, is a perennial with a 2 ft (600 mm) leafy stem and bright yellow flowers. The shape of the flowers and the two red-brown marks at the mouth give it the monkey look. It is hardy, blooms in early summer and has many striking varieties. But it must have really wet conditions where it will become lush in growth and prolific in flower.

This species is a parent of Monkey Musks in a variety of colours. The compact form known as 'A. T. Johnson' is so heavily blotched with wallflower-red that it appears to be of this colour but outlined with yellow.

Mimulus guttatus
A. T. Johnson

moschatus is a spreading woolly perennial with pale yellow flowers lightly dotted and splashed with brown, summer and autumn. The plant used to have a pleasant musky odour, but since about 1914 this appears to have been lost.

Nemesia. Began its career as a garden plant in the last years of the last century. Though rather untidy in habit, its orange flowers won acclaim, and since then it has been developed to the compact and colourful plants we have today. They are easily grown as half-hardy annuals and are unrivalled as bedding and edging plants. They also make lovely winter-flowering pot plants for a cool greenhouse. There are two groups, both descended from the species *strumosa*, small and tall.

Nemesia strumosa

compacta or *nana compacta*. These are 6–9 in. (150–230 mm) high, making neat compact little bushes with a mass of large brilliantly coloured flowers.

'Blue Gem', dwarf but with medium-sized flowers of forget-me-not blue.

'Triumph', the best dwarf mixed strain of all colours, 9 in. (230 mm) high.

suttonii, the taller type, has a more straggling habit but is still useful for bedding or the front of borders. The long-stemmed flowers are excellent for cutting, and the colours are available separately or in a mixture.

Ourisia. A genus inhabiting South America, New Zealand and Tasmania, the plants growing in open moist places by the sides of streams. They are dwarf creeping perennials, in dry gardens asking for some shade and preferring a cool peaty soil.

caespitosa forms tiny creeping mats of small leaves decorated with small white flowers on fine stems. The variety *gracilis* is even more compact and the pure white flowers elfin-like.

Ourisia elegans

elegans (*coccinea*) makes tufts of heart-shaped light-green leaves and has loose racemes of tubular red flowers on 8 in. (200 mm) stems.

microphylla has creeping mats of thin stems clad in tiny overlapping leaves and a profusion of relatively huge clear rose-pink flowers with a white eye throughout the summer.

× 'Snowflake' is a lovely little plant with neat mats of dark olive-green leaves above which hover large snow-white flowers with a yellow eye.

197

Penstemon. A group of about 150 species of beautiful plants invaluable for summer flowering, many for the border and several for the rock garden. The name (also spelt pentstemon) means 'fifth stamen', and this peculiarity distinguishes it from other like genera.

alpinus, clear blue funnel flowers with a white throat on 8 in. (200 mm) stems in June, rising from clumps of broad leaves.

barbatus, one for the border, 3 ft (900 mm) tall. The branching stems have many tubular flowers of bright scarlet touched with pink in the hairy throat, lasting all summer. There is a light pink form, 'Carnea', and a profusion of lilac-pink flowers in 'Catherine de la Mare'.

campanulatus, with pink, dark purple or violet flowers on branching stems 1–2 ft (300–600 mm) high. The variety *pulchellus* is for the rock garden, making low mats and having small but brilliant blue flowers.

gloxinoides is a group of half-hardy perennials which can be grown as half-hardy annuals, making superb bedding plants just as showy as antirrhinums, with the advantage of a long flowering period into autumn, the flower-spikes being long-lasting and useful as cut flowers. The variety 'Southgate Gem' is brilliant scarlet, and 'Sour Grapes' livid ash-purple.

hartwegii is also to be recommended for long-flowering hardiness. The variety 'Cherry Ripe' has warm red flowers on 2 ft (600 mm) stems. 'Garnet' has deep-red trumpets, and 'Pink Endurance' clear pink flowers.

scouleri makes bushes of narrow leathery leaves and purple flowers, 1 ft (300 mm) high. The albino form is a gem for the rock garden.

Scrophularia. A gift for the flower arranger in its species and variety *aquatica*

Penstemon hartwegii

'Variegata', which gives a vigorous display of bright foliage, green splashed and striped with cream. It forms a statuesque plant 2 ft (600 mm) tall and is best in semi-shade. The leafy stems last well in water.

Torenia. A genus of tropical plants to be raised in hothouse or warm greenhouse conditions. Transferred to pots or hanging baskets they can then decorate a cool greenhouse.

fournieri, a much-branched annual, is the most popular species, with pale blue and violet flowers. The variety 'Grandiflora' has larger flowers with a yellow throat.

198

Verbascum. Mullein includes biennial and perennial species, but it is the hybrids and their varieties which are mainly grown in gardens. All appreciate a well-drained soil in full sun. The leaves usually form a large basal rosette, and some are especially attractive for their soft silvery-green felt. The flowers of the biennials rise on single spires.

'Cotswold Queen' has branching stems with sprays of apricot-buff flowers, 3–4 ft (900 mm–1.2 m) tall.

'Gainsborough' provides clear light-yellow above grey foliage, 4 ft (1.2 m).

'Golden Bush' is bright yellow, in flower for months, 2 ft (600 mm).

'Mont Blanc' has pure white flowers, felty grey leaves, 4 ft (1.2 m).

'Pink Domino' is deep rose, 3½ ft (1 m).

Veronica. The Speedwell has some beautiful plants, from spreading mats to fine shrubs, all easy to grow in any well-drained soil in full sun.

exaltata, a most beautiful plant, its 4 ft (1.2 m) stems standing well without staking. The tiny flowers of a clear and lovely light blue make a plume in late summer. The jagged-edged leaves are arranged up the single stem.

gentianoides is mat-forming, with broad dark green leaves from which rise spires of palest blue flowers in May, 18 in. (450 mm) high. There is a white-flowered form, and one called 'Variegata', whose leaves are splashed with cream.

nummularia, small mats of rounded light green leaves and sprays of blue flowers, ideal as as a plant for crevices between paving stones.

prostrata (*rupestris*) makes spreading mats covered with brilliant deep-blue spikes in early summer. It is a lovely wall plant. Varieties are 'Spode Blue', delicate china-blue spikes; 'Royal Blue', with rich gentian-blue flowers.

teucrium gives us flowers of a true blue on 18 in. (450 mm) stems rising from dense tussocks. 'Crater Lake Blue' and 'Blue Fountain' are excellent varieties.

virginica, a valuable species with erect stems having whorls of horizontal dark green leaves and ending in erect spikes of flowers. Several tints are available: pale blue, pale lilac-pink, and a striking white.

Veronica nummularia

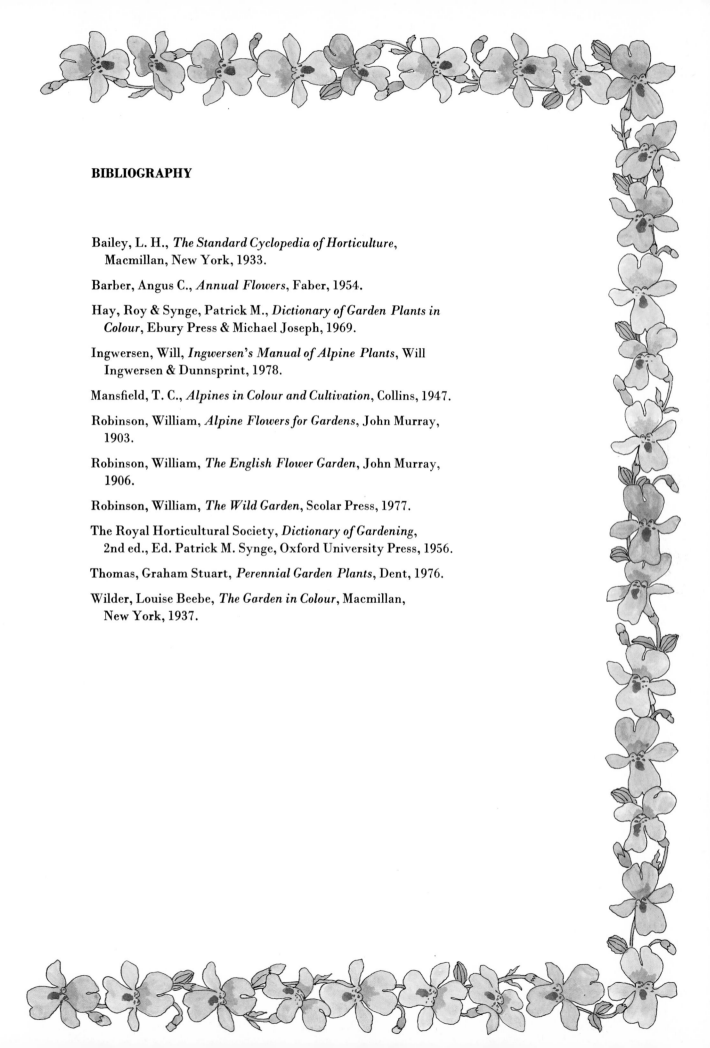

BIBLIOGRAPHY

Bailey, L. H., *The Standard Cyclopedia of Horticulture*, Macmillan, New York, 1933.

Barber, Angus C., *Annual Flowers*, Faber, 1954.

Hay, Roy & Synge, Patrick M., *Dictionary of Garden Plants in Colour*, Ebury Press & Michael Joseph, 1969.

Ingwersen, Will, *Ingwersen's Manual of Alpine Plants*, Will Ingwersen & Dunnsprint, 1978.

Mansfield, T. C., *Alpines in Colour and Cultivation*, Collins, 1947.

Robinson, William, *Alpine Flowers for Gardens*, John Murray, 1903.

Robinson, William, *The English Flower Garden*, John Murray, 1906.

Robinson, William, *The Wild Garden*, Scolar Press, 1977.

The Royal Horticultural Society, *Dictionary of Gardening*, 2nd ed., Ed. Patrick M. Synge, Oxford University Press, 1956.

Thomas, Graham Stuart, *Perennial Garden Plants*, Dent, 1976.

Wilder, Louise Beebe, *The Garden in Colour*, Macmillan, New York, 1937.

Index

(Separate bibliographies are given at the end of each chapter – these works and their authors are not so listed in this index)

203

204